3/29/12
$128.00

STUDIES IN AMERICAN POPULAR HISTORY AND CULTURE

Edited by
JEROME NADELHAFT

A ROUTLEDGE SERIES

STUIDES IN AMERICAN POPULAR HISTORY AND CULTURE

JEROME NADELHAFT, *General Editor*

PIETY AND POWER

Gender and Religious Culture in the American
Colonies, 1630–1700

Leslie J. Lindenauer

Routledge
Taylor & Francis Group
New York   London

Routledge
Taylor & Francis Group
270 Madison Avenue
New York, NY 10016

Routledge
Taylor & Francis Group
2 Park Square
Milton Park, Abingdon
Oxon OX14 4RN

Routledge is an imprint of the Taylor & Francis Group

Library of Congress Cataloging-in-Publication Data

Lindenauer, Leslie J.
   Piety and power : gender and religious culture in the American colonies, 1630–1700 /
Leslie J. Lindenauer.
     p. cm.
   Includes biblographical references.
   ISBN 0-415-93392-7
   1. Women in Christianity—United States—History—17th century. 2. Protestant churches—
United States—History—17th century. 3. United States—Church history—17th century. I. Title.
BR520.L56 2002
277.3'06'082—dc21   2002024899

FOR RANDY, LEO, AND ETHAN

contents

ACKNOWLEDGMENTS

T HIS BOOK COULD NOT HAVE BEEN WRITTEN WITHOUT THE GUIDANCE, SUPPORT, ADVICE, and good humor of people both inside and outside the academy. First and foremost, I owe a profound debt of gratitude to my advisor at New York University, Patricia U. Bonomi. It was a distinct honor and pleasure to study both early American history and the craft of writing with her; there could be no better mentor on both counts.

It was an honor too to share my graduate education with a terrific group of fellow students. The opportunity to experience the joys and trials of scholarship with them was the highlight of my graduate career. To them—and they know who they are—I extend my thanks and my love.

I am grateful to New York University and the History Department for their generous financial assistance as I pursued my degree. Balancing family, scholarship, and work is never easy; it would have been close to impossible without their support. In addition, a fellowship from the Pew Program in Religion and American History enabled me to finish writing in a more timely fashion. The Pew Fellows conference provided an invaluable and stimulating forum in which to exchange ideas.

I extend thanks and appreciation to my colleagues and friends at Hartford College for Women of the University of Hartford and the Connecticut Women's Hall of Fame. It has been a privilege to develop programs in women's history for the Hall of Fame, and to teach in the College's Women's Studies program. The Hall of Fame's support in the time since I completed the dissertation reflects their dedication to the careful scholarship at the heart of all public history programs. I also thank David Ader, who encourages me to reach ever higher, and whose own writing serves as a constant inspiration to me.

My parents, Jinx and Art Lindenauer, have been the greatest source of encouragement, love, and support from beginning to end. They have never doubted that I could accomplish my goals, nor questioned the value of my pursuits, even when I have expressed my own doubts about the paths I have chosen. For that, and for the gift of curiosity and a thirst for knowledge that they bestowed upon me and my sister, Thea, I am deeply grateful.

My children, Leo and Ethan, have most literally grown up with this project. Whenever I am in danger of losing all perspective in my work, they are there to pull me back down to earth. They are my light and my joy. My husband, Randall Rode, has accompanied me every step of the way. His patience, good humor, and love have sustained me. To him and to my two boys—feminists all—I dedicate this book with love.

Introduction
Gender and Protestantism in Early America

What Christian left Locked up and went his way,
Sweet Christiana opens with her key...
. . . Go then, I say, tell all men who thou art,
Say, I am Christiana, and my part
Is now with my four sons to tell you what
It is for men to take a pilgrim's lot.[1]

C HRISTIANA, A FEMALE CHRISTIAN. JOHN BUNYAN CAPTURED IN A NAME WHAT HISTORI-
ans over three hundred years later have only begun to explore: gender as a
category of analysis in the study of religious culture. We ask new questions of
our texts as we search for differences and similarities in the ways women and men
experienced and shaped religious culture and in the meaning they discovered in it.

This study will explore gender and religious culture in the seventeenth century
in three American colonies, each with a dominant religious tradition: Puritan
Massachusetts, Dutch Reformed New York, and Anglican Virginia. Though most
scholars acknowledge the centrality of religion in the earliest period of colonial history, few early American historians have been interested specifically in the meaning that women drew from their religious worlds as Christian wives, mothers,
neighbors, and church members. Fewer still have explored the relationship
between gender, religious culture, and power within the context of colonial patriarchy.

As this study will demonstrate, our notions of power and patriarchy change
when we explore the layers of meaning embedded in the rituals and practice of colonial religious culture. By so doing we will come closer to understanding the complex
avenues of influence open to women in the seventeenth century. For in the religious
arena above all others women found outlets that were personally empowering,

among their families, and in their communities. There they found ways to circumvent a socially constructed patriarchy that deemed them inferior to men.[2]

A number of historians have taken note of the relationship between religion, gender, and power in Catholic religious culture. In their studies of gender and the Catholic church, scholars have moved beyond mere doctrine to explore the meaning of Catholic symbols and their impact on the ways women and men perceived their roles in the earthly church. The symbolic importance of Mary, communities of women in the cloister, and female sainthood are seen as benchmarks of female authority in Catholic society. Protestantism, on the other hand, abolished these symbols and communities, which action has been read by many historians as an attempt by men to rein in on women who exercised power in their religious worlds. Yet within such a narrow interpretive structure, Protestant women are defined as little more than victims of a deeply ingrained patriarchy. To the degree that historians accept this view, I will argue, they have impoverished Reformed religion by turning a blind eye to *Protestant* rituals and communities which reflected, promoted, and sustained women as well as men in a "priesthood of all believers."[3]

The Reformation's radical conception of a "priesthood of all believers" is central to the arguments made in this study. Evidence suggests that the fundamental belief in the equality of the Protestant soul shaped women's conception of themselves as Christians, blurred distinctions between their roles in the public and private sphere, and gave them a voice in arenas often assumed by historians to have been closed to them. Analysis of religiously-charged community networks, Protestantism's complex system of symbols and rituals, and the secular as well as sacred arenas in which religious performance took place reveals shades of meaning that have proved elusive to historians of Reformed religious culture. When women raised their voices in song, testified to conversion, challenged or promoted the actions and words of their ministers, performed their neighborly duties, or catechized their children, they shared in a theology that blurred the socially-constructed roles of the two sexes. As I will argue, religious practice—in each colony and within the context of each Reformed denomination—provided women with a platform from which to assert their authority, even as Reformed doctrine itself lauded their submissiveness.

Historians such as Amanda Porterfield have noted that Puritan women did find a source of respect and "indirect" authority within the bounds of submissiveness. Indeed, the feminine qualities of submissiveness and humility were held up as the model for regenerate Christians of all denominations.[4] When we move beyond this simplistic notion of feminine virtue, however, which juxtaposes the temptress Eve against the pious and submissive Mary, the field for women's actions expands and deepens. For a woman's virtue and virtuous behavior, like a man's, was defined in part by her ability—her *duty*—to call to account those secular and religious leaders who would undermine the kingdom of God. If the actions of her husband, minister, governor, or king put her piety or the piety of her community in jeopardy, God called the Christian woman to action, both inside and outside the home.

This study is located at the juncture of two bodies of literature: women's history and the history of American religion. Too often, historians of colonial women have paid insufficient attention to the role of religious culture. Similarly, religious histories, which until just twenty years ago were largely denominational in focus, have rarely devoted substantial attention to the role of women.[5] Thus, to a considerable degree, histories of colonial women remain trapped within the confines of theoretical structures established by women's historians in the 1960s, especially the notion that men and women inhabit "separate spheres." Even those historians interested in religious culture incorporate into their arguments the trope of "separate spheres." Piety, when it has been examined at all, has been equated with domesticity. Though women often held sway in the home, they rarely, if ever, in this view, held authority in the public sphere. "How difficult it is to uncouple women from domestic life," wrote the French historian Joan Landes. "How much more difficult, once uncoupled, to imagine a world in which women's proper place is in the public sphere." When we examine colonial religious culture, however, we find how thin was the line was between private and public. Hence, we need to include in our understanding of colonial women places and events where they acted as Christians.[6]

Similar historiographic constraints have shaped colonial religious history as well. For upwards of half a century historians of seventeenth-century religion have used as their benchmark the works of Perry Miller. With notable exceptions, few historians have succeeded in effectively challenging Miller's narrow intellectual definition of Puritanism. The voices continue to emanate from the pulpit. Moreover, many scholars still accept published doctrine as evidence of religion as practiced. This elite-driven definition of religion directs historians of all denominations to a field of evidence in which women's voices are rarely audible.[7]

Related to the power of Miller's work to shape religious scholarship is the continued impact of the "evangelical synthesis" in American religious history, which views the seventeenth century through the lens of nineteenth-century religious revivals. Though the influence of the evangelical school, which originated in nineteenth-century interpretations of the second awakening as a resurrection of religion in severe decline, was mitigated by the changes wrought by community studies, women's history, and black history in the 1970s, it continues to hold sway in studies of all three colonial regions under examination here. This is owing, I believe, to a continued emphasis on clerical power as the prime element in shaping and maintaining religious culture, to the exclusion of popular religious impulses. In fact, as this study will argue, the "awakenings" of the eighteenth and nineteenth centuries have as much to do with seeds planted by women in the seventeenth century and with their role in the changing nature of faith as they do with a reaction to the supposed failure of early churches.[8]

The primacy of Miller's paradigm is reflected in another gap in the literature of colonial religion. Again, with notable exceptions, scholars have paid scant attention to early religion or religious culture in regions other than New England. The idea of a Puritan hegemony pervades the literature of other colonies, and has shaped our ideas of what might constitute the "American mind" and American culture.[9]

Central to this study's aims of mediating the distance between popular and elite religious traditions, and of examining dominant colonial traditions comparatively, is the search for what might be called "Protestant culture." Though denominational and demographic differences between colonies certainly existed—indeed, as this study will demonstrate, regional distinctions shaped the variant ways women mitigated the impact of patriarchy in each of the colonies—there were similarities in the religious culture as well, similarities grounded in the Reformed assumption of the equality of the soul. In each of the three Protestant denominations—Puritan, Dutch Reformed, and Anglican—as set in time and place, women could and did find avenues of self-expression and influence based on the fundamental belief that they were potentially as godly and therefore as likely to be saved as men.

Anthropology, literary criticism, and other interdisciplinary methodologies have begun to reshape historic inquiries into both women's history and religious history, and have proved especially useful to historians interested in the intersection of gender, religion, and power. Religious language in seventeenth-century Protestant culture—expressed in rituals and sermons, in public and in private— reflected and shaped new arenas for social, political, and cultural struggle. Where women's voices seem most elusive, as they do in Protestant doctrine, these methodologies provide the means to disclose social relationships of power, relationships more complex than the mere subjugation of women to a rigid colonial patriarchy. Close analysis of religious rituals will allow us to move beyond false distinctions between elite and popular religious traditions to examine religion as it was practiced and experienced rather than solely as defined and prescribed. In so doing we may add gender to our understanding of social relationships of power in the colonial period. Women were actors in Protestant society, and their actions reflected and shaped Protestant religious culture in early America.[10]

* * *

This study will explore gender and religious culture in Massachusetts, Virginia, and New York between 1630 and 1700, a period of profound change and of what one historian has called the "seasoning" of American religious culture.[11] Its conclusion suggests new directions for scholarship on the upheavals that marked the history of each colony under consideration: the Glorious Revolution in Massachusetts, Leisler's Rebellion in New York, and Bacon's Rebellion in Virginia.

Women played an integral part in the changing nature of faith, which, as evidence from the second half of the seventeenth century suggests, included in its practice a re-conceived imperative to action. Faithful Christians, regardless of gender, were "soldiers of Christ," bound by their religion to voice a militant concern about events that seemed to jeopardize their colony's place in the kingdom of heaven. This imperative to action, for women as for men, grew out of shifts in the relationship between an individual and her God. New questions about the meaning of grace, and the role of "works" in the in the salvation of an individual or her community went hand-in-hand with the social, political, and cultural reformation of the seventeenth century. Protestantism's imperative to root out the remnants of popish corruption at all levels of society, at its most stark in the English Civil War of the 1640s, seemed well-suited to the climate of change and upheaval in the colonies during the 1680s and 1690s.

Similarly, as this study suggests at its conclusion, the public roles women assumed during the Revolutionary War, in the Federal period, and with the emergence of the middle class in the nineteenth century—Liberty's daughters, Republican and moral mothers—found their roots in the seventeenth century. The language of religion pervaded eighteenth- and nineteenth-century public behavior. The religious context reflected not only specific events and mentalities—though events specific to time and place indeed defined the issues about which women and men articulated their concerns—but the gender-neutral ideas of moral duty and action that had found clear expression in the Protestant culture of the seventeenth century.

While it would enrich any study of religious culture in early America to examine additional colonies and to include Judaism, Catholicism, and other Protestant denominations, in the interest of time and focus this project is limited to three, each of which shares differences and similarities with the others. This has allowed for fruitful comparison. The study is also limited by the nature of the evidence available which, as historians of colonial religion know, tends to be skewed toward white, male members of the middling sort or above. I wanted to add race to my analysis of gender and religious culture. While I hold out hope that sources like those mined by Mechal Sobel for the eighteenth century exist for the seventeenth, I have found too little to allow me to draw any substantial conclusions.[12]

This study walks a fine line between perpetuating the view of the seventeenth-century American colonies as "New England writ large" and attempting to distinguish between the religious rituals and traditions of specific denominations. In its search for similarities in the experiences of women in three colonies, born of what might loosely be termed "Protestant culture," this project draws on the work of scholars who have attempted to restore to Protestantism its subjective meaning. European historians Steven Ozment, Natalie Davis, and J. Sears McGee, in analyzing Reformation culture, have mitigated the impact of nineteenth- and twentieth-century definitions of "reformed" and "Calvinist," definitions that have shaped our notions of seventeenth-century religious culture.[13]

Central to these new interpretations is the question "How revolutionary was the Reformation?" Scholars, few of whom incorporate gender into their analysis of the Reformation, have drawn conclusions that represent a range of opinions on the spectrum from radical to conservative. Lucien Febvre points to the emergence of a new kind of laity, no longer passive about the world or willing to accept unquestioningly church teachings, in his conclusion that the Reformation represented a historical watershed. Michael Walzer sees in English Puritanism the beginnings of a modern ideological revolution. Other historians, Jean Delumeau, Carlo Ginzberg, and John Bossy among them, conclude that, far from being revolutionary, the Reformation served to break family and communal ties that Catholicism had fostered.[14]

Those few historians who have questioned the Reformation's revolutionary nature with respect to women have reached similarly varied conclusions. As I stated from the outset, when gender is included as a category of analysis I believe the revolutionary nature of the Reformation is manifest in the Protestant denominations in the American colonies.[15]

Regardless of where they fall on the line between radical and conservative, scholars of gender and Reformation culture have addressed the role of John Calvin and his writings in shaping contemporary attitudes toward women. Calvinist doctrine is central to the thesis of this dissertation as well. Though it is nearly impossible to document the degree to which women in the American colonies had access to *The Institutes of Christian Religion* or Calvin's commentaries and published sermons on the Bible, Calvinist doctrine is at the core of Reformation notions about the equality of the soul and a "priesthood of all believers." It is the goal of this study, then, to mediate the distance between doctrine and religious experience and practice. Protestant men and women worshipped in many different ways; they prayed alone, with their families, in conventicles, and in church. And wherever they prayed, they did so secure in the thought that they needed no priest to intervene between them and God. A lay believer's voice would speak as clearly to God as a cleric's. Calvin's doctrine thus set Catholic interpretations of the Bible on end and recast the relationship between God and Christian men and women.

Implicit in the Reformation challenge to Catholic hierarchy and papal corruption was the conception of Christian freedom, freedom which, with regard to the potential for grace or salvation, liberated the regenerate Christian from the shackles of priestly control. All Christians stood on equal footing before God, a God solely responsible for determining whether one was saved. "Let it then be known by us," Calvin wrote in his Commentary on Paul's letter to the Corinthians, "that it is the property of faith to rest upon *God* alone, without depending on *men*. This cannot be accomplished unless we are fully persuaded that God has spoken to us, and that what we have believed is no mere contrivance of men." Moreover, though on earth the subservience of women to men might be necessary to maintain civic order, Calvin's rules of subservience to male authority were transient and historically conditioned. Female submission was neither necessary for salvation nor should it bind women's consciences. As Calvin wrote in his sermon on I Corinthians,

> . . . [Though Paul] says that women are not at all marked with the image of God like men, in regard to this temporal state which passes and vanishes with the figure of the world . . . we see that God has created us all in his image, both males and females, and that however much this image has been abolished by the sin of Adam, it is renewed by our Lord Jesus Christ; that when we are regen-

erated by the Holy Spirit, it is as if God declares that he dwells in us, that we are his temples.[16]

The "temporal state" thus had no bearing on the potential for grace for men or women. This gender-neutral tenet represented the theological underpinnings of Reformed religion.

The equality of the soul proved to be at the heart of Christian liberty for regenerate women. Calvin's message, translated and paraphrased in countless sermons by radical ministers, and encompassed in the sermons and homilies that formed the core of church ritual not only in the Calvinist North but in Anglican Virginia, made its way into lay conceptions of piety, and helped to shape colonial notions of self.[17]

Related to the question of the Reformation's revolutionary character, and central to a comparison of piety in Anglican Virginia with the more "Calvinist" Dutch Reformed Church in New York and Congregational churches of Massachusetts, is a discussion of the relationship between "Puritan" and "Anglican." A search for definitions of Anglican and Puritan and the related analysis of the English (as opposed to the Continental) Reformation has for some time dominated scholarly discourse about late sixteenth- and early-seventeenth-century England. Such scholarship is at the same time helpful and marginal to any examination of Protestant culture in the American colonies. For while events and theological shifts in England and on the Continent certainly shaped religious culture in America, theological shoots rooted in American soil also tended to grow in their own directions. As this study will demonstrate, the Anglicanism of seventeenth-century Virginia was not identical to that practiced in England. Nor were the differences between radical, moderate, and conservative Protestantism so clearly drawn. Changes in the ways religion was practiced and experienced on American soil had a profound impact on the roles women sought to play in both their secular and religious worlds.[18]

Among the most disturbing interpretations of the differences between "Puritanism" and "Anglicanism"—one casting a pall on studies of religious culture in colonial Virginia—is the assumption that Anglicanism was but the philistine step-child of the Reformation, that Anglicans, really closet Catholics, were somehow less religious than their Puritan neighbors. Grounded in the Oxford Movement of the 1840's, and successfully revived by the evangelical school in the mid-twentieth-century, numerous studies examined Puritanism and Anglicanism with an eye toward establishing a measure of the *degree* of each denomination's piety. Relying primarily on Puritan sources, scholars concluded that if Puritans found piety so lacking in the Anglican establishment, then surely it must have been so.[19]

One of the weaknesses in scholarship on Protestant culture lies in the fact that few historians have studied Anglicanism, amid a virtual flood of scholarship on Puritanism. Fewer still have attempted to study the religious cultures comparatively. Where scholars have explored differences and similarities between the predominant seventeenth-century English religions, it has been with respect to the role of religious differences in the English Civil War.[20]

Over the past two decades, a number of scholars—among them Patrick Collinson, J. Sears McGee, and Nigel Yates—have attempted to include Anglican conceptions of piety and salvation in their analysis of English Reformation thought. Their work has served to moderate the impressions left by scholars in the preceding decades in studies that stripped Anglicanism of much of its spiritual meaning. While all acknowledge fundamental differences between Anglicanism and Puritanism, each begins with the basic premise that both groups thought of themselves as "heirs of the Orthodox Protestant tradition in England." The differences, according to Puritan scholar Patrick Collinson, "were differences of degree, of theological temperature so to speak, rather than fundamental principle." Each religion had its own "ideal Christian" or "true Israelite." Each desired a moral reformation in England. They differed primarily in the proposed means for bringing that reformation about. And within the bounds of each religious tradition, bolstered by reformed notions of faith and the individual self, women found avenues of power.[21]

The centrality of the discourse on the meaning of "Puritanism" and "Anglicanism" in English history has had an impact on the way historians have perceived religious culture in colonial Virginia. Fueled by evidence of Virginia's demographic struggle—a skewed male-female ratio, a high mortality rate, parishes so sparsely populated as to be unable to support a minister—the impression left by most studies is one of a colony bereft of religious tradition and practice. Comparisons with the religious histories of New England's Puritan colonies seem stark indeed, just as Anglicanism seems to run a pale second to her more radical cousin. It is no wonder, then, that the relationship between gender, religion, and power has proved to be of little interest to most historians of seventeenth-century Virginia.[22]

With few exceptions (see note 22), most historians have defined early Virginia Anglicanism too rigidly, setting up misleading divisions between what has been labeled "elite" and "popular" religion. In so doing, they have ignored such things as the persistence of Catholic traditions, Puritan impulses, and the occult, all of which contributed to contemporary definitions of Anglicanism as it was experienced and shaped by male and female colonists. Once we begin to examine colonial Anglicanism within the context of Virginia's peculiar demographic circumstances and the nature of the established church there, we leave room to incorporate these diverse religious impulses. In the absence of a bishop and often a permanent minister, Virginia Anglicanism was practiced and experienced in ways far removed from the way it was practiced in England. Without the imposition of a rigid clerical hierarchy so often associated with the Anglican church, Virginia women could take their role in God's mission there to heart.[23]

From the earliest accounts of Virginia history to the present, most historians have focused on perceived weaknesses in the daughter church in Virginia. Drawing primarily on letters from unhappy ministers, complaints of too few clerics, too few parishioners, and inadequate pay, and the impressions of elite vestry members whose interests lay in protecting their control, scholars have turned a blind eye toward those sometimes elusive bits of evidence that challenge a one-dimensional view of Anglicanism. In inventories, vestry books, wills, and court records lie the materials that enable us to re-evaluate the place of religion in every-day life, and the power that women might have derived from it.

Though leaders in colonial Virginia recognized that a strong Anglican presence would provide the order and piety necessary for economic success, religion itself, unlike in Congregational Massachusetts, did not dictate the shape or conduct of the colony's communities. Attempts to create strong centers of economic, political, and social activity were thwarted by the decentralized impulses of the colony's developing tobacco culture. As labor shifted from white indentured servitude to black slavery, and plantations and small farms dispersed further from Virginia's tidewater roots, families lived lives of increasing isolation. How much more vital, then, to a sense of community were those days devoted to court, church, and market? And in a society that denied women access to the formal power inherent in public office or commerce, those opportunities to address personal and communal concerns in a public forum loomed large indeed.[24]

From court to church, from home to market, Virginia women expressed in vernacular language their role in the colony's power structure. That language, often ignored by historians or at best interpreted as part of women's economic or social concerns, was infused with lay notions of piety and salvation in the Reformed tradition. Whether they took their place at the center of the church's most sacred ordinance by donating ritual objects of communion, fought in court to suppress their neighbor's "unquiet" behavior, or criticized their ministers for ignoring parish duties, Anglican women shaped and responded to those duties taught in the Bible, the Book of Common Prayer, or in Episcopal homilies.

Like their more radical Puritan sisters, Anglican women, through God's grace, were bound to the Decalogue. Those duties toward God and humankind, as handed down by Moses, proved the foundation for the regenerate Christian life and lent shape to day-to-day events. And though Anglicans and Puritans might have agreed doctrinally on ideas of sin and salvation, they differed in which sins and virtues were the key to God's grace or punishment. For while the tenets of the First Table—duties toward God—defined the ideal Christian for Puritans, Anglicans emphasized the Second Table—duties toward fellow humans. Each table defined sin and virtue differently, and though both Puritans and Anglicans were to obey all commandments, their individual and communal concerns reflected most those tenets which stood at the center of their sacred worldview. Though the paths to salvation differed, as this study will demonstrate, each was in its own way as potentially empowering for women as the other.[25]

Within the bounds of their duties toward God, Puritan women in Massachusetts identified opportunities to wield authority in their communities. The rituals of Puritan culture—at home, in church, or in the town square—provided

women with a voice that both affirmed and challenged contemporary social order.
Yet despite scholars' recent attempts to interpret religion in ways that would seem
to encourage the inclusion of women, few have chosen to explore the role of gender
in the establishment or transformation of those many "cities upon a hill." While
some have challenged Miller's "declension" model, and others strive to find the
appeal of a religion so often associated with repression and fear, few have used gender to enhance their interpretations.[26]

New Amsterdam by 1664, the year of the English conquest, had a population of
upward of 9000 inhabitants, about 60% of whom were Dutch. The balance were
Scandinavians, Walloons, Germans, and French. Because most of New Netherland's
settlers remained after the English took control of the government, New York was
marked by a religious and ethnic diversity largely missing from New England and
the southern colonies. This diversity has proved particularly intriguing to colonial
historians, especially with regard to its role in the colony's political and economic
conflicts. Though scholars have done battle over whether diversity destroyed or
enhanced Dutch culture, few have incorporated gender into their interpretations.
One notable exception lies in the work of Joyce Goodfriend, whose books and articles have addressed exactly that issue.[27]

Though doctrinally allied with the Puritan church in Massachusetts, the religious culture in New York also shared similarities with that of Anglican Virginia. A
dearth of ministers, periods of benign neglect on the part of a mother country consumed with political conflicts at home, and an atmosphere of relative religious toleration all contributed to a religious culture shaped as much by popular practice as
by the teachings of the Dutch Reformed Church. Dutch women, drawing on the
same notions of piety available to their Calvinist neighbors to the North, and a sense
of authority derived from their role as keepers and transmitters of a religious culture threatened by political upheaval, found a voice in events and places traditionally associated with men.

In each of the three colonies discussed in this study, women, as heirs to God's
grace, found avenues of authority in a range of arenas. Each of the following four
sections, based loosely on the structure of John Calvin's 1536 edition of the
Institutes, considers those arenas as a series of ever-expanding spheres—from the
intensely private to the most public—where women exercised the voice of authority.
Part one, Faith and Self, establishes the demographic and geographic context for
Protestantism in the colonies, and addresses those most private moments in any
Christian's religious life when one had to contend with questions of personal grace
and salvation. In the privacy of her "closet,"—in the privacy of her thoughts—the
Christian woman defined herself according to the Bible, personal doubts and sure-
ty, and even her dreams. Part two, Prayer and Home, places the Protestant woman
at the center of the Christian home and family, the "little commonwealth." Much of
the authority that a woman wielded in her community was directly related to the
power she exercised at home as the transmitter of Christian ideals, the teacher of
her children, and the keeper of religious rituals. There the symbols of domesticity

and marriage central to the Bible's teaching on the relationship between men and women and the Trinity came to life. Part three follows women from the home into the church, arguably the most important social and political institution in communities across the colonies. There they applied their notions of Christian equality and Protestant duty to all manner of activities that shaped the church itself, its membership, and its ministry. Part four examines women's roles in public rituals and events that marked a community's passage from the seventeenth to the eighteenth century.

NOTES

[1] John Bunyan, *Pilgrim's Progress*, ed. Roger Sharrock (London, 1965), 215–216.

[2] Recent feminist theorists have suggested the need to redefine politics and power to encompass "symbolic" or "cultural" politics. Because women in the colonial period were denied access to formal political power, analysis of their symbolic and cultural power—in this case through their participation in religious culture—assumes a greater significance. For examples of recent scholarship which suggests the need to redefine political power, see Denise Riley, *"Am I That Name?" Feminism and the Category of "women" in History* (Minneapolis, 1988); Judith Butler, *Gender Trouble: Feminism and the Subversion of Identity* (New York, 1989); Joan Landes, *Women and the Public Sphere in the Age of the French Revolution* (Ithaca, 1988).

[3] For examples of studies which employ gender as a category of analysis in the study of Catholicism, see Penelope D. Johnson, *Equal in Monastic Profession: Religious Women in Medieval France* (Chicago, 1991); Caroline Walker Bynum, *Jesus as Mother: Studies in the Spirituality of the High Middle Ages* (Berkeley, 1982); Rudolph Bell, *Holy Anorexia* (Chicago, 1985); Bynum, "'...And Women His Humanity': Female Imagery in the Religious Writing of the Later Middle Ages," in Caroline Walker Bynum, Steven Harrell, and Paula Richman, eds., *Gender and Religion: On the Complexity of Symbols* (Boston, 1986), 257–288; Bynum, "Fast Feast, and Flesh: the Religious Significance of Food to Medieval Women," *Representations* 11 (Summer 1985):1–25. For examples of studies which juxtapose women's power in Catholicism with the supposed stripping of power from women with the coming of the Reformation, see William Monter, "Protestant Wives, Catholic Saints, and the Devil's Handmaid: Women in the Age of Reformation," in Renate Bridenthal, Claudia Koontz, and Susan Stuard, eds., *Becoming Visible* (Boston, 1987), 203–219.; G.R. Quaife, *Godly Zeal and Furious Rage: The Witch in Early Modern Europe* (New York, 1987), chaps. 6 and 7, passim. Margaret Spufford challenges the notion that women were victims in the shift from Catholicism to Protestantism in "Puritanism and Social Control?," in Anthoney Fletcher and John Stevenson, eds., *Order and Disorder in Early Modern England* (Cambridge, 1985). Merry E. Weisner also explores the possibility of adding gender to Reformation history without focusing on the victimization of women, but cautions that scholars have begun to ghettoize women's and family history: "Beyond Women and the Family: Towards a Gender Analysis of the Reformation," *Sixteenth Century Journal* 18 (1987): 311–321. Marilyn J. Westerkamp, in her book published after the completion of this dissertation *Women and Religion in Early America, 1600–1850*, adds much needed balance and nuance to the discourse: (New York, 1999). For examples of works which focus on women as victims of American Puritanism, see Lyle Koehler, *A Search for Power: The 'Weaker Sex' in*

Seventeenth-Century New England (Urbana, 1980); Ben Barker-Benfield, "Anne Hutchinson and the Puritan Attitude Toward Women," *Feminist Studies* 1 (1973): 65–96; Rosemary Skinner Keller, "New England Women: Ideology and Experience in First Generation Puritanism, 1630–1650," in *Women and Religion in America*, vol.2, *The Colonial and Revolutionary Periods* eds. Rosemary Reuther and Rosemary Skinner Keller (San Francisco, 1983), 132–192.

[4] Amanda Porterfield, *Female Piety in Puritan New England: The Emergence of Religious Humanism* (New York, 1992), 80.

[5] Colonial women's historians notable for their work with religious sources and their attention to religious culture include Laurel Thatcher Ulrich, *Good Wives: Image and Reality in the Lives of Women in Northern New England, 1650–1750* (New York,1983); Carol Karlsen, *The Devil in the Shape of a Woman: Witchcraft in Colonial New England* (New York, 1987). Recent scholarship on colonial religion which focuses on the role of women includes Porterfield, *Female Piety in Puritan New England*; Gerald F. Moran, "'Sisters' in Christ: Women in the Church in Seventeenth Century New England," in *Women in American Religion*, ed. Paul Boyer (Philadelphia,1980) 47-65; Joyce D. Goodfriend, "Social Dimensions of Congregational Life: Church Life In Colonial New York City," *William and Mary Quarterly* (*WMQ*), 3rd ser., 46 (1989):252–278; Goodfriend, "Recovering the Religious History of Dutch Reformed Women in Colonial New York," *de Halve Maen* vol.LXIV #4 (Winter 1991); Mary Maples Dunn, "'Saints and Sisters': Congregational and Quaker Women in the Early Colonial Period," *WMQ*, 3rd ser., 30 (1978). And see especially Westercamp, *Women and Religion in Early America*.

[6] Joan Landes,*Women and the Public Sphere in the Age of the French Revolution* (Ithica, 1988), 1. Even Laurel Ulrich, whose study of northern New England women in the early colonial era reshaped our understanding of the variety of spheres within which women operated, devotes relatively little attention to the relationship between power and piety, choosing instead to draw distinctions between the social and the "inner dimensions" of women as Christians. "As Christians," Ulrich states, "women enlarged the meaning of their own lives without really changing its dimensions." Ulrich, *Good Wives*, 239. Also see p. 226, and chap.12, *passim*. See also Mary Beth Norton, *Founding Mothers and Fathers: Gendered Power and the Formation of American Society* (New York, 1996). Norton's work does much to highlight the fluidity of the lines between the public and private spheres with regard to gender, and the potential for gendered power therein, though her interpretation relies only in small part on an examination of religious culture. See also Kathleen M. Brown, who incorporates the relationship between religious culture, gender, and power in Virginia in her book *Good Wives, Nasty Wenches, and Anxious Patriarchs: Gender, Race, and Power in Colonial Virginia* (Chapel Hill, 1996). For a helpful discussion of the impact of "separate spheres" on scholarship in women's history, see Linda Kerber, "Separate Spheres, Female Worlds, Woman's Place: The Rhetoric of Women's History," *Journal of American History* , 75 (June, 1988): 9–40.

[7] Perry Miller, *The New England Mind: The Seventeenth Century* (Cambridge, 1939); Harry Stout, in *The New England Soul: Preaching and Religious Culture in Colonial New England* (New York, 1986) writes in direct response to Miller's intellectual history. Though Stout successfully traces patterns of Puritan piety over two centuries, and thus challenges the notion of religious declension, he does not explore the ways in which sermons might have been heard and understood by parishioners, as opposed to the messages ministers intended to communicate. For a comprehensive discussion of recent shifts in scholarship on Puritan cul-

ture, see David Hall, "On Common Ground: The Coherence of American Puritan Studies," *WMQ*, 3rd ser., 64 (June 1987): 193–230. For examples of recent attempts to diminish the distance between "popular" and "elite" religion, see Hall, *Worlds of Wonder, Days of Judgment: Popular Belief in Early New England* (New York, 1989); Charles Hambrick-Stowe, *The Practice of Piety: Puritan Devotional Disciplines in Seventeenth-Century New England* (Chapel Hill, 1986); Charles Lloyd Cohen, *God's Caress: The Psychology of the Puritan Religious Experience* (New York, 1986); Patricia U. Bonomi, *Under the Cope of Heaven: Religion, Society, and Politics in Colonial America* (New York, 1986); Christine Heyrman, *Commerce and Culture: The Maritime Communities of Colonial Massachusetts 1690–1750* (New York, 1984). The work of Hall, Heyrman, and Bonomi is central to attempts to counter religious declension interpretation fostered by Miller's work. Richard Godbeer, in *The Devil's Dominion: Magic and Religion in Early New England* (Cambridge and New York, 1992) adds welcome complexity to our understanding of Puritan religious culture, particularly in his addition of magical practice to the narrative.

[8] For a review of the tension between the "evangelical synthesis" and recent revisionist scholarship, see Patricia U. Bonomi's review of Jon Butler, *Awash in a Sea of Faith: Christianizing the American People* (Cambridge, 1990) in *WMQ*, 3rd ser., (Jan., 1991): 118–124.

[9] On the importance of using a comparative approach in the study of American religion, see Jerald C. Brauer, "Regionalism and Religion in America," *Church History* 54 (Sept. 1985): 366–378. For welcome examples of studies which cross regional boundaries see Bonomi, *Under the Cope of Heaven*; Butler, *Awash in a Sea of Faith*. Karen Ordahl Kupperman adds complexity to our definition of Puritanism and Puritan culture in her examination of a Puritan colony outside of New England; her exploration of the failure of the Providence Island colony becomes a vehicle for understanding the common qualities of successful colonies, i e. New England and the Chesapeake: *Providence Island, 1630–1641: The Other Puritan Colony* (Cambridge and New York, 1993). See also Paula A. Treckel, *To Comfort the Heart: Women in Seventeenth-Century America* (New York, 1996).

[10] For examples of scholars who suggest that attention to ritual language and action might help to mediate the distance between popular and elite religion and create a category of "religious culture," see Natalie Zemon Davis, "From 'Popular Religion' to Religious Cultures," in *Reformation Europe* ed. Steven Ozment (St. Louis, 1982), 321–341; Davis, "Some Tasks and Themes in the Study of Popular Religion," in *The Pursuit of Holiness in Late Medieval and Renaissance Religion* eds. Charles Trinkaus and Heiko Oberman (Leiden, 1974); David Hall, "Toward a History of Popular Religion in Early New England," *WMQ*, 3rd. ser., (Jan. 1984): 49–55. Cultural historians Natalie Davis, Robert Darnton, Rhys Isaac, and Lynn Hunt have employed interdisciplinary methodologies to uncover symbolic meaning embodied in rituals, value systems, ideas, and institutional forms. Their work has had a tremendous impact on recent scholarship, particularly in the realm of religious history. See, for example, Robert Darnton, *The Great Cat Massacre* (New York, 1984); Davis, *Society and Culture in Early Modern France* (Stamford, 1975); Rhys Isaac, *The Transformation of Virginia* (Chapel Hill, 1982). For a comprehensive explanation of what is meant by "New Cultural History," see Lynn Hunt's introduction in Hunt, *New Cultural History* (Berkeley, 1989). For a discussion on the relationship between "language" and gender as a category of analysis, see Joan Scott, *Gender and the Politics of History* (New York, 1989).

[11] Bonomi, *Under the Cope of Heaven*, 40.

¹² Mechal Sobel, *The World They Made Together: Black and White Values in Eighteenth-Century Virginia* (Princeton, 1987). Marilyn Westerkamp has added substantially to the literature addressing both gender and race in evangelical Protestant culture: *Women and Religion in Early America* (New York, 1999), as has Treckel, *To Comfort the Heart.* See especially Catherine Clinton and Michelle Gillespie, *The Devil's Lane: Sex and Race in the Early South* (Oxford and New York, 1997). Several historians have uncovered substantial evidence for a complex web of relationships between white planters, black slaves, and free blacks in seventeenth century Virginia. Those studies, however, pay scant attention to religious culture, and devote little if any attention to gender. See, for example, James R. Perry, *Formation of a Society on Virginia's Eastern Shore, 1615–1655* (Chapel Hill, 1990); T.H. Breen and Stephen Innes, *'Mine Owne Ground': Race and Freedom on Virginia's Eastern Shore, 1640–1676* (New York, 1980). Though I have mined countless non-religious sources to re-create religious meaning for women in the 17th century, those sources offer little if any indication of the social or economic status of the subjects. Throughout, where possible, I draw conclusions based on inventories, wills, explicit or implied relationships between women and well-known members of their communities, or their relationship to the print culture of the time. For a discussion of women, and the culture of the book, see below, chapter two.

¹³ See, for instance, Steven Ozment, *Protestants: The Birth of a Revolution* (New York, 1992); Davis, "Some Tasks and Themes in the Study of Popular Religion"; Davis, "City Women and Religious Change"; McGee, *The Godly Man in Stuart England.* For reviews of scholarship which examines popular culture within the broad reform movements of the Reformation and the Counter-Reformation, see Davis, "From 'Popular Religion' to Religious Cultures"; David D. Hall, "Introduction," in Steven L. Kaplan, ed., *Understanding Popular Culture: Europe from the Middle Ages to the Nineteenth Century* (Berlin, 1984).

¹⁴ Carlo Ginzburg, *The Cheese and the Worms: The Cosmos of a Sixteenth-Century Miller,* trans. John and Anne Tedeschi (New York, 1980); Jean Delumeau, *Catholicism Between Luther and Voltaire: A New View of the Counter-Reformation* (London, 1977); John Bossy, "The Counter-Reformation and the People of Catholic Europe," *Past and Present* 47 (May, 1970): 51–70; Michael Walzer, *The Revolution of the Saints* (New York, 1968). Other scholars find the revolutionary nature of the Reformation in the rise of a secular culture. See Miriam U. Chrisman, *Lay Culture, Learned Culture:Books and Social Change in Strasbourg, 1489–1599* (New Haven, 1982); Max Weber, *The Protestant Ethic and the Spirit of Capitalism,* trans. Talcott Parsons (New York, 1958). For a concise overview of historiographic issues on this point, see Ozment, *Protestants,* 32–42 and 218–219. Sec also Merry E. Weisner, "Beyond Women and the Family: Toward a Gender Analysis of the Reformation," *Sixteenth Century Journal* 18 (1987): 311–321 for a discussion of the historiographic trends in the literature of gender and the Reformation.

¹⁵ For a discussion of the spectrum of opinions on the meaning of the Reformation vis a vis Catholicism in women's lives, see above, note 3. See also Davis, "City Women and Religious Change," in Davis, *Society and Culture in Early Modern France* (Stanford, 1975); Margaret Olofson Thickstun, *Fictions of the Feminine: Puritan Doctrine and the Representation of Women* (Ithaca, 1988). Those scholars who have studied Calvin with an eye toward the relationship between gender and doctrine have for the most part concluded that Calvinist doctrine restricted the freedom of women.

¹⁶ John Calvin, *Commentary on the Epistles of Paul to the Corinthians,* trans. Rev. John Pringle (2 vols., Edinburgh, 1848), I, 101; Jane D. Douglass, *Women, Freedom, and Calvin*

(Philadelphia, 1985), 35. Douglass is one of the few scholars to challenge the conventional interpretation of Calvin's writing as conservative and restricting, especially for women. She asks us to consider carefully the contradictions and qualifications in Calvin's work, for while he supported contemporary political and social constraints on women, these stood at odds with his own interpretation of the Bible. See also Douglass, 30–31, 50–51. William J. Bouwsma, a recent biographer of Calvin, acknowledges that Calvin did not believe that gender-based hierarchy was mandated by the need to maintain order in society. It was only one of many possible modes of social organization. In spite of that, Bouwsma focuses on Calvin's view of women as subordinate, weak-willed, fickle, vain, and superficial: Bouwsma, *John Calvin: A Sixteenth-Century Portrait* (New York, 1988) 52–54, 76–77. cf. Bouwsma, 194 and note, 284. For examples of other scholars who stress Calvin's qualified subordination of women, see John Bratt, "The Role and Status of Women in the Writings of John Calvin", in *Renaissance, Reformation, Resurgence* ed. Peter DeKlerk (Grand Rapids, 1976), 1–17; Willis DeBoer, "Calvin on the Role of Women," in *Exploring the Heritage of John Calvin* ed. David E. Holwerda (Grand Rapids, 1976) 236–272; Rita Mancha, "The Woman's Authority: Calvin to Edwards," in *The Journal of Christian Reconstruction* 6 (1979–1980): 86–98.

[17] For a discussion of private and public affirmations of the Calvinist/Reformed notions of equality in the American colonies, see below, chapters two and four.

[18] Several scholars have noted the inadequacy of using the terms "Puritan" and 'Anglican" to express contemporary religious practices. "The word Puritan...," states Christopher Hill, "is an admirable refuge from clarity of thought." Hill, *Society and Puritanism in Pre-Revolutionary England* (London, 1964), 13. For an historiographic review of the English Reformation, see Christopher Haigh, ed., *The English Reformation Revised* (Cambridge, 1987); Rosemary O'Day, *The Debate on the English Reformation* (London, 1986).

[19] On the influence of the Oxford movement on scholarship of the nineteenth and twentieth centuries, see Nigel Yates, *Buildings, Faith, and Worship: Liturgical Arrangement of Anglican Churches, 1600–1900* (Oxford, 1991), 2–3, 7–8.

[20] J.Sears McGee, *The Godly Man in Stuart England: Anglicans, Puritans, and the Two Tables, 1620–1670* (New Haven, 1976), 2–3. McGee suggests that scholars have either underestimated or overestimated the differences between Anglicanism and Puritanism, especially with regard to the role those differences played in the Civil War. McGee's own work has provided a much-needed balance. His careful study of Puritanism and Anglicanism as theological categories, which has done much to shape my own approach to colonial religion, explores the models that each religious tradition provided to those who sought to lead a life of piety.

[21] Patrick Collinson, *The Elizabethan Puritan Movement* (Berkeley, 1967), 26. Also see above, note 20. See also McGee, 242–243, 250; Yates, *Buildings*, 8; Sydney Ahlstrom, *A Religious History of the American People* (New Haven, 1972), 91. For a compelling discussion of the differences between Anglican and Puritan models for the "ideal Christian," see McGee, Chap. 3, "The Two Tables," 67–113.

[22] For a review of demographic evidence regarding the colonial Chesapeake, see Lois Green Carr and Lorena Walsh, "The Planter's Wife: The Experience of White Women in Seventeenth-Century Maryland," in *The Chesapeake in the Seventeenth Century* eds, Thad Tate and David Ammerman (Chapel Hill, 1979); Darrett B, and Anita H. Rutman, "'Now-Wives and Sons-in-Law': Parental Death in a Seventeenth-Century Virginia County," in *The Chesapeake in the Seventeenth Century*; Lorena Walsh, "'Till Death Us Do Part': Marriage

and Family in Seventeenth-Century Maryland," in Tate and Ammerman, eds.; James Horn, "Servant Immigration to the Chesapeake in the Seventeenth Century," in Tate and Ammerman. There are, of course, exceptions to the overall tendency to dismiss the impact of religion on the early history of Virginia, the most cited of which is Perry Miller, "The Religious Impulse in the Founding of Virginia: Religion and Society in Early Literature," *WMQ* 3rd ser. , 5 (1948): 492–522 and 6 (1949): 24–41. Miller is frequently criticized for over-estimating Puritan influence in Virginia (see below, note 23), though in the rush to supersede his interpretation, scholars run the risk of underestimating the variety of religious impulses that constituted Virginia's religious culture. Joan Gunderson has devoted much time and attention to the question of Anglican spirituality in Virginia. She offers a revisionist interpretation that counters the more conventional evangelical criticisms of the Anglican church and clergy, though she is concerned primarily with the eighteenth century. Gunderson, *The Anglican Ministry in Virginia, 1723–1766* (New York, 1989) and Gunderson, "The Non-Institutional Church: The Religious Role of Women in Eighteenth-Century Virginia," *History Magazine of the Protestant Episcopal Church*, 51 (1982): 347–357. See too her article "Kith and Kin: Women's Networks in Colonial Virginia" in Catherine Clinton and Michele Gillespie, eds., *The Devil's Lane: Sex and Race in the Early* South (Oxford and New York, 1997). James Horn suggests that there has been a tendency to overdraw the contrasts between the northern and southern colonies with respect to religiosity, among other measures: *Adapting to a New World*, 8–9. Also see Butler, *Awash in a Sea of Faith*; Bonomi, *Under the Cope of Heaven.*

[23] Several historians have acknowledged Puritan influences in Virginia Anglicanism, though none to my knowledge has studied the religious culture with respect to gender. See, for example, George Maclaren Brydon, *Virginia's Mother Church and the Political Conditions Under Which It Grew* (Richmond, 1947) 8–9, 20–29, 119–122. Though certainly an apologist's account of the Anglican Church in Virginia, Brydon's book remains one of the best narrative sources, full of useful evidence, and a much-needed balance to those evangelical accounts which categorically dismissed Virginia Anglicanism. Also see Ahlstrom, *A Religious History of the American People*, 185; John Frederick Woolverton, *Colonial Anglicanism in North America* (Detroit, 1984). Woolverton, an Episcopal minister, sees colonial Anglicanism as a breed apart, shaped by early laicization, Puritan ministries, and a singular lack of "theological explicitness." Woolverton, 21. See also 74–76 on laicization. And see Babette M. Levy, "Early Puritans in the Southern and Island Colonies," *American Antiquarian Society Proceedings* 70 (1960): pt.1, 69–348.

[24] For studies which examine Virginia's transition to slave labor and tobacco culture see Edmund Morgan, *American Slavery, American Freedom: The Ordeal of Colonial Virginia* (New York,1975); Allan Kulikoff, *Tobacco and Slaves:The Development of Southern Culture in the Chesapeake, 1680–1800* (Chapel Hill, 1986; T. H. Breen, *Tobacco Culture: The Mentality of the Great Tidewater Planters on the Eve of Revolution* (Princeton, 1985); Breen, "A Changing Labor Force and Race Relations in Virginia, 1660–1710," *Journal of Social History* 7 (1972), 3–25; Kevin P. Kelly, "'In Dispers'd Plantations': Settlement Pattern in Seventeenth-Century Surry County,Virginia," in *The Chesapeake in the Seventeenth Century: Essays on Anglo-American Society* eds. Thad Tate and David L. Ammerman; Darrett B. and Anita H. Rutman, *A Place in Time: Middlesex County, Virginia, 1650–1750* (New York, 1984); Russell R. Menard, "From Servants to Slaves: The Transformation of the Chesapeake Labor System," *Southern Studies* 16 (1977): 355–390. For rich descriptions of activities and

rituals surrounding church and court days eighteenth-century Virginia, see Rhys Isaac, *The Transformation of Virginia, 1740–1790* (Chapel Hill, 1982). Isaac contends that Sunday services were indeed one of the key moments of community affirmation, though women are sorely neglected in his analysis.

[25] I owe a great intellectual debt here and throughout the dissertation to the work of J. Sears McGee. In his effort to answer the question "are the terms 'Anglican' and 'Puritan' useful?," McGee created a compelling and workable structure for his analysis by using the Two Tables as a guide to the differences between the Anglican and Puritan models for the ideal Christian. Though his book makes no real attempt to address the way religion was *experienced* as a result of these differences—most of his evidence was drawn from clerical treatises, sermons, and tracts—it has proved tremendously useful to me as I sort out the differences between the ways women experienced religion in each of the three colonies. McGee, *The Godly Man in Stuart England*, especially chapter three.

[26] For examples of the "declension" interpretation associated with economic changes in New England in the mid-seventeenth century, see Miller, *The New England Mind*; Richard Bushman, *From Puritan to Yankee* (New York, 1970). For attempts to counter the declension interpretation, see Christine Heyrmann, *Commerce and Culture* (New York, 1984); Stout, *The New England Soul*; Bonomi, *Under the Cope of Heaven*; Robert G. Pope, "New England Versus the New England Mind: The Myth of Declension," *Journal of Social History* 3. For an analysis of church attendance as it relates to the notion of declension, see Patricia Bonomi and Peter Eisenstadt, "Church Adherence in the Eighteenth-Century British American Colonies," *WMQ*, 3d ser., 39 (1982), 245–286. For a discussion of Puritanism's appeal to New England women, see Amanda Porterfield, "Women's Attraction to Puritanism," *Church History* 60, #2 (June, 1991): 196–209. For examples of recent work which attempts to balance the more prevalent interpretations of Puritan repression with its more positive impact, see Charles Hambrick-Stowe, *The Practice of Piety: Puritan Devotional Disciplines in Seventeenth-Century New England*, (Chapel Hill, 1986) and Charles Lloyd Cohen, *God's Caress: The Psychology of the Puritan Religious Experience* (New York, 1986), though neither of these studies pays particular attention to the role of gender. For examples of those scholars who have taken note of the importance of religion in women's lives in colonial New England, see above, note 5.

[27] See especially Goodfriend, *Before the Melting Pot: Society and Culture in Colonial New York City, 1664–1730* (Princeton, 1991). See also Goodfriend, "Recovering the Religious History of Dutch Reformed Women in Colonial New York," *de Halve Maen*, LXIV (Winter, 1991). Goodfriend writes in direct response to historian Randall Balmer, who found that English culture virtually eclipsed the Dutch by the Revolutionary era. Both Goodfriend's work and this study suggest that if we look at the role of women in the Dutch Church we might wish to modify Balmer's interpretation of Reformed declension in the face of English political hegemony. See Randall Herbert Balmer, *A Perfect Babel of Confusion: Dutch Religion and English Culture in the Middle Colonies* (New York, 1989). Regarding a similar cultural confrontation in Albany, see Donna Merwick, *Possessing Albany, 1630–1710: The Dutch and English Experiences* (Cambridge, 1990). See also Firth Fabend, *A Dutch Family in the Middle Colonies, 1660–1800* (New Brunswick, N.J., 1991). Faband examines in detail the social, political, economic, and religious forces that shaped one family's history in the Hudson Valley.

Part I

FAITH AND SELF: GENDER AND THE PROTESTANT SELF-IMAGE

Chapter One
"IN THE BEGINNING": GENDER AND THE ESTABLISHMENT OF PROTESTANT CULTURE IN EARLY AMERICA

> He saith, women are froward, which the rib doth declare,
> For like as the rib, so crooked they are:
> The rib was her subject for body we find,
> But from God came her soul, and dispose of her mind.[1]

FEMALE PROTESTANTS THE WORLD OVER WOULD HAVE UNDERSTOOD THE GENDERED description of piety penned by Joan Sharpe, whose pamphlet "A Defense of Woman . . ." was published in London in 1617. Regardless of the source of a woman's body, her soul and her mind came from and belonged to God. The Reformation reinvigorated the concept of soul equality; if a pious woman could expect to stand alongside men in heaven, then she was duty-bound to conduct herself on earth according to standards set by God alone.[2] In order to adhere to those standards—to please God, to protect her own soul and that of her family and the community—a Protestant woman could expect to express and act on her piety in both private and public. In her struggle to maintain a pious life, the Protestant woman often acted with strength and autonomy unexpected of her sex in the seventeenth century. Within the context of a pious life, the Protestant woman thus challenged contemporary notions of female subservience.

Like the Protestant men who journeyed to America, Protestant women arrived with certain expectations about the practice of piety in their daily lives. Once they settled on American soil, however, English and Dutch Protestants confronted a religious culture that was shaped as much by peculiarities of colonial demography, geography, and regional influences as it was by preconceived theological notions. As Massachusetts, New Netherland, and Virginia each struggled to create a solid foundation for its predominant Protestant denomination, it became clear that no religious group could simply recreate itself in its English or Dutch image.[3]

Within the bounds of this uniquely American Protestantism, women identified new ways to express their piety. Congregational, Dutch Reformed, and Anglican women learned to navigate patriarchal waters, to express their religious convictions in unfamiliar environments and in unconventional ways. Though they carried with them specific denominational prescriptions that helped to shape their worship practices in the New World, little about their public or private religious experiences exactly replicated what they had left behind. In all three colonies, as Protestant men and women expressed concern over the spiritual health of their families and communities, they adjusted old patterns of worship to reflect and conform to specific colonial conditions.

"YOU, MADAM, WILL BE A HAPPY INSTRUMENT FOR THE HONOUR AND WELLFAIRE OF VIRGINIA . . ."

When Virginia Ferrar wrote those words to Lady Berkeley, wife of the Virginia's governor, there was little doubt in her mind that her friend would be an active architect of what she called a "Noble Christian Designe."[4] Despite Ferrar's conviction that the colony's honor was inextricably linked to its spiritual health, three and a half centuries later few scholars acknowledge the centrality of religion in seventeenth-century Virginia. Amidst discussions of dire ministerial shortages, sparsely populated counties, and dramatically skewed gender ratios, historians have often assumed that if it existed at all, Protestant faith and spirituality were at best lukewarm in Virginia. Yet those very conditions cited by some scholars as barriers to the planting of religion in fact laid the foundation for what was perhaps the most "exceptional" of all colonial Protestant cultures.[5]

Few would question that Virginia's founders and its earliest settlers expected to plant religion there. Both the Virginia Company and the crown recognized that the Church of England by necessity would have to play a role in the maintenance of social order and control in a colony settled so great a distance from the mother country. Among the earliest laws established by the Virginia Company, and in the royal charter granted in 1624, were a variety of statutes addressing the religious needs and health of the population. Beginning with the first settlements, colonial leaders enacted laws pertaining to ministers' duties, attendance at weekly sermons, births and baptisms, marriage, communion, catechism, and scandalous behavior.[6]

For all of that, however, the religion that settlers planted in Virginia was far from the high church Anglicanism scholars are wont to compare it to. What resulted in Virginia was a religion more fluid and malleable than that practiced in England's urban high churches; if it could be compared to any form of English Anglicanism, it most closely resembled religious practice in England's more rural villages, what one historian has called "folklorized Christianity." The 1624 act of the Virginia Assembly mandating uniformity in the church and adherence to the canons of the Church of England included the phrase "as neere as may be," acknowledging the difficulties the church would face reinventing itself in the New World.[7]

The fluidity of religious culture in Virginia resulted from four interrelated conditions, each of which allowed for varying degrees of female autonomy in the private and public sphere: the religious heterogeneity among colonists and in their established churches; the increase in power of the church vestry, the county court, and other local lay authorities; ministerial dearth; and demographic and geographic conditions that shaped both where and how religion flowered.

Several prominent historians have written monographs on the strength of Puritanism in early Virginia.[8] In fact, though several of England's "hotter sort" of ministers made Virginia their home, the colony attracted ministers from a wide spectrum of Anglican churches. Mass conformity to specific church ritual was no more a facet of popular religious culture in Virginia than it was in England.[9] As early as 1620, John Porey, a member of the Virginia Company, complained to its treasurer, Sir Edwin Sandys, that one colonial minister, Mr. Chesterton, "smells too much of Rome," while at the same time King James I denounced the Virginia Company as the "seminary of a seditious Parliament."[10] While several of Virginia's earliest ministers were trained at the non-conformist colleges of Cambridge, Anglican colonist Alexander Whitaker, in a letter to his cousin in London in 1614, wondered "that so few of our English Ministers that were so hot against the Surplis and subscription, come hither where neither are spoken of." Virginia Protestant culture varied dramatically from parish to parish.[11]

Like their ministers, Virginia colonists brought with them both high and low church traditions. Though Royal Governor William Berkeley instituted measures to insure conformity to the Church of England, and several parish churches sought to replicate high church rituals, by the 1640s Puritan sympathizers gathered in Upper and Lower Norfolk Counties, in Nancemond and Isle of Wight Counties, and in other pockets along the banks of the James River. Quakers settled Norfolk and York counties in the middle years of the century. In addition, nonconformist numbers swelled in Virginia with the arrival of Huguenot refugees after the revocation of the Edict of Nantes in France. And while Governor Berkeley attempted to control nonconformity in the colony as a whole—ironically, his attacks were the most vigorous during the Interregnum—without the support of a local episcopacy or an ecclesiastical court, "seditious sectaries" thrived alongside high church settlers who "smelled of Rome." One early visitor to the colony reported to a colleague in England that there was an "unhappie dissention fallen out" among settlers, "by reason of their minister, who being, as they say, somewhat a puritan, the most part refused to go to his service to hear his sermons, though by the other part he was supposed favored." The result was a Reformation culture that offered a variety of freedoms to its practitioners, including its women.[12]

The opportunity to exercise religious freedom was enhanced by the lack of commitment to maintaining Virginia's religious health on the part of the government in England, from the king and Archbishop Laud to parliament and Cromwell. This "benign neglect" with respect to colonial church affairs persisted through the Restoration period. Local authorities stepped into the vacuum. Increasingly, church vestries and county courts oversaw devotional practice and mediated conflicts that in England would have been handled by ecclesiastical authorities. And though women could hold seats on neither the vestry nor county or quarter courts, they soon found that those institutions provided effective forums in which to air and redress grievances, especially those grievances inspired by, or at least couched in, moral and religious language.[13]

The opportunities for lay men and women to shape and define religious practice and language in Virginia were enlarged by a periodic dearth of ministers in its parishes. Though colonists had established twelve churches by 1634, and another fifty by 1668, most parishes were forced to rely at one time or another—and sometimes for long periods—on lay readers. In 1680, of the thirty-five ministers serving in Virginia, several were responsible for services in more than one parish, two were serving parishes in more than one county, and one or two parishes were served by lay readers alone. In 1692, councilman Hugh Campbell noted that settlers in parts of Isle of Wight, Nancemond, and Norfolk Counties, "liveing att great Distances from any Churches or Chappells very Seldome have the oppertunity to bee att the publick worship of God." Cambell, "conceiving it would tend to the more Christian Liveing," directed that a lay reader be appointed every Sabbath "to Read prayers and a Sarmon Espicalay in the winter When it is Impossibell for them to goe to Church." As parishes in England scrambled to place ministers in the wake of the Restoration, the shortage in Virginia became increasingly acute. As late as 1707 the Society for the Propagation of the Gospel noted that fifteen parishes lacked ordained ministers.[14]

In the face of such ministerial dearth, colonists in some parishes agreed to raise substantial sums to secure a clerical leader (though disputes often arose between ministers and parishioners when the time came to actually pay the salary). In his request to John Ferrar in England to secure "Two or three more Orthodox Ministers" for Virginia, Edward Johnson assured his colleague that the ministers need not "Feare the Double Honour of Maintenance and respect: besides they shall be helped in any things that possibly may be acquired for there better welcome." In 1640, inhabitants of Norfolk County's Sewells Pointe, anxious to attract a suitable minister "to instructe them concerninge their soules health," agreed to pay Thomas Harrison one hundred pounds a year, to "testifie their zeale and willingness to promote gods service." The appointment of Harrison was not without conflict, however, a result of competing interests in churches located vast distances apart within the parish. The residents of Daniel Tanner's Creek, who agreed to shoulder thirty-six pounds of the minister's salary, did so only on the condition that "hee shall teach and Instruct them as often as hee shall teach at the pshe church...at Mr Sewells Pointe."[15]

Most scholars have cited ministerial dearth as a factor which contributed to an allegedly weak religious culture in Virginia. It is misleading, however, to assume that colonists practiced their faith and sought spiritual comfort only in those churches presided over by an ordained cleric; to do so betrays a narrow definition of religious experience and strips colonists—men and women—of the ability to adapt their spirituality to local conditions. Moreover, given the fluidity of Virginia's religious culture and the impact of nonconformity on religious practice, male and female parishioners often accepted the puritan-influenced notion of a voluntary, gathered church whose members might seek grace without the services of a minister. In 1648, residents of Elizabeth River Parish in Norfolk County turned to lay preacher William Durand, whose meetings attracted large numbers of people, "men women and children," who "assembled and mett together in the Church or Chapell of Elizabeth River." The sheriff, instructed by the court to stop Durand from preaching, testified that he found Durand "in the Deske Reading place...where as aloe in the pullpitt he hath customarily by the space of these three moneth...preached to the said people." The assembled worshippers were read a proclamation ordering them to disperse; two county commissioners who worshipped among the others refused to help the sheriff suppress Durand.[16]

With regard to gender issues especially, one could argue that the laicization of the Anglican church in Virginia mitigated the impact of the colony's male centered hierarchy and encouraged women to explore new avenues for autonomy. Without the continual guidance of an ordained minister, the use of lay readers reinforced the Calvinist conviction that all Protestants were capable of reading, comprehending, and sharing the gospel, whether in a public religious setting or in the privacy of their own homes.[17]

Just as ministerial dearth reinforced the importance of private, home-based worship in Virginia, demographic and geographic conditions in the colony also heightened religious autonomy. In spite of a rapid growth in population—from 8,000 in 1640 to 30,000 by 1670—colonists were dispersed over large areas, without a population sufficiently concentrated in any one county to support an adequate number of churches or ministers. Moreover, the colony's long, wide river estuaries created what amounted to a series of peninsulas. As a result, several Virginia parishes were as much as sixty miles long. In 1662, the Lancaster County Court "taking into consideracon the want of the Ministry that hath been in this Countie, and con[ceiv]ing it to arise from the smallness of the parishes, not able to give such a competency as may in[duce] mynisters to officiate amongst us," ordered the county's constables to arrange for a meeting place—if not in a church than in some other fitting place—and to act as readers for each parish "till such time as they may be able to maintain a minister themselves." As late as 1719, the vestry in one Virginia parish noted that some of its parishioners were "Seated very remote from the Upper church" and recommended that the minister preach at least one a month "on the Frontiers." In 1700 the vestry of St. Peter's Parish acknowledged the need to construct a second church as "the Lower Church Standeth very inconvenient for most of the Inhabitants." Five weeks later the "upper Inhabitants," perhaps weary of waiting for the vestry to take action on the matter, submitted a petition asking that "they may have a place apointed and preaching amongst them."[18]

Though colonists sought communal, church-based religious experiences, served by either ministers or lay readers, parishioners expected to discover and foster spirituality in the privacy of their homes as well. As one historian has noted, neither the shortage of ministers nor the distance from the churches necessarily meant the collapse of religion in Virginia; rather, religion in that colony took on a new and unique prominence at home. And the home—in Virginia, as in Massachusetts and New York—was frequently the domain of women. There, as wives and mothers, they shouldered responsibility for the education of their families. There too, as pious Christians, they established a personal relationship with their God, with countless examples of Biblical women to guide them.[19]

In addition to the dispersal of churches and a dearth of ministers, a dramatic sexual imbalance also contributed to women's authority with regard to their domestic religious experience. The ratio of men to women in the earliest migration was high, six to one in 1630. Though the proportion of women increased over the course of the seventeenth century, the ratio remained over two to one in 1700. The competition for wives—who, if they survived their childbearing years, were likely to outlive their husbands—was fierce. Relative to their position in England, Virginia women wielded more influence at home, in church, and in their communities.[20] Just as demographic destabilization resulted for a time in women assuming greater legal and mercantile autonomy in Virginia as compared with England, so too did it result in greater religious independence for women. That more prominent religious role persisted for women in Virginia even as the legal and mercantile patriarchy reasserted itself by the end of the seventeenth century.[21]

THE ESTABLISHMENT OF THE DUTCH CHURCH IN NEW NETHERLAND

Though doctrinally more closely aligned with the Congregational church in Massachusetts, the religious culture in New Netherland shared similarities with that of Anglican Virginia as well. A shortage of trained ministers, periodic neglect on the part of a mother country contending with political conflicts in Europe, and an atmosphere of religious toleration and diversity all contributed to the development of a religion shaped as much by popular practice as by strict adherence to the teachings of the Dutch Reformed Church. Drawing on notions of piety similar to those of their Calvinist neighbors to the north, and a sense of authority derived from their role as keepers and transmitters of a religious culture threatened by political upheaval, Dutch women in New Netherland found a voice in events and places traditionally identified as male-dominated.[22]

Like Virginia colonists, New Netherland's earliest settlers incorporated religious impulses into their first laws, and saw to the establishment of a state-sponsored church. By 1628 the Dutch West India Company—which obtained its charter for New Netherland in 1621—had established the Dutch Reformed religion in the colony and arranged for the services of two "comforters of the sick," assigned "to read to the commonality . . . on Sundays, text of the scripture and the commentaries." Within the year, New Netherland's first minister, Jonas Michaelius, had arrived. Soon after his arrival, he gathered his church for the first administration of the Lord's Supper, "which was observed not without great joy and comfort to many." Residents, long deprived of the sacrament, were anxious to establish it in New Amsterdam. As Michaelius reported, "fully fifty communicants—Walloons and Dutch" celebrated that first ordinance. Magistrates sworn in to the colony's court at Fort Orange in 1657 vowed to "maintain here the Reformed Religion according to God's word and the regulations of the Synod of Dordrecht, and not tolerate publicly any sects."[23]

Though most of New Netherland's first ministers had been trained in Calvinist universities in the Netherlands, they, like the population they served, represented a broad spectrum of religious beliefs, from the most orthodox to the most liberal. Tensions soon arose within the Dutch church, as each side grappled with just how to configure their religious institutions in the new colony. In addition, pressures from outside the Dutch church threatened to undermine what little cohesion ministers were able to encourage in their communities; New Netherland from the outset was among the most diverse colonies. As the Jesuit priest Isaac Jogues noted in the 1640s, though "no religion is publically exercised but the Calvinist . . . there are in the colony Catholics, English Puritans, Lutherans, Anabaptists, here called [Mennonites] etc." In 1671 the deacons of the Dutch church in New York complained that their coffers were being drained in the care of poor Lutherans; they accused Lutheran deacons of mismanaging funds. They brought their complaint to the court, which ordered "that each Church should for the future Maintaine theire owne Poore."[24]

The Dutch church itself fostered heterogeneity by admitting a high percentage of non-Dutch worshippers to its ranks. German, French, English, and Scandinavian Protestants joined the Dutch in Sabbath-day services. In 1628, the Reverend Jonas Michaelius acknowledged that "the Walloons and French have no service on Sundays, otherwise than in the Dutch language, for those who understand no Dutch are very few." Michaelius did make some attempt to accommodate cultural differences; he noted that "the Lord's Supper is administered to them in the French language, and according to the French mode, with a sermon preceding, which I have before me in writing." Later in the century, the Reverend Samuel Drisius wrote to the Amsterdam Classis that every two months he traveled to Staten Island to preach and administer the Lord's Supper to French families there.[25]

Confronted with such vast diversity, Dutch women and men struggled to maintain their religious traditions. And though Dutch colonists are accused by scholars of being "indifferent" to religion, evidence suggests that, far from indifferent, Dutch Protestants in New Netherland adapted their piety to the colony's unique conditions and fought at every turn to control the direction their religious culture would take. Women played a large role in those battles.[26]

Dutch men and women often struggled to sustain their religious traditions without the support of a properly ordained clergy. From the outset, New Netherland, like Virginia, was plagued by a perpetual shortage of ministers and profound professional inconsistencies among those who at last arrived to serve the colony's diverse population. In Albany in 1681, residents wrote to the Amsterdam Classis to request a minister to assist the Rev. Gideon Schaets, old and infirm. Though Schaets provided some comfort to his congregation, they lamented so "small number of laborers for so large a harvest." The Classis, they prayed, would "take pity on us in this our emergency, and see that a proper person shall be sent over, who will feed our congregation, consisting already of 400 members." Throughout the seventeenth century, ministers were required to serve more than one congregation, and were sometimes asked to tend to settlements many miles apart, on schedules to be determined jointly by the minister and the colony's governor.[27]

Dutch congregations frequently exerted pressure on their ministers to serve them more often or at more convenient locations. For instance, when Director General Kieft in 1654 called upon the Amsterdam Classis to provide a minister for the towns of western Long Island—Midwout (Flatbush), Brooklyn, and Amersfort—the congregation in Brooklyn complained that they hardly got their money's worth. Reverend Johannes Polhemus, they claimed, served his hometown of Flatbush most thoroughly, reserving little time or energy for his other congregations. By the time he arrived to preach in Brooklyn, he rendered "a prayer instead of a sermon, that was finished before they could collect their thoughts, so that he gives small edification to the congregation." When the governor and the Classis subsequently ordered Polhemus to alternate preaching between the three towns, the congregations at Amersfort and Gravesend lodged their own complaints. After months of squabbling, the Reverend Henricus Selyns arrived to answer the needs of the Brooklyn congregation, provided that he also agree to preach for Governor Stuyvesant and local residents at the Bouwerie on Sunday evenings.[28]

So prevalent was the ministerial shortage that New Netherland's early ecclesiastical regulations included specific instructions for comforters of the sick, who were to be allowed "on the Lord's Day and on other proper occasions, to deliver sermons out of God's Word, for the instruction, admonition, comfort and further enlightening (or easing) of the people." In 1670 the Dutch Church in Manhattan reported that, in the absence of a minister, "each Sunday morning and afternoon, the usual prayers are offered, and the Word of God and a sermon are read by the chorister, Evert Pieterse." As they complained to the Amsterdam Classis, they were "destitute of preaching and the regular administration of the Sacraments." Like their Anglican neighbors to the south, Dutch Protestants in New Netherland were accustomed to sharing their Sabbath worship with lay readers, whose presence enhanced the Calvinist belief that each congregant belonged to "a priesthood of all believers." Dutch worshippers—regardless of sex or status—saw that they needed no ordained minister to establish a house of the Lord; their personal relationship with God transcended church walls and ecclesiastical hierarchy.[29]

Without the support of a sufficient number of trained clergy, however, the pressures generated by New Netherland's cultural diversity often loomed large.

Civic leaders struggled to maintain control of lay worship, fearing that the increase in conventicles and unauthorized preaching signaled grave denominational schism and heresy. In 1656, New Amsterdam's Director General and the City Council articulated their concern that "unqualified persons in such mtgs assume the ministerial office, expounding and explaining the word of God without being called or appointed thereto by ecclesiastical or civil authority." As a result, they forbade all conventicles and meetings "whether public or private, differing from the customary and not only lawful but scripturally founded and ordained mtgs." The Council made it clear, however, that they did not intend to constrain private conscience; they encouraged the continued "reading of God's holy word, family prayers and worship, each in his household."[30]

Fears of religious degeneration intensified with the conquest of New Netherland by the English in 1664. All aspects of Dutch culture—language, religion, law—were threatened as the English established supremacy in the colony. In spite of the Articles of Capitulation, instituted to guarantee the Dutch the right to liberty of conscience and public worship, New York ministers informed the Amsterdam Classis that "the particular circumstances of our churches are such that they cannot expect much help from the civil authorities here, or from the government of such a nation . . . .They differ much in spirit, form of Church Government, and usages."[31]

A number of historians have concluded that Dutch culture—including religion—faded and ultimately disappeared in the face of English conquest.[32] While there is little question that the English conquest of New Netherland exacerbated long-standing tensions between the two nations, New Netherlanders found in the Dutch Reformed Church an effective institution through which to preserve Dutch culture. Amidst increasing heterogeneity church membership remained one of the strongest supports for ethnic identity. And, as subsequent chapters will demonstrate, Dutch women played an active and key role in attempts to protect, preserve, and purvey their religious culture. It was, I will argue, a mantle they assumed with relative ease. Colonial religious conditions enhanced Protestant notions of the power and responsibility of a lay priesthood. Those notions, played out during times of intense cultural conflict, resulted in women assuming active roles in their homes and communities.[33]

"NOT THE MINISTERS ALONE MUST WORKE HERE, BUT THE CHURCH WITH HIM . . ."[34]

Nowhere did these words of Puritan Dudley Fenner's—a testament to the importance of communalism—ring more true than in New England. And nowhere were they as fraught with meaning for women. Though Fenner referred in his treatise specifically to the communalism of the Lord's Supper, his words echo throughout the religious culture of seventeenth-century Massachusetts.[35]

Communalism—the presumption that the strength of the church depended directly upon collective ownership of and responsibility for the covenant—combined with the Calvinist position on soul equality to create a religious culture that encouraged women to exert their opinions both publicly and privately. In addition, conditions peculiar to colonial settlements in Massachusetts fostered an environment in which women were free to accept the rights and responsibilities of membership in the "priesthood of all believers."

According to Calvinist theology, the gathered church needed neither walls nor a minister. Its legitimacy depended only on the consent of its members, who, by their very nature, would be knowledgeable in their faith. Under the conditions of a gathered church, godly men and women determined the shape and meaning of church membership, a responsibility they shared with their clergy. The power to identify and separate the pure from the corrupt rested in lay as well as clerical hands.[36]

Nowhere did the differences between pure and corrupt seem as stark—and as grounded in experience—as they were in New England in the 1630s, among Puritans who had embarked on the treacherous journey across the vast Atlantic. Many of the "hotter sort" of men and women who migrated to the colony in the years before the English Civil War did so firm in the belief that theirs was the way of the righteous; though not all colonists had chosen to separate entirely from the Church of England, most agreed that the purity of the church could no longer be sustained in their mother country.[37]

For many men and women, the journey itself proved to be a transforming experience, laden with symbolic meaning for both the individual and the community . Theirs had been a cleansing voyage, a test of their will to pursue a covenant with God as individual saints and within a gathered church. Confessions of conversion experiences—required for admission into membership in many early Massachusetts churches—are filled with references to the trials endured during the crossing, and the impact of such experiences on a hopeful saint's worldview. Goodwife Stevenson, a member of Thomas Shepard's Cambridge congregation, confessed in 1648 that "having way made to New England, I desired God would glorify himself by my coming." Dorcas Downey, a member of the same congregation, related that "when I came in ship, many [were] afflicted with disease and pestilence, and I prayed for sparing till I came to this place. And when I was here I rejoiced to live here." Richard Eccles revealed both the symbolic and literal weight of his ocean passage when he confessed, "by sea I was sick and at land I did not find that delight in His company and fellowship. But . . . although my soul did doubt, yet my soul was a ship at anchor." Mr. Haynes acknowledged in his relation that "we had some sad expressions of God's providences in our passage hither when, if we had perished in storms, I thought I should go to hell. But after the storms I went on as before." Women and men alike shared the experience of the passage. The responsibility and authority to gather a church and form a covenant rested with all hopeful saints, regardless of sex.[38]

Membership in the church covenant was by its nature lay-defined. Because the legitimacy of the church depended on the consent of its members, the opportunity to establish a new church in the wilderness—with or without the aid of an ordained minister—must have been especially liberating and empowering. Though clerical shortages were not nearly as acute in early Massachusetts as they were in New Netherland or Virginia, most colonists experienced a period of lay control in the months between a minister's calling and his ordination. Godly men and women gathered in private homes to study scripture and pray in the months before the minister arrived. Home and neighborhood meetings, which often persisted after a minister's ordination, were vital to the establishment and organization of a church in most Massachusetts towns in the seventeenth century. Women both hosted and led these meetings.[39]

Though John Brock, a minister, perhaps in a fit of pique at a family member, proclaimed, "sisters are not so prudent in their Meetings. . . . My Sister El. is not so humble or heavenly," most colonists accepted the presence of women's private meetings. In spite of the decision by Massachusetts magistrates to abolish female leadership of mixed-sex meetings in the aftermath of the trial of Anne Hutchinson in 1636–1637, women's private prayer meetings persisted. On a December Friday in 1706 Cotton Mather wrote "the Afternoon of this Day, I visited a Society of devout Women, who were keeping this, as a Day of private and solemn *Thanksgiving* unto God." Mather prayed with the women, and preached to them out of I Sam. 2:1. His choice of biblical passage was most appropriate, for the verses extol Hannah's supplication to God.[40]

❊ ❊ ❊

In 1690, another Hannah offered her prayers to God, deep in the Maine wilderness, far from the relative safety and comfort of a Massachusetts prayer meeting. Hannah Swarton, taken captive by Indians from her home on Casco Bay, feared her captivity was a punishment for having left her church and minister in Beverly, Massachusetts to settle on the Maine frontier. Her punishment, however, was a blessing, not unlike the blessings experienced by New England's earliest settlers on their passage to the New World; the days and nights lived in fear and isolation left Hannah with a vision of God's grace and the authority she might derive from that grace. "I had very often a secret persuasion," Hannah wrote, "that I should live to declare the works of the Lord. And 2 Chron. 6. 36,37,38,39 was a precious scripture to me in the day of evil. We [Hannah and a fellow captive, Margaret Stilson] have read over and prayed over this scripture . . . and talked together . . . how the Lord had promised though they were scattered for their sins yet there should be a return if they did bethink themselves and turn and pray."[41]

Captivity narratives, like that written by Hannah Swarton, were among the texts second- and third-generation Puritan divines employed to combat what they perceived as declension. Though the audience ministers hoped to attract to their churches had in large part been born in New England, and had no first-hand experience with the fear, hope, and faith that drove their parents or grandparents to abandon England's unholy shores, ministers recognized that captivity stories might recreate the powerful pull of the spiritual journey and reiterate the gap between the corrupt and the pure, the spiritually lazy and the pilgrim.[42]

The pilgrims in these narratives, most frequently women, valiantly struggled to escape their impure captors. Through their trials, they hoped to find or regain their covenant with God. Held aloft by ministers as examples of the power of faith to lead the Christian to a better place, these women exhibited many of the same qualities found in the earliest settlers: they prayed, alone or with fellow captives, with no minister to guide them. Theirs was a "gathered church," as holy as any led by a minister. God, they knew, would hear their prayers in the wilderness. Moreover, like the earliest pilgrims to America, they recognized that their pilgrimages bestowed upon them the responsibility to bring evidence of God's grace back to their settlements. For like Hannah Swarton, women who settled the colonies in the seventeenth century were persuaded that they "should live to declare the works of the Lord."

NOTES

[1] Joan Sharpe, "A Defense of Women Against the Author of the Arraignment of Women" (London, 1617), in Angeline Goreau, ed., *The Whole Duty of a Woman: Female Writers in Seventeenth-Century England* (Garden City, N.Y., 1985), 81.

[2] On the origins and meaning of soul equality, see above, introduction.

[3] For a discussion of the concept of colonial exceptionalism as it applies to religion, see Patricia U. Bonomi, "Religious Dissent and the Case for American Exceptionalism," in *Religion in a Revolutionary Age*, eds. Ronald Hoffman and Peter J. Albert (Charlottesville, 1994), 31–51.

[4] Virginia Ferrar to Lady Berkeley, 10 August 1650, Ferrar Papers, Virginia Colonial Records Project, Reel 573. Virginia Ferrar (1626–1687) learned the art of silkworm cultivation from her father and brought the skill with her to Virginia. Though most of the Ferrar family remained in England, they had many ties to the colony, initially through the Virginia Company: Ibid., Reel 573; See also A. M. Williams, ed., *Conversations at Little Gidding* (Cambridge, 1970), xiii-xvi.

[5] Bonomi, "Religious Dissent and the Case for American Exceptionalism," 48. For an opposing viewpoint on the issue of American exceptionalism, see James Horn, *Adapting to a New World: English Society in the Seventeenth-Century Chesapeake* (Charlottesville, 1994), 10, 15, and *passim*.

[6] See, for instance, George Maclaren Brydon, *Virginia's Mother Church and the Political Conditions under Which it Grew* (Richmond, 1947), 424–425; William Hening, ed., *Statutes at Large: Being a Collection of All the Laws of Virginia* vol. 1 (New York, 1823), 155–160.

[7] Barry Reay, "Popular Religion," in *Popular Culture in Seventeenth-Century England*, ed. Barry Reay (London and Sydney, 1985), 111.

[8] See Introduction, note 23.

[9] For a discussion of the flexibility of the post-reformation Church of England, see Patrick Collinson, *The Religion of the Protestants*, 282, and Barry Reay, "Popular Religion," 94.

[10] John Porey to Sir Edwin Sandys, June, 1620, Ferrar Papers, Virginia Colonial Records Project, reel 573; Sydney Ahlstrom, *A Religious History of the American People* (New Haven, 1972), 185, 187.

[11] Quoted in Brydon, *Virginia's Mother Church*, 24. J.F. Woolverton notes that by 1680 Virginia had attracted 107 ministers, most graduates of Cambridge's Puritan colleges or Magdalen College at Oxford. Woolverton, *Colonial Anglicanism in North America* (Detroit, 1984), 37. As late as 1697 Anglican minister Nicholas Moreau complained to a colleague in England that "Your clergy in these parts are of a very ill example, no discipline or Canons of the Church are observed. Chamberlayne, C.G., ed., *Vestry Book of St. Peter's Parish* (Richmond, 1927), 619. Joan Gunderson has written of eighteenth-century Virginia Anglicans that they stressed a "practical morality" in the face of the influence of other Protestant denominations. This religious "middle ground," she posits, contributed to a unique form of Anglican spiritualism: Gunderson, *The Anglican Ministry in Virginia, 1723-1766 A Study of Social Class* (New York, 1989), 160. Thomas C. Parramore notes that even within the bounds of one parish, religious sentiments might shift from decade to decade. Early in the history of Norfolk County, Lynnhaven Parish was served by the Oxford-educated Anglican priest William Wilkinson. In 1640 Wilkenson abandoned his post, "opening the way for the spread of more solidly non-conformist practices." : *Norfolk: The First Four Centuries* (Charlottesville and London, 1994), 31–32.

[12] [John] Beaulieu to William Trumbull, 1613 (?), VCRP, Reel 554, Parish Records; Horn, *Adapting to a New World*, 389–392; Brydon, *Virginia's Mother Church*, 119–122; Edward James, ed. *Lower Norfolk Virginia Antiquary*, vol. 2, 83; Thomas C. Parramore, *Norfolk: The First Four Centuries*, 31–34; Louis Manarin and Clifford Dowdy, *The History of Henrico County* (Charlottesville, 1984), 72. On Quakers in early Virginia see Kathleen M. Brown, *Good Wives, Nasty Wenches, and Anxious Patriarchs: Gender, Race, and Power in Colonial Virginia* (Chapel Hill, 1996), 141–144; Susie M. Ames, *Studies of Virginia's Eastern Shore in the Seventeenth Century* (Richmond, 1940), 231–241.

[13] See below, chapters six and seven. On the development of local mechanisms to monitor religion and morality—especially the church vestry and civil court system—see for instance Brydon, *Virginia's Mother Church*, 67–68, 87–88, 125–144; Woolverton, *Colonial Anglicanism*, 15–21; Manarin and Dowdy, *The History of Henrico County*, 37, 63–64; Horn, *Adapting to a New World*, 406. For a thorough description of the development of the Virginia General Assembly, Council, Quarter and county court system see Warren Billings, John Selby, and Thad Tate, *Colonial Virginia* (White Plains, 1986), 69–73.

[14] Edward James, ed., *Lower Norfolk Virginia Antiquary* (5 vols., 1895–1904), I, 65–6. For statistics on numbers of ministers/parishes, see Horn, *Adapting to a New World*, 382–383; *Colonial Records of Virginia* (Baltimore, 1964), 10[3?]-10[4?]; and Brydon, *Virginia's Mother Church*, 173, 187–190; *The Vestry Book of St. Paul's Parish*, 96–97. Society for the Propagation of the Gospel in Foreign Parts, Lambeth Palace, "Fulham Papers," Reel 739. Sydney Ahlstrom estimates that as late as 1720 only about half of the seventy churches in Virginia's forty-four parishes had ministers. Ahlstrom, *Religious History of the American People*, 190.

[15] Edward Johnson to John Ferrar, 25 March 1650, Ferrar Papers, 1640–1663; *Lower Norfolk Virginia Antiquary*, I: 83–84. See also VMHB I (1893): 327.

[16] *VMHB*, II:14–15, 61–62.

[17] See below, chapter two, for a discussion of the importance of private prayer in Protestant worship.

[18] Lancaster County, VA Court Records: Orders etc. 1655–1666, Reel 24; Chamberlayne, C. G., ed. ., *The Vestry Book of St. Paul's Parish 1706–1786* (Richmond, 1940), 85; Chamberlayne, ed., *The Vestry Book of St. Peter's Parish*, 68. On geographic conditions in early Virginia, see Kevin Kelly, "'In Dispers'd Country Plantations': Settlement Patterns in Seventeenth-Century Surry County, Virginia," in Thad W. Tate and David L. Ammerman, eds., *The Chesapeake in the Seventeenth Century: Essays on Anglo-American Society* (Chapel Hill, 1979). On the relationship between geography and religious experience in Virginia, see Ahlstrom, *Religious History*, 192; Horn, *Adapting to A New World*, 383.

[19] Horn, *Adapting to a New World*, 402–403. For a discussion of the importance of female biblical exempla, see below, chapter 2.

[20] Russell Menard, "British Migration to the Chesapeake Colonies in the Seventeenth Century," in *Colonial Chesapeake Society*, eds. Lois Green Carr, Philip Morgan, and Jean Russo (Chapel Hill, 1988), 130. See also James Horn, "Servant Emigration to the Chesapeake in the Seventeenth Century," in Tate and Ammerman, eds., *The Chesapeake in the Seventeenth Century*; Darrett B. and Anita H. Rutman, "'Now-Wives and Sons-in-Law': Parental Death in a Seventeenth-Century Virginia County," in Tate and Ammerman, eds., *Chesapeake in the Seventeenth Century*; Lois Green Carr and Lorena S. Walsh, "The Planter's Wife: The Experience of White Women in Seventeenth-Century Maryland," *WMQ*, 3d ser., XXIV (1977). Carr and Walsh speculate that a majority of women chose to migrate to the Chesapeake region in the hope of finding a husband once their servitude was over or they found men capable of buying out their contracts. Chesapeake women married later and bore a smaller number of children on the average than women in Old or New England. See also H. R. McIlwaine, "The Maids Who Came to Virginia...," *Reviewer*, I (1921).

[21] For a comprehensive discussion of early female commercial and legal autonomy in Virginia relative to England, and the subsequent reinvigoration of patriarchy by the end of the seventeenth century, see Terri L. Snyder, "' Rich Widows are the best Commodity This Country Affords': Gender Relations and the Rehabilitation of Patriarchy in Virginia, 1660–1700" (Ph.D. diss., University of Iowa, 1992). While Snyder's evidence for the reinstitution of patriarchy in Virginia by century's end is compelling, she pays no attention whatsoever to the place of women in religious culture, and thus does not consider the possibility that women maintained some autonomy in that realm.

[22] On the relationship between religious tolerance and anti-Catholicism during Dutch and English rule, see Frederick J. Zweirlein, *Religion in New Netherland: A History of the Development of the Religious Conditions in the Province of New Netherland, 1623–1664* (Rochester, 1910), 10–35; David W. Voorhees, "'In Behalf of the true Protestants religion': The Glorious Revolution in New York" (Ph.D. diss., New York University, 1988), 47, 60, 63–64, 68.

[23] A.J. van Laer, ed., *Minutes of the Court of Fort Orange and Beverwyck* (2 vols., Albany, 1920–1923), II: 9; "Wassenaer's 'Historisch Verhael'," in Jameson, ed., *Narratives*, 83; Gerald F. DeJong, *The Dutch Reformed Church in the American Colonies* (Grand Rapids, 1978) 9–10; Frederick J. Zweirlein, *Religion in New Netherland: A History of the Development of the Religious Conditions in the Province of New Netherland, 1623–1664*, 40–42, 66–67. For a description of the duties of "*ziekentroosters*," or comforters of the sick,

see Edwin T. Corwin, ed., *Ecclesiastical Records of the State of New York* (7 vols.; Albany, 1901–1916), I, 93–95; and DeJong, 11–12. For a description of the first celebration of the Lord's Supper, see "Letter of Reverend Jonas Michaelius," in *Narratives of New Netherland*, 124–125, and De Jong, *Dutch Reformed Church*, 18.

[24] De Jong, *Dutch Reformed Church*, 5–7; Isaac Jogues, "Novum Belgium," in *Narratives of New Netherland*, 259; Fernow, ed., *Records of New Amsterdam*, VI, 352–353; Zweirlein, *Religion in New Netherland*, 61, 64, 138–142. See Voorhees, "In Behalf of the true Protestants religion," 19–24, for a discussion of the doctrinal conflict within the Dutch church on both sides of the Atlantic.

[25] On the diversity of the pre-1664 Dutch church, see Joyce Goodfriend, *Before the Melting Pot: Society and Culture in Colonial New York City, 1664–1730* (Princeton, 1992), 16. "Letter of Reverend Jonas Michaelius," in *Narratives of New Netherland*, 125; "Letter from Reverend Samual Drisius," *Ecclesiastical Records*, I, 554–555.

[26] With little evidence to support his conclusions, Frederick Zweirlein wrote of early members of the Dutch church in New Netherland that they "never manifested great zeal in the practice of their faith." Zweirlein, 60. Firth Fabend and Joyce Goodfriend offer a welcome salve to Zweirlein's and others' contention of irreligiosity in the early colony. See Goodfriend, "Recovering the History of Dutch Reformed Women in Colonial New York," *de Halve Maen*, LXIV, 4 (Winter, 1991). According to Goodfriend, religion was the foremost shaper of Dutch women's lives. See also Goodfriend, "The Social Dimensions of Congregational Life in Colonial New York City," *WMQ*, 3d. ser., 46 (1989): 275; Firth Fabend, *The Dutch Family*, chapter 7, on religion and the church.

[27] *Ecclesiastical Records*, II, 770; Zweirlein, *Religion in New Netherland*, 93–100; De Jong, *Dutch Reformed Church*, 19. For evidence of the constant shifting of ministers from one settlement to another, see *Ibid.*, 17–19, 65–67; *Ecclesiastical Records*, I:227–260, *passim*. In 1682 Albany residents were still in search of a minister to assist Rev. Schaets, whose "voice is also becoming feeble, so that people sitting far back cannot well understand him.": *Ecclesiastical Records*, II: 826. See also Zweirlein, *Religion in New Netherland*, 73–74; *Narratives of New Netherland*, 412.

[28] Records of the Reformed Protestant Dutch Church of Flatbush, Vol. 1–A, Consistory Minutes, 28; Charles T. Gehring, trans. and ed., *Council Minutes, 1655–1656* (Syracuse, 1995), 20–21, 271–272. See also De Jong, *Dutch Reformed Church*, 30–31.

[29] *Ecclesiastical Records*, I: 93–95, 610. For evidence of the existence of an "informal" church in one newly settled Hudson River community—where services and prayer meetings were offered in a private residence until the congregation could build a suitable house of worship see Fabend, *Dutch Family*, 135.

[30] Gehring, trans. and ed., *Council Minutes, 1655–1656*, 209–210.

[31] De Jong, *Dutch Reformed Church*, 48–54; *Ecclesiastical Records*, II, 754.

[32] See, for instance Randall Balmer, *A Perfect Babel of Confusion: Dutch Religion and English Culture in the Middle Colonies* (New York, 1989). Balmer assumes that declining economic circumstances for Dutch parishioners, coupled with disputes with clergy who sided with the English, necessarily signaled the decline of the Dutch religion. See also Linda Briggs Biemer, *Women and Property in Colonial New York: The Transition From Dutch to English Law, 1643–1727* (Ann Arbor, 1983). Biemer makes a compelling case for the decline of women's *legal* rights in the shift from Roman-Dutch law to the English Duke's Laws. However, not only

does the work suffer from a deliberate focus on case studies drawn only from the lives of wealthy women, but Biemer ignores other avenues for autonomy that might have persisted through the conquest, including religion. Similarly, Thomas Archdeacon equates the English economic and political supremacy with the dissolution of Dutch culture. Archdeacon, *New York City, 1664–1710: Conquest and Change* (Ithaca, 1976).

[33] Once again, Joyce Goodfriend's work stands in direct opposition to studies which point to the dissolution of Dutch culture. See above, note 24, and Goodfriend, *Before the Melting Pot*, esp. chap. 5. See also Willem Frederick Nooter, "Between Heaven and Earth: Church and Society in Pre-Revolutionary Flatbush, Long Island," (Ph.D. diss., Vrije Universiteit Van Amsterdam, 1994). Nooter examines the strength of the Dutch church in a community outside of Manhattan. The church in Flatbush not only maintained its strength in the face of diversity, it increased its services to the community. Evidence of the role Dutch women played—as wives, mothers, and church and community members—in the preservation of Dutch religious culture will be presented in subsequent chapters.

[34] Puritan Dudley Fenner, from a 1588 work published on the continent, quoted in E. Brooks Holifield, *The Covenant Sealed: The Development of Puritan Sacramental Theology in Old and New England, 1570–1720* (New Haven, 1974), 37.

[35] See David Hall, "On Common Ground: The Coherence of American Puritan Studies," *WMQ*, 3d ser., (1987), for a comprehensive review of scholarship on American Puritanism. One of the best description of Puritanism as a devotional movement remains Charles Hambrick-Stowe, *The Practice of Piety: Puritan Devotional Disciplines in Seventeenth-Century New England* (Chapel Hill, 1982). See also Patrick Collinson, *The Elizabethan Puritan Movement* (Berkeley and London, 1967) for a classic account of the rise of Puritanism in England, and Collinson, *The Religion of the Protestants* (Oxford, 1982), and Collinson, "Toward a Broader Understanding of the Dissenting Tradition," in *Godly People* (London, 1983) for the origins and meaning of communalism in Puritanism.

[36] Holifield, *Covenant Sealed*, 37; Collinson, *The Religion of the Protestants*, 250; Anne S. Brown and David D. Hall, "Family Strategies and Religious Practices in Early New England: An Essay in the History of Lived Religion," (Unpublished paper, 1994), 14–15. Brown and Hall also provide a concise analysis of the criticism contemporary English Puritans leveled on the "Congregational Way": Brown and Hall, 15–17.

[37] It has been noted, too, that not all Puritans were as "pure" as scholars have assumed. For example, Thomas Parker and James Noyes of Newbury, Massachusetts duplicated the reformed English parish system, and admitted all but the most sinful to the sacraments: Robert Pope, ed., *The Notebook of the Reverend John Fiske, 1644–1678* (Boston, 1974), Introduction, 16.

[38] Goodwives Stevenson and Downey's confession are found in Mary Rhinelander McCarl, "Thomas Shepard's Record of Relations of Religious Experience, 1648–1649," *WMQ* 3d ser., 48 (July, 1991): 442–443, 461; Richard Eccles and Mr. Haynes confessions are in George Selement and Bruce C. Woolley, eds., *Thomas Shepard's Confessions*, Colonial Society of Massachusetts, *Publications*, vol. 58 (Boston, 1981), 115–116. See also David Cressy, "'The Vast and Furious Ocean': The Passage to Puritan New England," *New England Quarterly*, (December, 1984). The classic text on the migration as a cleansing journey of biblical proportions is Perry Miller, *Errand into the Wilderness* (Cambridge, MA, 1956). For further dis-

cussion of the role of the conversion experience in private and public expressions of faith, see below, Chapters two and five.

[39] For a discussion of the importance of the conventicle in Puritan culture, see Collinson, *The Religion of the Protestants*, 250–251, 252, 265–268. Collinson suggests that conventicles were attended by many who were not included among the "hotter sort" of Puritan; rather, the acceptance of such voluntary, private activities lent the church the legitimacy sought by those godly who declined to separate entirely from it. See also *The Notebook of the Rev. John Fiske*, x; Mary M. Ramsbottom, *Religion, Society, and the Family in Charlestown, Massachusetts, 1630–1740* (Ph.D. diss., Yale University, 1987), 7, 22, for accounts of the role conventicles, or private meetings, played in the founding to churches in Wenham and Charlestown, respectively.

[40] "Memoranda of John Brock ," in *Puritan Personal Writings: Autobiographies* (New York, 1983), 101; *Diary of Cotton Mather* (New York, 1957) I: 679; see also Hambrick-Stowe, *Practice of Piety*, 140–141. For examples of private meetings held at women's houses (though presumably not led by them), see M. Halsey Thomas, ed., *Diary of Samual Sewall* (New York, 1973), I: 28–29, 32–33, 119, 139, 179, 183, among others.

[41] Alden T. Vaughan and Edward W. Clark, cds., *Puritans Among the Indians: Accounts of Captivity and Redemption, 1676–1724* (Cambridge, 1981), 157; c.f. Laurel Thatcher Ulrich, *Good Wives: Image and Reality in the Lives of Women in Northern New England, 1650–1750* (New York, 1980, reprint, New York, 1983), 180, 181.

[42] Hambrick-Stowe, *Practice of Piety*, 246.

Chapter Two

Gender, Private Prayer, and Protestant Self-Image

Christ our Lord, when he willed to lay down the best
rule for prayer, bade us enter our bedroom and there,
with door closed, pray to our father in secret,
that our father, who is in secret, may hear us.[1]

JOHN CALVIN, IN HIS REFERENCE TO A PASSAGE FROM MATT. 6:6, REAFFIRMED THE IMPORtance of private prayer in the lives of reformed men and women. From the seclusion of their bedroom, in private conversation during moments of solitude, Protestants established a personal relationship with God. As important as it was to conduct oneself with piety and prayer in church, God was to be found most easily in solitude, for prayer's "principal place is in the mind and heart." And few places fostered the desire for, indeed, the necessity of, private prayer more than the seventeenth-century American colonies. There, in the face of ministerial shortages, isolating terrain, and dispersed churches, Protestants turned to private prayer with renewed vigor.[2]

The relationship with God, initiated without the intervention of minister or spouse, stood at the heart of Protestant piety and paved the way for pilgrims who sought evidence of their salvation. "Petition is a Prayer where the Desire is poured out before God," wrote Puritan Edward Taylor, minister in Westfield, Connecticut. Private prayer constituted one facet of petition, "that which is Carried on by persons in a Private Capacity."[3] And God heard the prayers of all pious Christians; in God's ears, women's voices resonated with strength equal to men's. With no fear in private of being censured for their speech, Protestant women could establish a relationship with God that no man could tear asunder.

It is possible, moreover, that women who engaged in private prayer found greater comfort there than men. Regarded as the weaker sex, women had reason to hope that God might single them out for his use; as Massachusetts Puritan Thomas

Shepard noted in his journal, "God doth shew his power by the much ado of our weakness to do anything . . . . the more weak I, the more fit I to be used." In addition, discouraged as they were from some aspects of public worship, Protestant women were less likely to fall prey to the hypocrisy of engaging in prayer "for the sake of ostentation," or for "the applause of the world," motivations frowned upon by God.[4]

Suffering motivated all pious men and women to engage in private prayer. Whether in response to death—omnipresent in the American colonies, especially among young children and women of childbearing years—sickness, the travail of childbirth, or the adversities associated with life in a hostile environment (weather, epidemics, attacks by Indians), suffering lay at the heart of colonists' private supplications to God. The rhetoric of suffering was shared by all Protestants, from the most radical Puritans and Dutch Calvinists to the more moderate Anglicans. Suffering was caused by man's sins; out of love for His children, God afflicted the sinful individual or community with all manner of trials. Protestants acknowledged that God's chastisement was a necessary part of the journey toward salvation. The greater the trial, the greater God's test of an individual's will and faith. Moreover, though suffering was a sign of God's displeasure, it might also be a sign of His ultimate favor, saving grace. Only the truly faithful could recognize and make use of God's tests. Through private devotion pious Protestants found the means to come to terms with and soften God's blow.[5]

The seventeenth-century poet Anne Bradstreet revealed in her work poignant reflections on suffering and private supplication. In the throes of a grave illness in the 1660s, Bradstreet wrote of the comfort she found in prayer:

> In anguish of my heart repleat with woes,
> And wasting pains which my body knows,
> In tossing slumbers on my wakeful bed,
> Be drencht with tears that flow'd from mournful head . . .
> And looking up unto his Throne on high,
> Who sends help to those in misery;
> He chac'd away those clouds and let me see
> My Anchor cas i'th' vale with safety.
> He eas'd my Soul of woe, my flesh of pain,
> And brought me to the shore from troubled Main.[6]

A number of Puritan memoirs make specific reference to the importance of private devotion. An integral part of the conversion process, which itself caused suffering among those who followed its path, private devotion allowed Christians moments of pure honesty, contrition, and penitence. Captain Roger Clap noted that in the privacy of one's own closet, "you may tell God your very Hearts, and lay open to Him your worst Plague-Sore, your vilest, lewdest, most notorious wickedness." Clap went on to assure those who sought to pray in secret that they might do so "though you have not a Closet or Door to shut; you need none: you may Pray alone in the Woods, as Christ did in the Mountain . . . And when you are alone at any Time Think with your self, assuredly God is present tho' none else." Joseph Green, in his commonplace book of 1696, instructed his sister Bethiah Green Hicks to "live in the constant exercise of secret prayer; do not neglect it for one day in the world; be not ashamed to let your husband or your family know that you make conscience of praying in secret dayly: but let your conversation be such as may win many to be Christians." In a conversation in his study with his nine-year-old daughter, Katy, Cotton Mather charged her *"to pray in secret Places,* every Day, without ceasing." If she performed that duty wisely and well, Mather promised, "the People of God, would much observe how shee carried herself." A pious woman, then, *by her own example,* might encourage devotion in others.[7]

Private devotion did not always come easily, however, especially to Puritans riddled with doubts about their own piety. When asked by the ruling elders whether "she sought God in private," Mary Angier, a member of Thomas Shepard's congregation, admitted that she had not, "for some weeks." Aware of the profound importance of private prayer, Mary "set upon it again but continued worse and worse." Samuel Sewall's daughter, Betty, found little comfort in her constant prayer. In his journal Sewall recorded the fifteen-year-old Betty's trials and her struggle to find solace in private devotion. In January of 1696, Betty confessed to her mother that she "feared her prayers were not heard because her Sins not pardon'd." In May of that year, Sewall noted that "Betty can hardly read her Chapter For weeping; tells me she is afraid she is gon back, does not taste that sweetness in reading the Word which she once did, fears that what was once upon her is worn off." The struggle to hear God's voice in private plagued pious Puritans throughout their lives.[8]

"THE BIBLE . . . WILL AFFORD UP MANY PRECIOUS PROMISES AND QUICKENINGS . . ."

Protestant men and women acknowledged the importance of the Word of God as they sought a personal relationship with Him through prayer. Scripture was God's language; it signified his presence on earth. All who sought God's approbation—whether from the privacy of their chamber, in church, or as a member of the community—did so by virtue of their familiarity with His Word. According to Calvin, God's Word in the scriptures was not obscure; the Bible was within reach of all Christians prepared to devote themselves to mastering the tools needed to uncover its riches. So it was that Reformed men and women alike recognized the importance of learning to read at an early age. Women, for whom literacy was deemed unimportant and even suspect in worldly matters, found ample justification for learning to read as members of the "priesthood of all believers."[9]

According to Calvin, the command to pray from the Scriptures linked all mankind. Through prayer and knowledge of the Bible, pious individuals emulated the apostles, the holy patriarchs, and the prophets. Devout men and women who learned and lived by Scripture were "partakers of the same common faith" as the ancient divines; their reliance on the Divine Word linked them to the ancients with whom they shared this privilege. Moreover, pious Protestants were encouraged to replicate through their reading the process ministers used to lead their congregations through church services. Cotton Mather acknowledged the obligation to treat private reading as an intellectual exercise in a sermon delivered in Boston two weeks after his marriage. "Oh! That the God of Heaven would effectually perswade every Person here, every Day without fail," Mather exhorted, "to read a Portion in the Bible...not customarily, but with suitable *Observations*, and *Application*, and *Ejaculations*, during the whole Exercise." Once a woman learned to read, she had access to knowledge that might challenge the spiritual authority of her minister.[10]

From the outset, Protestant women undoubtedly met with objections to their attempts to master reading, especially if it was seen to pose a threat to male order. In the years following the flowering of Calvinism in Europe and England, men expressed their discomfort with women whose reading skills equaled their own. Puritan propagandist Robert Granjon, in his 1562 pamphlet "The Way to Arrive at the Knowledge of God," condemned such discomfort when he wrote: "You say that women who want to read the bible are just Libertines? I say you call them lewd merely because they won't consent to your seduction." Women who no longer needed the aid of their fathers, husbands, or ministers to share in God's glorious Word might be less vulnerable to other controls in their spiritual lives as well.[11]

Fears about teaching women to read notwithstanding, Protestant theologians acknowledged that girls as well as boys must learn to worship appropriately. In his commentary on the thirty-first chapter of Deuteronomy, Calvin noted that Moses specifically singled out women and children in his command to gather together to learn the ways of the Lord. "He especially mentions 'women and children,' lest their age or sex might be an excuse." Calvin decried the "villainy and dishonest of those who would debar not children only but women also, from religious learning."[12] Religious instruction was vital not only to enable each child to read the Bible, but to expose them to all facets of private and public devotion necessary to lead a pious life. According to Luther, "a girl or boy of fifteen knows more about Christian doctrine than did all the theologians of the great universities in the old days. For among us the catechism has come back in use . . . all that one should know about . . . how to live and how to die...so that each will know how to live and to serve God in his appropriate role." While parents bore the primary responsibility for teaching their offspring the rudiments of reading and prayer, clerical and civic institutions soon supplemented their efforts.[13]

There is ample evidence that colonial churches and local governments placed a premium on teaching young people of both sexes to read. Catechism was available throughout the colonies, though the evidence of extra-family instruction—which took place at church or in the private residence of a minister or teacher—is strongest in New York and Massachusetts. And though much has been written on colonial catechism, few scholars have noted the role it played in reinforcing in young girls the notion that they were as capable of learning religious principles as boys.[14]

In New York, evidence of the importance of religious education and the partic-ipation of girls in catechism exercises abounds. Among both Dutch and English set-tlers, religious education was a priority, from the earliest moment of settlement, and sometimes from the moment of embarkation from the mother country. The Classis of Amsterdam issued instructions for any schoolmaster who was to accom-pany colonists aboard ship to New Netherland. "He is to instruct the youth, both on shipboard and on land, in reading, writing, ciphering, and arithmetic...he is also to implant the fundamental principles of the true Christian religion and salvation by means of catechizing." Jasper Dankaerts recorded in his journal in October of 1679 a visit paid to observe a catechism class taught by schoolmaster Abraham Lanoy. At Lanoy's house Dankaerts found "a company of about twenty-five persons, male and female, but mostly young people." Throughout the colony, schoolmasters were to minister to the religious needs of both boys and girls, "in accordance with the Reformed religion."[15]

Not all catechism classes in New York were conducted by schoolmasters. The Reverend Henry Selyns, for example, conducted his own catechism classes, first with the children of his congregation in Brooklyn in the 1660s, and later in Manhattan. In 1662, Selyns' catechism class, held on Tuesday evenings, attracted thirty-eight students who performed with "diligence and extraordinary willing-ness." Close to half of those catechumens were female. Perhaps the best example of the success of female catechumens in New York occurred in Selyns' congregation late in the seventeenth century. Early in 1698, Selyns class consisted of thirty cate-chumens who, after reciting all of the Psalms on the second day of Easter, "excited such a desire and zeal among other pupils, that the number has increased to sixty-five." Forty-four boys and twenty-one girls, all between the ages of seven and four-teen, repeated the exercise. In September, Selyns wrote to the Classis to proclaim his success. The boys repeated 227 Psalms and Pauses, the girls, 213; a difference, Selyns noted, of not more than fourteen, leading him to conclude that the girls "although fewer in numbers, had learned and recited more, in proportion, than the boys."[16]

Though several scholars have noted that literacy rates for women were lower than those of men—true in all three colonies in question—we must take into account varying definitions of literacy before we can arrive at a considered picture of the role reading and private prayer played in the lives of colonial women. Many women who could not write their names—the measure of literacy in early studies of the subject—could in fact read. And while David Cressy hastens to point out that mere possession of a Bible (see below) did not necessarily indicate literacy, it did serve to join its owner to a "literary culture"; the world of print extended well beyond those who could read.[17]

The Bible stood at the heart of seventeenth-century Protestant private devo-tion. Though the Church of England mandated the use of *The Book of Common Prayer* in church services—a directive some Anglican churches chose to ignore in Virginia—most Reformed men and women prayed from the Bible at home. So important was home worship that often one of the first requests religious and civic leaders made in their correspondence with the mother country was for additional Bibles to be used not only in church services but to be lent to families in their congregation. The Geneva Bible, first printed in 1560, was probably the version used by most early Puritans. Though 140 editions of the Geneva Bible or New Testament were printed in English, by the mid-seventeenth century the King James version surpassed the Geneva in popularity. Similar in tone and language to the Dutch Bible, the King James version, published in 1611, was at the core of New England biblicism.[18]

Images of Women in the Bible

When Protestant men and women turned to the Bible in search of God's Word, they encountered many examples of the power of faith and the meaning of personal spiritual authority in the Old and New Testaments. Some of the Bible's most compelling figures, held aloft as examples by Calvin and by scores of Protestant ministers in the seventeenth century, were women.

Those chapters of the Bible in which women played key roles resonated in the minds and hearts of seventeenth-century women intent on absorbing God's Word in the privacy of their home. But while biblical messages regarding spiritual equality were clear—"there is no longer male and female; for all of you are one in Jesus Christ" (Gal. 3:29)—a woman's earthly role was more ambiguous. From Eve to Lot's wife, the scriptures provided fuel to spiritual and secular leaders intent on preserving patriarchal authority.[19]

Throughout the Bible, however, faithful women—wives, mothers, prophetesses, supplicants, and even soldiers—proved that their faith, equal to a man's, served them well in the eyes of God. Women in the Bible acted autonomously, with courage, strength, and humility.

Humility, for which all devout Christians were to strive, was considered a feminine trait, and found its greatest examples in biblical women. "That she fell to the ground at Christ's feet and lay there prostrate revealed her shame and humility," John Calvin wrote in his praise of the penitent woman in Luke 7. "She expressed by the ointment," Calvin continued, "that she offered herself and all she had to Christ as a sacrifice. *We should imitate her in all these things*." In 1686, Reverend Noyes in Salem echoed Calvin's prescription when he preached of humility, "from the woman's washing Christ's feet."[20]

Not all women in the Bible exhibited such feminine meekness as a hallmark of their piety. Some, like Jael, exhibited all the fortitude and courage of a man. These women were capable of physical endurance, blessed with a keen wit, and thus able to do battle with God's foes. Judges 4:2–23 and The Song of the Prophetess Deborah (Judges 5:2–31) each celebrate God's use of Jael to slay the wicked Sisera: "Most blessed of women be Jael,/ the wife of Heber the Kenite,/ of tent-dwelling women most blessed . . ./She put her hand to the tent peg and her right hand to the workmen's mallet;/ she struck Sisera a blow, she crushed his head, she shattered and pierced his temple."(Judges 5:24–26). When God demanded and duty called, women, like men, could bear arms against their enemies.[21]

The historical writings of the Bible, including Judges and the other books of the Prophets, provided additional models of feminine devotion. Many of the Bible's faithful women were, like Abigail, prudent and resourceful wives, capable of action, though solely on a husband's behalf (1 Sam 25:2–42). Others, like the wise woman of Tekoa (2 Sam 14:2–20) and Bathsheba (1 Kings 1:11–31), cleverly masked their gifts of persuasion, intelligence, and wisdom under a veneer of subservience. Women appear in the Bible as prophets: Deborah (Judges 4:4–16) and Huldah (2 Kings 22:14–20) offered female and male readers evidence that God used men and women alike to deliver His messages to their communities.

God chose women to deliver to His people the central message of the New Testament: Jesus' resurrection, power and grace. Mary Magdalene and Mary, the mother of James and Joseph, not only attended Jesus at the cross, but were sent by an angel of the Lord to deliver the news of his resurrection to his disciples (Matt. 27, 28). "There is in them," Calvin wrote of the women at the cross and the tomb, "more audacity than in men, even those who had been elected to publish the gospel in all the world." These women recognized the power and glory of God when all others, including the apostles, failed to do so. They, and scores of others, provided spiritual guidance and inspiration to those pious Christians who sought their own personal relationship with God.[22]

POPULAR LITERATURE AND PRIVATE DEVOTION

The Bible was by no means the only source of spiritual guidance available to devout Christians.[23] Printed versions of English and American sermons regularly circulated among friends and neighbors, and frequently turned up in the wills and inventories of men and women in all three colonies. Nineteen editions of Massachusetts minister Thomas Shepard's collected sermons, *The Sincere Convert*, were printed in England. Sewall noted in his diary numerous instances when he shared with friends printed editions of sermons. In many cases, female acquaintances and friends reaped the benefit of his generosity. In 1692 Sewall paid a call on a sick friend, Mrs. Pool, and gave her "one of Mr. Willard's Cordials [the Reverend Samuel Willard's *The Mourners Cordial Against Excessive Sorrow* . . .]." With Mary Rock, widow of both South Church founder Joseph Rock and the Reverend Samuel Danforth of Roxbury, Sewall shared "the 2d half of Dr. Sibb's Sermon Glance of Heaven." In 1689, Sewall wrote to Mrs. Hannah Tuckey, a friend in England, and enclosed "four of Mr. Cotton Mather's sermons." Printed sermons and other devotional material clearly played a key role in Sewall's private worship. As a faithful Christian and a good neighbor, he perhaps felt duty-bound to share the tools of his spiritual development others.[24]

Devotional manuals, among them Lewis Bayly's *The Practice of Piety* and Arthur Dent's *The Plaine Mans Pathway to Heaven* were enormously popular both in England and throughout the colonies. Bayly, the Anglican Bishop of Bangor, wrote that he conceived of *The Practice of Piety* as "a devotional guide for house-holders." It was popular with Anglicans and Puritans alike, with almost sixty editions in print by the end of the seventeenth century. By 1648, twenty-seven editions of Dent's *The Plaine Mans Pathway*, written in 1610, were in print.[25]

Like other popular devotional tracts, *The Plaine Mans Pathway* served as a roadmap for pious pilgrims intent on discovering signs of their own salvation. *Plaine Mans Pathway* appealed to Puritans riddled with doubts about the state of their souls, and to all faithful Protestants who, owing to the vagaries of geography or weather, could not always find solace in church. In easily-memorized verse, accessible to men, women, and children, Dent laid out "eight infallible notes and tokens of a regenerate mind." Two of the eight signs were "A delight in His Word" and "Often and fervent prayer." Dent's treatise could provide comfort to Dutch and English Protestants who often faced a daunting thirty-mile ride through snow or rain to worship in church. While devotional tracts were no substitute for church worship, they supplied readers with hope and inspiration during those weeks when they were unable to attend services.[26]

Other genres of popular literature also captured the imagination of pious colonists. Chapbooks—cheaply printed, often shorter versions of more ponderous devotional works—were widely distributed by book traders, who found a ready market among the godly in England and the American colonies. Thirty percent of all chapbooks printed during the Restoration were religious in character; their numbers indicate that they were designed to be shared by an audience that far exceeded the limited group of radical dissenters. Protestants of all stripes devoured the products of the popular press.[27]

PILGRIM'S PROGRESS, GENDER, AND PROTESTANT SELF-IMAGE

Among the most popular books by the end of the seventeenth century was John Bunyan's *Pilgrim's Progress*, written in 1678 and revised and continued, with the pilgrimage of the protagonist's wife, Christiana, added in 1684. Thousands of copies of the book were printed and distributed in Old and New England. By the turn of the century, the book had gone through twenty printings, and by 1684 it too had been published as a twenty-two-page chapbook, accessible intellectually and economically to a broad spectrum of the population. Bunyan made note of the book's popularity when he wrote in the introduction to Part Two "So comely doth my pilgrim walk, That of him thousands daily sing and talk." And of its acclaim abroad Bunyan wrote "'Tis in New England under such advance, Receives there so much loving countenance, As to be trimmed, new clothed, and decked with gems." So popular was *Pilgrim's Progress* that the English publisher, John Dunton, issued a counterfeit version of the second part, the tale of Christiana's journey. Christiana's tale held special meaning for women, who, as pious Christians in their own right, prepared to make their own pilgrimage to the Celestial City.[28]

As compelling as Bunyan's tale was to colonial women, many of whom could draw parallels between Christiana's journey toward salvation and their own harrowing voyages across the Atlantic, *Pilgrim's Progress* in many ways reflected Bunyan's ambivalence about women's roles in seventeenth-century society. Bunyan shared with other Puritan leaders a condemnation of separate women's meetings, doubts about the female intellectual capacity to interpret scripture, the conviction that a wife must submit to the will of her husband, and fear of a woman's propensity for weakness in the face of temptation. Those opinions pervade *Pilgrim's Progress*. The paradox between spiritual equality and social inequality would not have been lost on women intent on defining their own relationship with God.

Women, the "weaker sort," carry no burdens in Part Two of Bunyan's allegory. Bunyan portrays Christiana and her companion Mercy as less capable of fighting their own battles than Christian had been on his pilgrimage. The Reliever, who rescues Christiana and Mercy from the Ill-ones at the Gate to the Celestial City, reflects Protestant ambivalence when he states, "I marvelled much when you was entertained at the Gate above, being ye knew that ye were but weak women, that you petitioned not the Lord there for a Conductor." The Interpreter, in whose company Christiana vows to embark on her pilgrimage, specially designs his parables to make them more accessible to women. Great-Heart is assigned to accompany Christiana and Mercy on their pilgrimage, for as women they require a guide. *Pilgrim's Progress*, then, did little to challenge a Protestant social hierarchy that defined a woman's place according to notions of the weaknesses inherent to her sex. Yet that Bunyan felt compelled to add Christiana's journey to later editions of his book reveals something about the market to which it appealed.[29]

Pilgrim's Progress reflected and inspired a more complex definition of spirituality, one that by its nature required women to redefine themselves as Christians and reshape their relationship to society. Women in Bunyan's world held responsibility for their own salvation, and were as capable of taking action to preserve their souls as men. Like Chrisitan, Christiana and Mercy choose to leave behind friends and family to make their pilgrimage. In her decision to abandon the City of Destruction, Mercy challenges both the authority of men over women and parents over children. She is, according to the Interpreter, an heir to Ruth, "who did for the love that she bore Naomi, and to the Lord her God, leave her father and mother and the land of her nativity." Women who were called to salvation were obliged by God to answer their hearts, even if they had to leave an unregenerate husband in the process.[30]

According to Scripture, women followed their faith and opened their hearts to God long before men, as exemplified by the women who attended Christ at the cross and who proclaimed his resurrection. Throughout Part Two, Bunyan acknowledged women's privileged spiritual status. Though the disciple Gaius expresses his concern for Christiana and Mercy, heirs to female weakness and evil, he also admits that

> when the Savior was come, women rejoiced in him before either man or angel.
> I read not that ever any man did give unto Christ so much as one groat, but the

women followed him and ministered to him of their substance. 'Twas a woman that washed his feet with tears, and a woman that anointed his body to the burial. They were women that wept when he was going to the Cross. . . . They were women that was first with him at his resurrection morn, and women that brought tidings first to his disciples that he was risen from the dead. Women therefore are highly favoured, and show by these things that they are sharers with us in the grace of life.[31]

Protestant women thus found hope in their place within God's kingdom. In some of the most popular literature of the seventeenth century they found assurance that they not only shared in God's grace, but were perhaps better prepared to receive it.

"THESE WORDS DID SUPPORT ME VERY MUCH. . . .": GENDER AND PRAYER IN MASSACHUSETTS

The evidence for private prayer and reading among women in the seventeenth century is more accessible for Massachusetts than for Virginia and New York. Many clues to female piety are embedded in conversion narratives, some of the richest sources available to scholars interested in public and private devotion. Throughout much of the seventeenth century, many men and women who applied for membership in Massachusetts congregations were required to relate the story of their journey toward saving grace, a journey which frequently included intense periods of private prayer and study. These narratives, shared privately with a minister or publicly before the entire congregation, provide evidence that women not only read the Bible at home, but that they memorized substantial passages from it. They internalized the material enough to create their own personal "sermons," a record of their journey through sin to the blessing of salvation. Many women related that it was the Bible that provided them with their earliest comfort. It was to the Bible they turned when they confronted their ever recurrent crises of doubt.[32]

Puritan conversion is one of the most profoundly complex religious experiences for which we have a record. Though some work has been done on the significance of gender in nineteenth-century conversions, the gendering of religious language in the seventeenth century, and on seventeenth-century conversion in general, little attention has been paid to the meaning seventeenth-century women drew from the conversion experience within the context of private devotion. Above all else, for the purposes of this study, the Puritan conversion experience represented the first opportunity a woman had to account for—if not control—her own spiritual development. A woman who sought evidence of her own salvation did not need to look to her minister or her husband to tell her when she had slipped and fallen into sin; God told her in His own words. Only God was able to lead her to renounce her wickedness and reconstruct a new self. And while a minister's sermons on sin and salvation certainly helped to guide all Christians down the right path, any woman with access to the Bible or other devotional materials could find solace and kindle hope.[33]

One Puritan conversion narrative in particular, the subject of considerable scholarly attention (and some skeptical scrutiny), includes passages that ably illustrate the centrality of private prayer in the lives of pious Christians. Mrs. Elizabeth White, in a narrative published over seventy years after her death, wrote

> I remember the Scriptures were these: Isa. 51.10 . . . John 15.16. Ye have not chosen me, but I have chosen you, and ordained you, that ye should go and bring forth much Fruit, and that your fruit shall remain &c. Lamen.3.25. . . . These Words did support me very much, therefore I writ them out and laid them in my Closet, that they might still be in my Eye, that I might when I looked upon them be incouraged to hope in, and wait upon the Lord.[34]

Though plagued by periods of intense doubt, Elizabeth White found comfort in Scripture. So profound was her joy in God's Word that she engaged in the intellectual—and physical—act of writing out biblical passages to adorn her place of private devotion and to enhance her ease.

Mistress Mary Gookin, one of Thomas Shepard's flock, derived strength and ease from reading Isaiah 42, "A bruised reed will not break." Through His scripture, Mary related, the Lord showed "in this blessed promise a suitable good to all my wants, and the Lord gave me a heart to stay upon him." Dorcus Downey confessed that "the Lord spoke to me by word after I was so smitten with sadness for dishonoring God." It was God, she said, who "brought that Scripture, 'Come to me, ye that are weary and heavy laden, and I will ease you.'" Elizabeth Dunster, also of Shepard's congregation, confessed "when I was reading John, This is will of him, that whoever come, I'll not cast them off. This sunk deep into my soul, and encouraged me to come boldly." Joan White, a member of John Fiske's congregation, related that "reading on Rom. 10, faith cometh by hearing, put her affections onward the desire of the means." In White's case, her quest for the "means" led directly to her migration to Massachusetts from England. Other hopeful female converts referred in their narratives to verses from Psalms, Genesis, Isaiah, Kings, Jeremiah, and Luke. Devout Puritan women read broadly and deeply in the Old and New Testaments.[35]

Conversion narratives are laden with peculiarly female language. Conversion itself was a "deliverance," toward God, and away from sin. The process of conversion was often referred to as "travail." Words that could evoke the emotions, pain, and joy associated with labor and birth resonated deeply with Puritan women. Moreover, the passion that regenerate Christians experienced as they neared rebirth was referred to as "quickening," a word also applied to a physical sensation with which only a woman who had felt a baby move in her womb could identify. The use of such gendered language might well have signaled the special relationship a woman could hope to establish with God in the process of her regeneration.[36]

Gender and Prayer in New Netherland

Dutch Reformed women, like their Calvinist sisters in Massachusetts, assumed the mantle of spiritual equality and conducted themselves in private and public in ways that they hoped would strengthen their bond with God. As in Massachusetts, private prayer played a central role in that process. In moments of solitude, Dutch women withdrew from worldly distractions to prepare for Sabbath services and communion, and, most importantly, to seek evidence of their own salvation.

Jasper Danckaerts, writing in his journal in May of 1680, recorded the experiences of a woman "who had undergone, several years ago, some remarkable experiences; of a light shining upon her while she was reading in the New Testament about the sufferings of the Lord Jesus, which frightened her very much." The woman overcame her fear; her conversion, facilitated by her devotion to God's Word, left her with "such a joy and testimony in her heart as she could not describe."[37]

The moments of private devotion might well have assumed added importance in New Netherland, where a recurrent scarcity of ordained ministers meant that families might not be assured of regular Sabbath-day services. Even in communities well-served by a cleric, church leaders acknowledged the importance of private prayer as a means of preparation, "that the weekly sermons may be listened to with profit and greater edification." Dutch women, like their fathers, husbands, and brothers, took responsibility for their own spiritual development. A substantial part of that spiritual growth took place in the home, in the company of the Bible, printed sermons, and other devotional tracts.

To the dismay of worshippers and church officials, however, many Dutch communities had too few religious books to serve their congregations. Some churches, like the one in Flatbush, made a concerted effort to supply their congregation with adequate reading material. In 1679, the Flatbush consistory, in order to remedy "a great scarcity of books, which are . . . necessary with other things for the instruction of old and young," asked the church deacons to advance money to the towns "to purchase a bill of exchange therewith and with such bill procure books from the fatherland." The consistory also encouraged individuals to take the opportunity to purchase books for their own private libraries at the same time. Flatbush and two neighboring towns pooled their money, and individual members of the congregation contributed additional sums. "For this money were ordered through captain Jacob Mauritez various Bibles in folio and also octavo, Psalm Books, New Testaments, Prayer Books, Catechisms, ABC Books, &c." While the books must have been used during family devotions or in weekly meetings and lectures, some of them surely rested in the hands of individuals for use in private devotion.[38]

Certainly few members of the Dutch Church in New Netherland had a private library of religious books as extensive as Mrs. Bronck's. The widow of a wealthy Dutch settler, Mrs. Bronck's inventory included a Bible in folio, Calvin's *Institutes*, Bullinger's *Works*, Luther's Psalter and complete catechism, and eighteen Dutch and Danish pamphlets, among dozens of additional books and pictures depicting religious themes. While Mrs. Bronck's library included books in Dutch, German,

Danish, Latin, and English, few colonists, male or female, would have found any language but Dutch accessible. Several wills from the seventeenth century specify "Dutch Testament," "Dutch Bibles," or "great Dutch Bible." Ownership of a Dutch Bible might well have taken on added significance in the face of the English conquest, when language itself proved to be a point of cultural contest. When printed in the native tongue, the Bible could serve as an able vehicle for the preservation of Dutch language and an expression of Dutch culture.[39]

As Protestants, the Dutch in New Netherland recognized the importance of the Word. Bibles frequently appear in the wills of both women and men. Daughters and wives also appear in men's wills as the recipients of family Bibles. An inventory of the estate of Mr. Gysbert Van Imbroch, taken in 1665, included among numerous books one referred to only as "a woman's Testament with silver clasps." Even more telling, religious books were at the center of at least two court cases in the seventeenth century. In both, women fought to retain ownership of the books, clearly significant and prized possessions. In June of 1674 Willemtie van Lyden appeared in court as a plaintiff against Albertus Ringo. Ringo, she claimed, had bartered a testament and a psalm book away from her son, Pons Jansen. The court ordered Jansen to appear to explain the transaction, and though the record is silent on the outcome of the case, Willemtie's willingness to stand before the court attests to the significance she assigned to the books. We can only imagine the words that passed between mother and son when the barter was uncovered.[40]

Nine years earlier, in 1665, tensions between the Dutch and English surfaced in a case involving Mary Verplanck, who purchased from some English soldiers a Bible which allegedly belonged to the town's sheriff, Jacob Kip. Court officer Allard Anthony demanded that Mary return the testament. Though she admitted to purchasing the Bible from the soldiers, who said they had brought the book with them from the south, Mary refused to return the property. Instead, she spent the next three months fighting for the right to retain what was clearly a prized possession. She challenged the *schout* and the *schepen*, both men of authority in town, and demanded clear proof that the book belonged to Kip. The court at last admitted that it could not bring charges against Mary, but instead had to institute action against the thieves themselves, presumably the English soldiers. Until that case was resolved, Mary was to place the Bible in the hands of the court, which she did. Two months later, however, frustrated with the delay, she returned to court to demand her book. The following month, the court decreed that the Bible be returned to Jacob Kip, but held him—and not the English soldiers—responsible for repaying Mary her money. Though money, and not piety, might have been the prime motivating factor in Mary's dogged pursuit of the book—she had lost not only the Bible but the ten guilders it had cost her—this case, like the latter, provides evidence of the involved trade in religious books engaged in by both men and women, Dutch and English.[41]

Like many of the most radical nonconformists in Massachusetts, some Dutch colonists chose to separate themselves from what they deemed a corrupt society, rendered even more corrupt by the English conquest. The conquest, which followed closely on the heels of the restoration of the crown and the re-establishment of the Church of England, heightened anti-Catholic sentiments in New Netherland. For those Dutch colonists who abandoned New York for isolated settlements in Delaware or New Jersey, private devotion took on added significance.

One such migrant, Elizabeth van Rodenburgh, relocated to Newcastle with her husband Ephraim Herman in the winter of 1679. Jasper Danckaerts, a radical Labadist dissenter in his own right, and not entirely welcome by Dutch Church officials in town, accompanied Rodenburgh and Herman on their journey south. Danckaerts revealed in his journal that Elizabeth had "the quietest disposition we had observed in America." He expressed admiration for her devotion and private piety when he noted that she "has withdrawn herself from the idle company of youth, seeking God in quiet and solitude. She professes the reformed religion, is a member of that church, and searches for the truth which she has found nowhere except in the Word and preaching." In order to encourage Elizabeth at her private devotion, Danckaerts, upon his return to New York, translated Labadie's *Verheffinge des Geestes tot God* [The Lifting up of the Soul to God] into Dutch and sent it to her at Newcastle. According to Danckaerts, Elizabeth "had evinced a great inclination for it and relished it much, when sometimes we read portions of it to her." A month later, in May of 1680, Elizabeth reported that in reading the book on her own, "she had experienced great enjoyment, and had been sometimes tenderly affected." Even when they left the shelter of their church and removed to the isolated frontier, Dutch Reformed women carried with them the texts to foster their own spiritual development.[42]

Gender and Private Devotion in Seventeenth-Century Virginia

As we have seen, a recurrent scarcity of ministers and the dispersal of settlements plagued Anglicans in Virginia as well as the Dutch in New Netherland. Though there were certainly ample religious, legal, and social reasons to attend Sabbath services— for women especially, with little if any access to male-centered gaming or market activities, the church served as the central social event in an otherwise often isolated existence—church worship alone could not meet the spiritual needs of pious Virginia Protestants.

In parishes where the distance to church might exceed thirty miles, the journey easily could prove daunting, especially for the very old, the very young, or pregnant women. At best, the distance would be covered in a horse-drawn cart, over rough, uneven terrain. Though much of the tidewater was relatively flat, travelers were often forced to clamber down from their carts to ford one of the many rivers and streams that divided parishes and often rendered the local church or chapel inaccessible. Such terrain could be hazardous, especially during spring thaws and rainy seasons. At worst, parishioners might be forced to make the journey on foot, a formidable task during the winter or in the humid summer months. Even if environmental conditions did not discourage attendance at Sabbath services, women with several small children were expected to remain at home with them until they were old enough to attend church with a minimum of disruptive behavior. In addition, though some of the most radical nonconformists in Virginia and throughout the colonies condemned the churching of women, in some congregations a new mother would not return to services for six weeks following the birth of a child. Private prayer could fill the void.[43]

For most Anglican men and women, many of whom attended Sabbath services organized around *The Book of Common Prayer*, the Bible served as the primary source for private devotion. In spite of (or perhaps because of) the difficulties experienced establishing parishes and securing the services of an ordained minister, colonists in Virginia had ready access to the Bible, the basic source of spiritual development and inspiration. Bibles appear in the inventories of Chesapeake planters far more frequently than in England during the seventeenth century. In Lower Norfolk—admittedly more Nonconformist than other counties in the colony—planters' inventories between 1640 and 1680 included fifty-five Bibles, one out of every five planter estates. Bibles appear in inventories of estates in all counties for which seventeenth-century records survive.[44]

Women understandably are underrepresented in any accounting of book ownership in colonial Virginia. Few women's inventories or wills are extant, though the wills of husbands and fathers who included wives and daughters among the recipients of their books help to paint a more accurate picture of Virginia's literary culture. In 1643 John Holloway of Accomack County specified that "If it please God my child should out live my wife That my said Loveing wife would give my best Bible to it my said Child." Jane Perle's estate, inventoried in Northumberland County in 1650, included three Bibles; to her daughter Elizabeth she left one Bible and a *Practice of Piety*. Jane Hall, widow of Oswin Hall, provided for the education of her daughters by mandating in her will that a part of their estate was "to be equally divided amongst them toward their schooleing if need require or if I shall endeavour to educate them myselfe then they shall enjoy each her sev'rall propor'con." In a case brought before the Charles City County court in 1664 to determine whether the estate of Selby Sparrow had been appropriately distributed, Captain Grey revealed that "he had two bookes, one whereof was a small bible wch he gave to my daughter Elizabeth." The estates of Widow Heath and Widow Hayes each included "1 ould Bible." Mary Freme of Charles City County willed each of her children—two sons and a daughter—a religious book, including two testaments and a *Practice of Piety*. In 1716, Mary Degge, wealthy and unmarried, bequeathed to her nieces her private library, including *The Whole Duty of Man*, *Meditations on Eternity*, *The Book of Common Prayer*, a Catechism, *The Ladies Calling*, and *The Practice of Piety*.[45]

Lewis Bayly's *The Practice of Piety* appeared in many seventeenth-century Virginia wills and inventories, evidence of its popularity beyond New England, among Anglicans as well as Puritans. In fact, works by some of the sixteenth- and seventeenth-centuries' most ardent nonconformists could be found among the possessions of Virginia colonists, male and female. And though few private libraries could rival Mrs. Sarah Willoughby's, similar in breadth and depth to Mrs. Bronck's in New Netherland, colonists had access to a wide variety of devotional literature. Private collections in Norfolk County alone included Calvin's *Institutes*, Bunyan's *Pilgrim's Progress*, Dr. Sibbes' *Sermons*, and works by Puritan writers Dr. John Preston and William Perkins. Psalm books and catechisms also appear with regularity. Virginia women who learned to read found solace in all manner of books and pamphlets. Though the ministers in their parish churches might demand the use of the Prayer Book in weekly services, in the privacy of their homes Anglican women were free to explore their own path toward regeneration.[46]

* * *

Whether colonial women and men relied on their "ould Bibles"—well-used, worn, bindings broken, pages tattered and soiled from a lifetime's use—as their sole source of inspiration, or they had access to vast private libraries of devotional literature, their pilgrimage toward salvation began at home, in moments of solitary contemplation. Only there could God speak to the faithful Protestant without the mediation of minister, parent, or spouse. Each pious Protestant, man and woman, took responsibility for his or her own salvation; the will to establish a personal covenant with God belonged to the individual alone, regardless of gender. In the privacy of their closets, then, Protestant women came to understand what it meant to own a soul equal in God's eyes to any man's. And as we shall see, with God's Word as their guide, Protestant women often crossed the thin line between private piety and public action.

NOTes

[1] John Calvin, *Institution of the Christian Religion [1536]*, trans. F.L. Battles (Atlanta, 1975), 100. cf. Calvin, *Institutes of the Christian Religion* [1559], trans. and ed. John Allen (2 vols., New York, 1936), II, 140.

[2] Calvin, *Institutes*, trans. John Allen, II, 138.

[3] Thomas and Virginia L. Davis, eds., *Edward Taylor's "Church Records" and Related Sermons* (Boston, 1981), 92, 93.

[4] Michael McGiffert, ed., *God's Plot: The Paradoxes of Puritan Piety Being the Autobiography and Journal of Thomas Shepard* (Amherst, 1972), 117, 106–107, 139; Calvin, *Institutes*, II, 138–139.

[5] J. Sears McGee offers a compelling analysis of the rhetoric of suffering shared by all Protestant denominations. He does find distinctions, however, in the degree to which each group believed itself capable of overcoming God's displeasure, the level of optimism with which they approached the potential for personal saving grace. "Puritans," writes McGee, "made [justification] *sound hard*, Anglicans made it sound easy." McGee, *The Godly Man in Stuart England: Anglicans, Puritans, and the Two Table, 1620–1670* (New Haven, 1976), 59. Also see McGee, Chapter 2, "The Rhetoric of Suffering," especially 42, 48–49, 51, 55, 59–60.

[6] Robert Hutchinson, ed., *The Poems of Ann Bradstreet* (New York, 1969), 56. See also Bradstreet's "Religious Meditations," poems never meant for publication, written as an expression of her private relationship with and love for God: *Ibid.*, 61–69.

[7] "Captain Clap's Memoirs," in *Puritan Personal Writings: Autobiographies and Other Writings* (New York, 1983), 31; "Commonplace Book of Joseph Green," in *ibid.*, 226–227; Worthington Chauncy Ford, ed., *The Diary of Cotton Mather* (2 vols., New York, 1957), I,239–240. See also "The Commonplace Book of Joseph Green," 203, 211.

[8] *Thomas Shepard's Confessions*, 67; *Sewall's Diary*, I, 345–346, 348.

[9] Louis Bouyer, *Orthodox Spirituality and Protestant and Anglican* Spirituality (London, 1969), 88. Several scholars have written extensively on the relationship between religion and literacy in England, Europe, and the American colonies. See for instance Margaret Spufford, "First Steps in Literacy: The Reading and Writing Experiences of the Humblest Seventeenth-Century Spiritualized Household," *Social History* 4 (1979): 407–435; Natalie Zemon Davis addresses the appeal that reformed religion held for women especially with respect to literacy in "City Women and Religious Change," in *Society and Culture in Early Modern France* (Stanford, 1975), 65–96, see especially 72, 76–78, 79–80, 92. Also see David Cressy, *Literacy and the Social Order: Reading and Writing in Tudor and Stuart England* (Cambridge, 1980), 2–5, 204n. For a thorough discussion of the relationship between literacy and Puritanism in early New England, see David D. Hall, *Worlds of Wonder, Days of Judgment: Popular Religious Belief in Early New England* (New York, 1989), Chap. 1, esp. pp. 31–43. See also Hall, "The World of Print and Collective Mentality," in *New Directions in American Intellectual History* eds. John Higham and Paul S. Conkin (Baltimore, 1979).

[10] Calvin, *Institutes*, I, 113; *Diary of Cotton Mather*, I, 127; Charles E. Hambrick-Stowe, *The Practice of Piety: Puritan Devotional Disciplines in Seventeenth-Century New England* (Chapel Hill, 1982), 49.

[11] Quoted in Davis, "City Women and Religious Change," 78.

[12] John Calvin, *Commentaries on the Last Four Books of Moses...*, Rev, Charles William Bingham, ed. and trans. (4 vols, Edinburgh, 1852), I, 373.

[13] Gerald Strauss, "Success and Failure in the German Reformation," *Past and Present* 67: 33.

[14] It is not my intention to discuss the specific history of catechism in the American colonies, nor that of the development of public education. The role of schoolmaster varied from colony to colony, as did the use of specific catechisms as readers. For general treatments of colonial education see Lawrence Cremin, *American Education: The Colonial Experience, 1607–1783* (New York, 1970); Bernard Bailyn, *Education in the Forming of American Society* (Chapel Hill, 1960); for a comprehensive analysis of colonial education in Massachusetts see James Axtell, *The School Upon a Hill: Education and Society in Colonial New England* (New York, 1974).

[15] *Ecclesiastical Records*, I, 98; *Kingston Papers*, II, 433; *Journal of Jasper Dankaerts*, 63. On the role the Dutch church played in providing educational services to its members see Willem Frederik Nooter, "Between Heaven and Earth: Church and Society in Pre-Revolutionary Flatbush, Long Island (Ph. D. diss., Vrije Universiteit Van Amsterdam, 1994), chapter 5.

[16] A. P. G. Van der Linde, ed., *Old First Dutch Reformed Church of Brooklyn* (Baltimore, 1983), 55; *Ecclesiastical Records*, II, 1231–1235. For examples of catechism practices in other New York towns see *Ecclesiastical Records*, II, 728–729; *Kingston Papers*, II, 433; *Dutch*

Reformed Church of Brooklyn, 23; Records of the Reformed Protestant Dutch Church of Flatbush, Vol. 1–A (Unpublished transliterations and translations, Holland Society), 39–40, 49. It is interesting to note that in Flatbush, under certain conditions catechism classes could be taught by a woman, usually the schoolmaster's wife: see below, chapter 6.

[17] Cressy, *Literacy and the Social Order*, 50–52. As evidence of the distinction between reading and writing in early New York, for instance, girls and boys attending school in Flatbush paid three guilders for a quarter year of reading or spelling, four guilders if they wished to write: Records of the Reformed Protestant Dutch Church of Flatbush (transliterations and translations) Vol. 1–A, Consistory Minutes, 51. For a revised definition of literacy, one which includes the concept of a "world of print" accessible to non-readers through pictures, storytelling, and sermons, see Hall, "The World of Print and Collective Mentality." Tamara Plakins Thornton, in her book on the history of handwriting, does make note of the difference between learning to read and learning to write in colonial America. She does not speculate fully, however, on how those differences might lead scholars to reevaluate literacy rates, especially among women: *Handwriting in America: A Cultural History* (New Haven and London, 1996), 5–6. Marilyn Westerkamp, in an important book published after the completion of this dissertation, argues that the emphasis on literacy in relationship to biblical scholarship in fact may have reinforced male authority by disenfranchising women religiously. Compelling though that argument is, it is also important to bear in mind the degree to which women were capable of drawing on the biblical erudition of ministers as they shaped their own pious statements, from conversion narratives to captivity narratives. Westerkamp, *Women and Religion in Early America, 1600–1850: The Puritan and Evangelical Traditions* (New York, 1999), 20–1.

[18] Harry Stout, "Word and Order in Colonial New England," in *The Bible in America: Essays in Cultural History*, eds. Nathan O. Hatch and Mark A. Noll (New York and Oxford, 1982), 20–26. For evidence of Bible ownership in each colony, see below.

[19] See above, Introduction, for a more detailed analysis of the relationship between biblical images of Eve and culturally-constructed female subservience. Also see Laurel Thatcher Ulrich, *Good Wives: Image and Reality in the Lives of Women in Northern New England, 1650–1750* (New York, 1983, reprint of 1982 edition), 106–107.

[20] Calvin's Commentary on Luke 7:44, quoted in William J. Bouwsma, *John Calvin: A Sixteenth-Century Portrait* (New York, 1988), 200, italics added; M. Halsey Thomas, ed., *The Diary of Samuel Sewall* (2 vols., New York, 1973), I, 116.

[21] All Biblical citations are taken from *The New Oxford Annotated Bible* (New York, 1991), unless otherwise noted. On Jael, c.f. Ulrich, *Good Wives*, 168–171.

[22] John Calvin, *Sermons de la passione*, quoted in Jane Douglass, *Women, Freedom, and Calvin* (Philadelphia, 1985), 58.

[23] See Hall, *Worlds of Wonder*, 43–61, for a discussion of the extensive book trade in seventeenth-century New England.

[24] Hambrick-Stowe, *Practice of Piety*, 49. Thomas, ed., *The Diary of Samuel Sewall*, I, 225, 287, 471. On the role of books in Sewall's life, see Hall, *Worlds of Wonder*, 234–237.

[25] Winton U. Solberg, *Redeem the Time: The Puritan Sabbath in Early America* (Cambridge, 1977), 64; Hambrick-Stowe, *Practice of Piety*, 49; Bouyer, *Orthodox Spirituality*, 155.

[26] Bouyer, *Orthodox Spirituality*, 155–156.

[27] Bernard Cap, "Popular Literature," in *Popular Culture in Seventeenth-Century England* ed., Barry Reay (London and Sydney, 1985), 218; Hall, *Worlds of Wonder*, 49, 50, 52–53.

[28] Christopher Hill, *A Tinker and a Poor Man: John Bunyan and His Church, 1628–1688* (New York, 1989), 374; Hall, *Worlds of Wonder*, 53; John Bunyan, *Pilgrim's Progress*, ed., Roger Sharrock (London, 1965), 213.

[29] Bunyan, *Pilgrim's Progress*, 243, 249.

[30] *Ibid.*, 255.

[31] *Ibid.*, 316.

[32] See below, chapter five, for a discussion of the meaning of public confession of conversion experiences.

[33] One example of a compelling treatment of gender and late eighteenth- and nineteenth-century conversion is Susan M. Juster, *Sinners and Saints: The Gendering of Evangelical Culture in Revolutionary New England* (Ann Arbor, 1992). Also see her article in *American Quarterly*, 41 (1989), 34–63. Juster also offers a concise description of the gendering of religious language and a review of the most recent literature in "The Spirit and the Flesh: Gender, Language, and Sexuality in American Protestantism," in *New Directions in American Religious History: The Protestant Experience*, eds. Harry Stout and Daryl Hart (New York, 1997) Also see Margaret Masson, "The Typology of the Female as a Model for the Regenerate: Puritan Preaching, 1690–1730," *Signs* 2 (1976): 304–315. And see Patricia Caldwell, *The Puritan Conversion Narrative: The Beginnings of American Expression* (Cambridge, Eng.,1983) and Amanda Porterfield, *Female Piety in Puritan New England* (New York, 1992) for gendered treatments of the conversion experience. Charles Lloyd Cohen and Charles Hambrick-Stowe each devote substantial portions of their books to an analysis of the conversion experience in Puritan New England: Cohen, *God's Caress: The Psychology of the Puritan Religious Experience* (New York, 1986); Hambrick-Stowe, *The Practice of Piety*. Standard collections of Puritan conversion narratives include George Selement and Bruce C. Woolley, eds., *Thomas Shepard's Confessions*, Colonial Society of Massachusetts, *Publications*, vol. 58 (Boston, 1981); Mary Rhinelander McCarl, ed., "Thomas Shepard's Record of Relations of Religious Experience, 1648–1649," *WMQ*, 3d. ser., 48 (July, 1991): 432–466; Robert G. Pope, ed., *The Notebook of the Reverend John Fiske, 1644–1675*, Colonial Society of Massachusetts, *Publications*, vol. 47 (Boston, 1974).

[34] Elizabeth White, "The Experiences of God's Gracious Dealing with Mrs. Elizabeth White As they were written by her own Hand, and found in her Closet after her decease Dec. 5, 1669." (Boston, 1741), 6–7. Mrs. Whites text serves as a focal point for Patricia Caldwell's monograph on the Puritan conversion narrative: Caldwell, *The Puritan Conversion Narrative*.

[35] McCarl, ed., "Thomas Shepard's Record of Relations," 458–460, 461, 465–466; Pope, ed., *The Notebook of the Reverend John Fiske*, 30, 8–9, 29; McCarl, "Thomas Shepard's Record," 441–443, 446–450.

[36] See Caldwell, *Puritan Conversion Narrative*, 8, 11–12, for a discussion of female imagery in conversion narratives. For a more complete discussion of the relationship between conversion and the birthing experience, see below, chapter four.

[37] *Journal of Jasper Danckaerts*, 231.

[38] Records of the Reformed Dutch Protestant Church of Flatbush, 1–A, Consistory Minutes, 10.

39 *Ecclesiastical Records*, I, 168; *Abstract of Wills, 1665–1707*, New York Historical Society *Collections*, vol. 25 (1892), 60, 209; David E. Narrett, *Inheritance and Family Life in Colonial New York City* (Ithaca, 1992), 156.

40 *Kingston Papers*, II, 566; Berthold Fernow, ed., *The Records of New Amsterdam, 1653–74*, VII, Minutes of the Court of Burgomasters and Schepens (New York, 1897), 95.

41 Fernow, *Records of New Amsterdam*, V, 196.

42 Bartlett Burleigh James and J. Franklin Jameson, eds., *Journal of Jasper Danckaerts* (New York, 1913, 1959 reprint), 146, 170, 233.

43 On the dispersal of churches and the dearth of ministers in tidewater Virginia see above, chapter one. On the ritual of churching, see William Coster, "Purity, Profanity, and Puritanism: The Churching of Women, 1500–1700," in *Women in the Church*, eds., W. T. Sheils and Diana Wood (London, 1990), 377–387. Even in Puritan Massachusetts, women absented themselves from church after the birth of a child: see, for example, "The Diary of John Hull," in *Puritan Personal Writings: Autobiographies and Other Writings* (New York, 1983), 147.

44 Edward James, ed., *Lower Norfolk Virginia Antiquary*, I, 104–106, 121–123; II, 33–36; James Horn, *Adapting to A New World: English Society in the Seventeenth-Century Chesapeake* (Chapel Hill, 1994), 402–403; Norfolk County Deed Book A, 1637–1648, Reel 1; Susie M. Ames, ed., *County Court Records of Accomack-Northampton, Virginia, 1640–1645* (Charlottesville, Va., 1973), 61, 71, 79, 181, 337; J. Walter, trans., *Book 'B', Lower Norfolk County*, 42, 44, 46, 49–50, 85–87, 88–89; Vincent Watkins, trans., *York County: Deeds, Orders, Wills Book 3, 1657–1662* (Poquosan, Va., 1989), 11.

45 Ames, ed., *County Court Records of Accomack-Northampton*, 35, 302; Northumberland County Records, 1652–1655, Reel 1; Ames, ed., *County Court Records of Accomack-Northampton, Virginia, 1632–1640* (Washington, D.C., 1954), 112; Charles City County Court Orders, Deeds, Wills, Orders, Etc. 1655–1665, Reel 1; *WMQ*, 1st ser., 21: 194–197.

46 For Sarah Willoughby's will, see James, ed., *Lower Norfolk Antiquary*, I,122. For a list of books in other libraries, see *ibid.*, I, 104–106, 121–123; II:33–36; see also Norfolk County Wills and Deeds, 1675–1686, Reel 1. On the preponderance of Puritan literature in colonial Virginia, see below, chapter five.

Part II

Prayer and Home: Piety and Power in the Protestant Family

Chapter Three
PIETY and THE Marriage BOND

> ... so it is with every believing soul, you have matched against the minds of your
> carnal friends, or master, or husband, yet comfort thyself, though thou hast the
> ill will of an earthly husband, yet now God will be a husband in heaven. . . .[1]

PURITAN MINISTER THOMAS HOOKER, IN HIS 1638 SERMON *THE SOUL'S EXALTATION*,
acknowledged the duty of the godly woman to challenge evil, though she
might in the process strain, or even shatter the bonds of the marriage contract. While earthly marriage and the family constituted the foundations of
Reformed society, regenerate men and women looked forward to that day when they
would join Christ in heaven in a holy bond of matrimony. That such a glorious end
to the journey to the Celestial City was accessible to all Christians regardless of sex
enhanced the position of a woman in her earthly role as wife and mother. Firm in
her faith, the Christian woman might boldly act to insure that those closest to her
would follow the path of the righteous. Should her best efforts fail, however, and her
husband stray from God, the Protestant wife acted to preserve her own soul, and that
of her children.

"THE LOYALL SPOUSE OF CHRIST": Marriage Imagery in Protestant THEOLOGY

According to John Calvin, marriage between a man and a woman was symbolic of
the holiest of unions, that between the faithful Christian and Christ. The earthly
institution of marriage was therefore deserving of the greatest respect. "Christ has
been pleased," Calvin wrote in his condemnation of the papal injunction against
priestly marriage, "to put such honour upon marriage, as to make it an image of his
sacred union with the Church. What could be said more, in commendation of the
dignity of marriage?" By employing images of earthly marriage to describe the

regenerate Protestant's bond with Christ in heaven, Reformed theologians honored the earthly institution and made the heavenly bond seem more accessible.[2]

Ministers, diarists, and correspondents from Massachusetts, New York, and Virginia frequently employed marriage imagery in their discussions of the relationship between the faithful and Christ. In 1696, Puritan diarist Samuel Sewall, filled with contrition for what he believed was his unseemly behavior at Communion, entreated God to "help me entirely to give my self to thy Son as to my most endeared Lord and Husband." John Hull, in his public diary entitled "Some Observable Passages of Providence," likened the Puritans' voyage to New England to the journey of a newly betrothed bride and the groom Christ to their heavenly mansion. "Make this wilderness as Babylon was once to Israel, as a wine-cellar for Christ to refresh his spouse in." Similarly, Thomas Shepard, minister of the Congregational Church in Cambridge in the middle years of the seventeenth century, exhorted his parishioners to seek a blessed union with Christ. "If thou consenteth to match with Christ, he doth so with thee, and so I pronounce Christ and you married." According to Shepard, gender was inconsequential in this heavenly marriage. "Man or woman," he preached, "thou art in a Heavenly condition already, and shall enjoy him forever." Shepard's congregation clearly heeded his words; in a confession of faith, a young woman known only as "Brother Jackson's maid," quoted scripture on heavenly betrothal from Hosea 2. She acknowledged that "Christ would be better than an earthly husband," adding, perhaps in reference to a recent loss of her own, "No fear there of widowhood." Sarah Smith, in her confession before Shepard's congregation, accounted for her passive reaction to her husband's death when she quoted Isaiah 54:5, "Thy maker is thy husband." "And the Lord" she added, "made me set a higher price upon him than a husband." Once betrothed to Christ, the faithful Christian woman would not be deserted. No such guarantees existed in earthly marriage.[3]

Dutch Reformed colonists in New York and Anglicans in Virginia were also familiar with spousal images of Christ. As they faced the threats of disease, starvation, and Indian attacks, male and female settlers in early New York and Virginia took comfort in the image of Jesus as husband and protector. In a letter to the Amsterdam Classis describing an Indian massacre at Esopus in New York in 1663, Domine Blom, minister of Kington's Dutch Church, wrote "Should we no more see each other there, may we see each other hereafter in our Bridegroom's chamber, securely sheltered behind the blue curtains of the Heavens." Faithful men and women could expect to find greater security and comfort in a heavenly marriage than they would ever find in their perilous lives on earth. In order to reap the benefits of a holy union with Christ, however, all brides, male and female, had to enter the marriage prepared to assist their protector. In a letter written in 1621 to Edwin Sandys in James City, Virginia, Anglican William Powell admitted that "my defenses are weak and they who attend the Bridegroom worthily must have oyl in theire lamps." The faithful helpmeet, man or woman, had to keep an orderly house for their groom. Mrs. Grace Gray of Charles City County, Virginia, employed a spousal image of Christ when she accused her husband of repudiating his own marriage vows. The proper treatment of a Christian wife should be self-evident, Grace Grey proclaimed, "there being so glorious a comparison betwixt Christ & his Church of wedded matrimony."[4]

Protestant women and men recognized that all Christians, regardless of gender, were *brides* of Christ. And as such, regenerate Protestants knew they must submit to Christ's love and God's fatherly authority. "The loyall Spouse of Christ," wrote Francis Cornwall in his dedication to one of John Cotton's sermons, published in 1646, "hath no Head, no Husband, no Lord, no Law-giver, but royall King Jesus." Protestant theologians often assumed that women, from whom submission to a male figure was expected in their earthly roles, were better equipped than men to accept their submissive status to God. After all, it had been women, not men, who had best demonstrated their humility and subservience when they tended to Christ at the cross and anointed him with their tears.[5]

As a reward for their humility and submission, Christ addressed his faithful spouses in the language of seduction and love. So clear to Protestants was the link between earthly and divine love that Puritan poet Edward Taylor, in his 1670 Foundation Day sermon, equated Christ's devotion to that of the lovers in the Song of Solomon: "Consider, Soule that thou art called to enter here, if Prepared, Christ Speakes unto thee in his language to his Spouse, Cant. 2.10,11,12,13, arise, my Love, my fair one, & Come a way." Romantic language appealed to Protestants in search of spiritual love.[6]

"FaITH, noT VIrGInITY, FILLS ParaDISe": GenDer, reLIGIon, anD EarTHLY MarrIaGe

Most historians acknowledge that one revolutionary aspect of the Reformation was the idealization of a woman as a Christian wife and mother rather than as a saint or virgin. The first generation of Protestant theologians rejected virginity as the highest state attainable on earth. Calvin and other early reformers cautioned that men and women who maintained chastity were not all as pure of heart as they were of the body; libidinous desire might infect the heart and the mind. "Let not him who refrains from actual fornication, flatter himself, as though he could not be charged with unchastity," Calvin wrote in his 1536 *Institutes of the Christian Religion*. The only solution for men and women who battled such desire was marriage. The seventh commandment on adultery impelled men and women to marry. "To avoid fornication," wrote Calvin in his commentary on that commandment, "let every man have his own wife, and let every woman have her own husband." And though scholars note that Protestant reformers, in their drive to sanctify marriage, bolstered patriarchal authority by closing down the convent—one of the few Medieval and early modern institutions controlled by women—Calvin interpreted marriage as an institution to be ruled by men and women equally.[7]

In his commentary on Paul's Epistle to the Corinthians, Calvin addressed the issue of marital mutuality from several angles. The husband and wife were "bound to mutual benevolence." Moreover, mutual benevolence extended beyond the expectation that spouses would honor one another with love, kindness, and respect; neither partner could claim dominance over the other's body or soul. That control belonged to God alone. And as intimacy played a vital role in any marriage, neither husband nor wife was free to withhold sex from the other unless they did so with consent, for "mutually spiritual" reasons. According to Calvin, with regard to mutual benevolence in marriage men and women were "upon a level."[8]

All Protestant denominations encouraged the "companiate marriage," grounded in loving respect and the knowledge of spiritual equality. "Women are Creatures without which there is no Comfortable Living for a Man," proclaimed John Cotton in a sermon preached in New England in 1694. Though Protestant men and women were cautioned to love no other above God, the love between husband and wife should surpass all other *earthly* love. As Boston cleric Benjamin Wadsworth wrote in his early eighteenth-century treatise on marriage and family, "This duty of love is mutual, it should be performed by each, to each of them. They should endeavour to have their affections really, cordially and closely knit, to each other. If therefore the *Husband* is . . . not kind, loving, tender in his words . . . he then shames his profession of Christianity, he breaks the Divine Law, he dishonours God. . . . The same is true of the *Wife* too." The Christian spouse would "share the sweets and sours" of day-to-day life.[9]

Thomas Shepard confirmed his search for mutual love when he confessed in his journal that, prior to his migration to New England, "I had been praying three years before that the Lord would carry me to such a place where I might have a meet yoke fellow." The Lord answered Shepard's prayers, and shortly before his departure "gave me her who was a most sweet humble woman, full of Christ, and a very discerning Christian." On a mid-summer day in 1697, Samuel Sewall and two friends, Edward Taylor and Mr. Fitch, wandered the streets of Boston exchanging opinions about the qualities they sought in a "meet yoke fellow." "We sat down on the great Rock," Sewall recorded, "and Mr. Taylor told me his courting his first wife, and Mr. Fitch his story of Mr. Dod's prayer to God to bring his Affection to close with a person pious, but hard-favored." When John Chew filed a pre-nuptial agreement with the York County, Virginia court in 1651, he did so "out of the singular love and affection that I beare unto Mistress Rachell Counstable whome I intend (by God's grace) shortly to make my wife.[10]

Evidence of the expectation of mutual love and respect in marriage is sometimes best illustrated in cases when its absence was a point of contention between husband and wife. In certain cases, the colonial court provided a forum for troubled couples attempting to negotiate their way through the trials of married life. During an extraordinary session of the court in Albany in April, 1681, Anneke Schaets, daughter of the minister at Albany, Gideon Schaets, accused her husband of failing to honor the call to mutual love and companionship. Thomas Davidtse admitted to his shortfall. Before the court, he promised, "to conduct himself well and honorably towards his wife; to love and never neglect her." To insure that he maintain his demeanor, "and for better assurance of his real Intention and good resolution," Davidtse requested that "two good men be named to oversee his conduct at New York toward his said wife, being entirely disposed and inclined to live honorably and well with her as a Christian man ought." By the same token, Anneke Schaets agreed not to desert her husband, but "with him to share the sweets and sours as becomes a Christian spouse." Another Dutch Calvinist, Jeronimos Douwersen, responded to his wife's accusation of desertion, made before the court in Kingston in 1672, with the counter-charge that she "cannot serve him as a wife," and that she "has said that she never loved him." Though he swore that he had never said he would leave her, Douwersen recognized that if, in fact, he chose to do so he would have had ample justification; no marriage could be sustained without mutual love. Similarly, Francis Howard, Anglican governor of Virginia, confessed that it was in his wife's absence that he felt most acutely the value of his companiate marriage. He wrote frequently to Philadelphia Pelham Howard, bemoaning the loss of her fellowship and Christian conversation. Late in the winter of 1684, he wrote "I misse your good example, assistance, and Company in my devotions at night as wee used to do, and at other times on speciall occasions, but you never misse my prayers."[11]

In spite of the Protestant emphasis on the "companionate" marriage, however, sermons, treatises, and pamphlets reinforced the notion of wifely submission in the marriage bond. Indeed, contemporary tracts on marriage frequently characterized women as overly passionate, irrational, and potentially profane, in dire need of the control and direction they might expect from a good husband. Reformers from William Gouge to William Perkins emphasized the need for male authority in the home; most were careful to distinguish between a husband's and wife's spiritual and civil relationships with one another. Though the former might be based in equality, the latter most certainly was not.[12]

Yet the gap between prescriptive formulas and the realities of day-to-day life introduced a number of complexities into the marital bond. Husband-wife relationships varied from household to household, shaped by the family's economic needs, demographic considerations, and personal philosophy. Moreover, the impact of patriarchal rule was mitigated by a revolutionary change in the legal and religious definition of marriage. As sacred as the Protestant church deemed the relationship between husband and wife, according to Reformed doctrine marriage was redefined as a contract rather than the sacrament it had been in the Catholic Church. If either party disobeyed the terms of their marriage contract—spiritually, economically, physically—the marriage could be thrown out of balance, subject to community and legal scrutiny, and, under certain circumstances, dissolved. Neglect, gross misbehavior, and infidelity were all grounds for divorce in the seventeenth-century colonies. And since men were more likely to misbehave than women, women were more likely to be the spouse petitioning for the dissolution of the marriage[13].

Some Protestant divines, among them Thomas Hooker, whose words on the subject are quoted at the beginning of this chapter, counseled women to bear with impious spouses, obey their wishes, and find comfort in the fact that holy marriage to the Lord would be their reward in heaven. His advice was in keeping with Calvin's own instructions to troubled spouses. In the end, the best weapon against the impiety of a spouse was profound personal faith. "The piety of the one," Calvin promised, "has more effect in sanctifying marriage than the impiety of the other in polluting it." Moreover, it was possible that by her example a wife might be the agent of her husband's salvation. God, in his wisdom, "condescends to make us ministers of his grace for the salvation of his brethren." In God's eyes, wives were no exception; he could bestow upon the wife the means by which she might save her faithless husband. "If Men are so wicked" wrote Cotton Mather in a 1692 sermon directed toward women, "as to deny your being *rational* creatures, the best Means to confute them, will be by proving yourselves *religious* ones." The religious wife would be "matched against the mind" of her carnal husband, who, if he refused to follow his wife's example, would be justly punished on his day of reckoning. As the New England minister Michael Wigglesworth wrote in his poem *The Day of Doom*, "The godly wife conceives no grief, nor can she shed a tear/ For the sad state of her dear Mate, when she his doom doth hear." The Christian wife could obey her unbelieving spouse and leave his punishment up to God.[14]

The promise of a better marriage in the hereafter, however, did not always provide sufficient solace to the Protestant wife who daily confronted an evil spouse. Some wives chose to challenge the authority of their husbands. Katherine Chidley, a radical Non-Conformist writing in England on the eve of the Civil War, equated the misplaced authority of a sinful husband with that of a corrupt church; neither was to be suffered for long:

> O! that you would consider the text in 1 Cor.7. which plainly declares that the wife may be the beleever, & the husband an unbeleever, but if you have considered this text, I pray you tell me, what authority this unbeleeving husband hath over the conscience of his beleeving wife; It is true he hath authority over her in bodily and civill respects, but not to be a Lord over her conscience.

In the name of her conscience, a godly wife might disobey the will of her unbelieving husband, or, under certain circumstances, separate from him altogether.[15]

Within the bounds of even the healthiest marriage, the promise to "love and obey" was tempered by spiritual belief. Since Christians owed their fealty to God above all others, the faithful wife knew that she need not submit to the will of a husband she deemed profane. As Francis Cornwall preached 1645, "in all things appertaining to conscience," the pious Christian was beholden to "no Husband . . . but the royall King Jesus." God's Word, above all others, ruled in the Christian home. And with equal access to the Word of God, the Christian wife could arm herself against her husband's profanity.[16]

Properly armed, the believing wife could denounce her husband's impiety and use the opportunity to publicly distance herself from him. Early in the eighteenth century, Hannah Abrahams proclaimed her repentance before the elders of the First Church in Salem and begged to be restored to the congregation. Newly widowed, she had been suspended for becoming pregnant with the child of a man who subsequently became her second husband. Hannah had asked the congregation many times to forgive her, but admitted that the only thing that had prevented her from full repentance was "the perverseness of her Husband, who would not suffer her to make a confession, least they should be presented." In the throws of a grave illness, however, she vowed to God that if He should spare her life "she would brake through all the difficultys." Rather than obey the will of an impious husband who feared the shame of public exposure, Hannah confessed her sins before the church, "that she might dye in their favor." Fear for her own salvation weighed more heavily upon her than the wrath of a disapproving husband.[17]

PIETY AND THE MARRIAGE BOND IN MASSACHUSETTS

Foremost among the decisions a husband and wife expected to make when they settled in colonial Massachusetts was when, where, and in what capacity they would join a church congregation. While Puritan women remained subservient to their husbands in many aspects of civil life, they frequently acted independently with regard to the pursuit of full membership in the church. For example, though the founding members of churches in Charlestown and Cambridge were composed largely of co-covenanting couples and married or single men who joined alone, within a few short years women began to exercise greater independence. By the mid-1630s, with the advent of conversion requirements in Charlestown, for instance, women began to take the lead in the decision to profess. In the years 1635–1637, wives initiated their family's ties to the church in 55% of cases; some 45% of their husbands chose to follow them into the fold. Of a group of forty new church members from 1640–1644, eleven wives joined without their husbands, and ten other wives initiated membership for the family. Two couples co-covenanted during those years. The feminization of the Protestant church in the colonies, most striking in Puritan Massachusetts, rests as a clear sign that, with regard to their own salvation, wives increasingly acted autonomously.[18]

The feminization of the church in Massachusetts presented elders with a new problem: how to contend with female members who depended upon non-member husbands to supply their contributions for the support of the minister and the administration of the sacraments. Wenham minister John Fiske noted "with reference to the sisters of the church whose husbands were not of us," that one Mr. Shipley had declined to make payments for his wife for the maintenance of the elements of the Lord's Table. Fiske suggested that such "neighbors . . . may be lovingly persuaded to contribute the proportion of their wive's parts." If community pressures could not be brought to bear, however, the deacons were instructed to supply the necessary money out of the general church fund. The church would see to it that a non-member husband would prove no barrier to his wife's full participation.[19]

Even within the bounds of a pious marriage, where both spouses were full members of a congregation, Puritan wives found opportunities to proclaim spiritual independence. Sometimes the threat to pious marriage came not from their husbands, but from church leaders. Thus when duty called, pious wives were prepared to challenge their ministers' authority. In Boston in the winter of 1669–1670, female church members called upon both their spiritual authority and the sanctity of the marriage bond to justify their requests for dismission from the First Church. In the search for salvation, loyalty to God and family outweighed obedience to church elders or their minister. When a group of men abandoned the First Church to form their own congregation, twenty of their wives petitioned for dismissal. The elders dragged their feet, unwilling, perhaps, to honor a petition presented by women. As days turned into weeks, the women, of their own accord and against the wishes of the church leadership, attended communion with their husbands in the newly-established Third Church of Boston. They made it clear to the elders in their petition that it was within their rights both as wives and as free Christians to worship where they pleased. "Wee humbly intreat you . . . " they wrote, "to release us from our Covenant engagement unto yourselves, that we may . . . have liberty so to provide for our own peace and spirituall comfort as may, in our own consciences be most suitable to our duety for our oedification in the Lord." Moreover, as loyal Christian wives, the petitioners sought only to avoid "the confusion, disorder, and disturbance which will unavoidably follow, when husbands goe to one place and wives to another to worship." Rather than rely on their husbands to do battle for them, the dissenting women of Boston's First Church took matters into their own hands. Their piety allowed them certain liberties to challenge authority, even within the context of their male-dominated worlds.[20]

Piety and Marriage in Early New York

By comparison with religiously homogeneous Massachusetts, where throughout the seventeenth century husbands and wives usually worshipped at the same church (even if only one spouse was a full member of the congregation), in Dutch New Netherland, wives and husbands contended with religious diversity within their own churches and families. Especially in the wake of the English conquest of New Netherland, Dutch women and men confronted profound threats to their religious culture, as colonists married outside of their faith and ethnic background.[21]

Even in the years prior to the English conquest of New York, the colony's clerical leaders expressed some concern over the pressures that so great a religious diversity placed on their Dutch families and on the institution of marriage. The Dutch church itself was home to French, German, English, and Scandinavian Protestants; the colony's economic health depended upon the contributions of and tolerance for settlers from outside of the Netherlands. As a result, Dutch religious culture seemed threatened from all sides. Domines Megapolensis and Drisius of the Dutch Church in New York City expressed to that town's burgomasters their concerns about the negative impact religious toleration might have on the families in their congregation. "We feel sure that great contention and discord will develop therefrom," they wrote in the summer of 1657, "not only among the inhabitants and citizens in general, but also in families, of which we have had proofs and complaints . . . .Some husbands have forced their wives to leave their own church, and attend their conventicles."[22]

The Domines' fears were in large part unfounded, however. Rather than cede responsibility for their salvation to their husbands, or bow to the social and political pressures that accompanied English rule, Dutch women responded by becoming even stronger advocates of the Dutch Reformed Church. And as pious purveyors of the Dutch Protestant tradition, Dutch women proved capable of protecting their own—and their family's—spiritual inheritance and ethnic identity.[23]

Even as the rate of English and Dutch intermarriage increased, Dutch women expressed their ethnic consciousness through worship in the Reformed Church, regardless of their husbands' affiliation. Out of twenty-five female members of the Dutch Church who married English men in the 1680s, twenty remained members even when their husbands chose not to affiliate. According to Henricus Seleyn's list of the members of his congregation in 1686 (a period of increasing strife between the English and Dutch), there were 179 married couples, 100 wives of non-members, thirty-three single men and thirty-one single women. Forty-four percent of the households in Selyns' congregation were represented by female members alone. From the middle of the seventeenth century on, Dutch women took the lead in directing their family's religious affiliation, and demonstrated time and again the depth of their piety in the face of increasing diversity and cultural conflict.[24]

Cultural competition and other trials of daily life in the colony could, in fact, inspire a woman to greater spiritual heights. Radical non-conformist Jasper Danckaets noted in his journal several occasions when a wife's piety equaled or exceeded that of her husband's, in spite of grave odds. One woman, referred to only as Illetie, was born of a Dutch father and an Indian mother. She converted to the Dutch religion and joined the church in Schenectady. In the years preceding her conversion, Illetie explored with increasing urgency and interest the teachings of the Dutch church. She found comfort among Christians, she told Danckaerts, though she had been brought up by her mother to distrust their doctrines. She married a Dutch man who, according to Danckaerts, was "not as good as she is, though he is not one of the worst; she sets a good example before him, and knows how to direct him." Danckaerts was especially impressed with the piety of Elizabeth Roderburgh, the wife of Ephraim Hermans. Though both Elizabeth and her husband shared a deeply pious, contemplative life together, it was to Elizabeth that Danckaerts chose to send a Dutch translation of Labadie's 1667 treatise, *The Liftings Up of the Soul to God*, noting that "she had evinced a great inclination for it, and relished it much." Danckaerts also took pains to describe Maria van Rensselaer, as "polite, well-informed, and of good life and disposition." Maria, the widow of Jeremias van Rensselaer, had suffered much with her parents' deaths and had been gravely ill as a result of the birth of her last child. Danckaerts noted that in spite of, or perhaps because of the pain, Maria had "experienced several proofs of the Lord." While few Dutch Protestants could meet Jasper Danckaerts' rigid standards (his journal is filled with self-congratulatory comments that reveal his strong ego and his evangelical bent), he was especially sensitive to female piety, and the odds against which a woman had to struggle to maintain it.[25]

A woman's piety could easily be threatened by the actions of an impious spouse. Dutch wives turned to the courts for protection against their impure husbands. Like Puritan jurisprudence, which respected lay pleading and promoted the individual's adherence to God's rules, the Dutch courts offered women—married and single—a forum in which to air their complaints. Obedience to God was paramount; women were encouraged to seek punishment of men who abused their authority and acted sinfully. Especially in pre-conquest New Netherland, where wives benefited from Roman-Dutch law that treated them as *feme sole*, the court aided women who, in the name of piety, acted independently.[26]

When in the winter of 1674 Annetie Cornelis brought suit against her husband, a former Lutheran minister, Jacob Fabritious, she knew she faced a court that was predisposed to take her part; civic and clerical leaders in New York had long been wary of Fabritious, whose rough ways and blatant proselytizing were notorious among Dutch and English alike. Even with that advantage, Annetie Cornelis made careful use of pious language to justify her attempts to shatter the marriage bond *and* wrest control of substantial property.

Court minutes noted that Cornelis approached the bench "with very great humility," a positive trait among pious women. Her husband, she declared, was "a drunken and constant prophaner of God's name, a ci-devant Lutheran preacher . . . married but unfaithful." Forced by him to move out of her own house—property she had intended to give to her son—she was obliged to spend the winter in a garret, which, she pleaded, "truly is a very hard thing to happen to an old woman." The house, Cornelis told the court, belonged "to her and her children from God and nature," and she was bound and determined to take possession of it. Her husband's behavior and his continued control of the property "ought not be tolerated in a place where law is maintained." The laws of both God and man should surely protect her best interests. The court apparently agreed; Annetie Cornelis's petition was granted, and Fabritious was forced to vacate the house. As winter turned to spring, Fabritious tried several times to reclaim both wife and property. On more than one occasion he pushed his way into the house, against the will and consent of his wife and the court. In July Cornelis called the sheriff to remove Fabritious from her property. The sheriff, in language similar in tone and meaning to Cornelis's, recommended that Fabritious "be banished forever . . . as a person unworthy to live in a well regulated Burghery." Though the Burgomasters and Schepens agreed that a more severe punishment was in order, they fined Fabritious Fl. 100, and demanded that he keep his distance from his wife.[27] Throughout the ordeal, Cornelis had successfully juxtaposed her humility with her husband's arrogance, her piety with her husband's profanity. It was language the court and the community understood.

Ten years earlier, in March of 1665, the court served as the stage for another battle between husband and wife. Arent Juriaenson Lantsman approached the New York Court of Burgomasters and Schepens to demand that his wife, who had retreated to her parents' house when her husband mistreated her, return to her rightful place at home with their children. The court, having heard testimony from both parties, decreed that Lantsman must promise "before God and justice to keep a peaceable house," or forfeit his rights as a husband. Spousal rights were the privilege of only those who adhered to God's demand for mutual respect.

The court's judgment apparently did not satisfy Lantsman's wife, Beletje Post, who used the occasion of her husband's suit to press her own case. She had absented herself with good reason: her husband frequently treated her in an "Unchristian and insufferable" manner. Submitting her own remonstrance to the court, she requested a divorce from Lantsman, with whom she declared she could not "keep house." The defendant denied mistreating his wife, but could find no witnesses to testify on his behalf. The court recommended that "some honorable and fitting person" be brought in to mediate between the warring husband and wife, with the hope of facilitating a speedy reconciliation. In desperation, they turned to New York City Ministers Megapolensis and Drisius. Should either party refuse to submit to the Domines' advice, the court vowed, the couple would be held up as an example to other "evil householders." Try as they might, however, the ministers failed to reconcile the two. The court, in the hope that the family might be preserved, ordered Beletie to attempt once more to cohabit with her husband, a ruling with which she complied.

Peace, alas, was temporary; Beletie filed several complaints against her husband over the ensuing few years. Six years after the original suit, Lantsman, in contempt of the court's order to live peaceably and piously with his wife, "aggravated his evil behavior by blasphemy," for which, the court declared, he deserved, "to be severely punished as an example to others." A year later, Beletie remained quartered away from her husband, still in pursuit of a divorce.[28]

Though the record is silent on the ultimate outcome of the case, the court seemed by then far less inclined to encourage the wife to forgive her perpetually wayward husband. Though the burgomasters and schepens of New York clearly did everything in their power to honor the wishes of the husband—including giving him several opportunities to alter his behavior—they were equally willing to hear Beletie's complaints against her blasphemous and unchristian spouse, complaints she clearly felt she had every right to make. Court records make no mention of physical violence. In Beletie's eyes—and the court's—her husband's blasphemous, insufferable behavior, and his inability to keep a Christian house with her, were grounds enough to defend her separating from him.

Gender, Piety and Power in Virginia Marriage

In seventeenth-century Virginia, demographic conditions joined religious practice to enhance the position of a woman *vis-à-vis* her husband. The dramatic sexual imbalance made a wife a valuable "commodity." Among the first few generations of colonists, who generally married several years later on average in Virginia than in England, a woman's labor was necessary to the financial health of the family. Moreover, the high mortality rate, which by some accounts persisted throughout the seventeenth century, also destabilized patriarchal control. Married women, once they survived their childbearing years, were more likely to outlive their husbands and remarry; the property they brought with them to a second or third marriage made them even more marketable.[29]

Because women were in short supply, they exercised a certain degree of autonomy through their marriage options. The marketability of a marriageable woman sometimes led her to overstep the bounds of law and propriety. In June of 1624, spring fever apparently got the better of Ellinor Sprage, who contracted herself in marriage "to two severall men at one tyme." The court ordered that on the next Sabbath day Ellinor Sprage "shall publickly before the Congregatione, Acknowleg her offence . . . and penitently Confessing her falte shall aske God and the Congregations forgiveness." Moreover, to prevent a similar offense in others— which the court seemed to believe was a distinct possibility—every Virginia minister was ordered to give notice to all his parishioners that the act of promising oneself to more than one person was punishable by whipping and by fine, "or other wyse Accordinge to the quallitie of the person offendinge." Though Ellinor Sprage had not legally contracted a marriage with any man, her words of promise "soe as may entangle and breede scrouple in theire Consequences," constituted a breach of piety, decorum, and ultimately law. The law regarding marriage made no distinctions based on gender; both men and women were expected to adhere to the same standards of piety and decorum with regard to promises of betrothal. This was in spite of demographic conditions that clearly indicated women would have a greater opportunity and inclination to make false promises than men.[30]

Once a man and woman contracted a legal marriage in Virginia's Anglican Church, they were as likely to expect companionship and love as Congregational or Dutch Reformed Protestants to the north. Captain Francis Page's eulogy for his wife, Mary, who died in Bruton Parish in 1690, attests to the respect and love he bore her during what was probably a short marriage (she died in her thirties):

> Thy modest, meek, and pious soul did shine
> With well-temper'd nature, and grace divine:
> One to excell in beauty, few could find;
> Yet thy rarest features were of the minde.
> Thou was a faithful and virtuous wife;
> Thou greatly loved peace and hated strife;
> Thou was a prudent and tender mother,
> A true-loving sister to each brother,
> A choice friend, a kind neighbor [illegible]
> A good Christian, ready at God's call [illegible]
> Thou lived and died, upon Christ relying;

Thou died to rise, and now livith by dying,
Thy faith doth yeild, thy piety doth give,
Restoratives to make thee ever live . . .

Respected (at least in death) for her profound piety, kindness, and grace, Mary Page was the epitome of the Christian wife. Her short but faithful life rendered her, in the eyes of her husband, family, and community, as likely as any in the parish to ascend to heaven and gain life ever lasting.[31]

William Byrd II and his wife Lucy Parke Byrd also shared such companionship. Byrd's diary includes dozens of references to activities he engaged in with his wife, many of them at least tangentially religious. William and Lucy Byrd spent many an evening discussing sermons, reading aloud from religious treatises, or quarreling about the singing of psalms. Their discussions strayed to the weightiest of matters as well, including such issues as the infallibility of the Bible.[32]

Even when an ocean separated husband and wife, they might continue to pursue companionship, love, and spirituality. Francis Howard, Baron Effingham, Governor of Virginia in the 1680s, wrote long, effusive letters to his wife, Philadelphia, who had remained in England with their children. She in turn wrote "Kind and endearing letters" which he read "with great affection, and delight." A devout member of the Anglican high church, Effingham's demeanor toward his wife exhibited nothing of the patriarchal bent with which the church has long been associated. He yearned for her pious counsel, and dismissed the notion that a wife was in constant need of guidance and control. "I misse your good example, assistance, and Company in my devotions at night as we used to do, and at other times on speciall occasions," he wrote Philadelphia in March of 1684. A month later he begged of her, "Pray remember me particularly on Easter day in Your prayers, or any other holy time that our prayers may meet at the Throne of Grace for Each other though our bodys do not." Through their letters Philadelphia and Francis Howard tried to preserve their spiritual bond, in spite of the tests of time and distance.[33]

Of course not all Virginia marriages were as affectionate as the Effingham's. And when ties between husband and wife broke down, in the south as well as in Massachusetts or New York, the injured spouse knew she could rely on one of several avenues to redress her grievances with her husband. Though patriarchal control arguably reasserted itself by the second half of the seventeenth century in Virginia, aggrieved wives continued to look to the courts for satisfaction, and the courts listened to their complaints.

Savvy wives demonstrated that they knew how to manipulate language to their advantage. Often, the words they chose to use in bringing charges against their husbands spoke to their relative piety, regardless of what their complaint was really about. In the summer of 1665, Grace Grey of Charles City County lodged a complaint in the county court against her husband, Captain Francis Grey, "for sevrall missusages of her & denyall of...food & raymt [raiment] according to her quality." This initial complaint, justified on the grounds of relatively mundane deprivations foreign to a woman of Grace Grey's "quality," resulted in the decision to allow her to separate from her husband and collect an allowance from him "for her dyet & habit." Final resolution in the case could be made only after the court had the time to examine the evidence at length. This action apparently did not satisfy Grace Grey, who took her complaint to the highest authority in the colony when she petitioned Governor William Berkeley for a separation and a divorce. In that forum, Grace Grey reconfigured her charges; she carefully chose language that emphasized her piety and patience, her exemplary behavior as a Christian wife, and the unacceptable *un*christian behavior of her husband.[34]

Though Grace Grey did not deny the material motivation for her complaints against her husband—she had, she claimed, "brought him considerable estate of wch he was then destitute"—she tempered her petition with language designed to reflect her commitment to a benevolent, loving, Christian marriage. She had lived "in the Honoble Estate of wedlock wth her sd husbd foure & twenty yeares...In all wch tyme...yor petisonr hath not failed in the least requsite in a Loveing & obedient wife, but hath diligently served him wth all possible care paines love loyalty & true obedience." In spite of her love and loyalty, "the sd Capt Grey hath for many years abused yor petisonr by private & unspeakable devises." Treated like "a most contemptible slave in the hands of an Imperious tyrant," Grace Grey nevertheless tried to forebear, the duty of all Christian wives. Furthermore, she expected no legal recourse, for, as she slyly noted

> even the most brutel & savage, & therefore much more all Christian law makers
> have thought it needlesse to prescribe rules & lawes, how men should use their
> wives, there being so glorious a comparison betwixt Christ & his Church of
> wedded matrimony that the divell might be thought to want [torn: cunning?] to
> persuade the worst of men to abuse a Loveing & obedient wife.

In a few carefully chosen sentences, Grace Grey not only forgave the lawmakers for not protecting her from an unchristian oaf—after all, why should they believe, any more than she had, that a Christian husband would willfully undermine a relationship so profoundly symbolic of the union between Christ and church—but she reasserted he own innocent behavior and pious comportment in the process. Grace Grey closed her petition with words designed to flatter the Governor: just as she had begun to lose hope of relief, she added, "it hath pleased God, to put us undr yor Honors Christian & Happy govment who is a knowne reliever of the distressed."[35]

Not all complainants were as well-connected or articulate as Grace Grey. Just months after Alice Clawson had suffered the humiliation of having her husband William deny paternity of her newborn child, she petitioned the Accomac, Virginia court for separation. In her petition she labeled William "a very Extravigant unworthy person in his life and Conversation, Spendinge his tyme amongst the Indyans, and demeaneinge himselfe in a most Lettigious, Leawd, dishonest manner." Alice claimed to have suffered his behavior long enough, and swore that if William continued to bother her she would "take the Assistance of the Sherriff (or neighbors) to rescue her." Upset with her husband, Alice was perfectly willing to air her grievances before the court, the law, and her neighbors alike. And she apparently knew how best to garner the court's sympathy, for she was granted not only a separation, but a divorce, on the grounds that "William Clawson . . . hath lived in an Adulterous life amongst the Indyans, the greatest part of the tyme hee hath been marryed." Furthermore, the court claimed, William Clawson was "so Naturalized to the pagans That hee is known by the name of . . . sonne in lawe to . . . the kinge of the Nanticoke." No wife should be required to live with a pagan husband who worshipped among the Indians. Alice effectively played upon fears of Indian paganism, at a time when tales of local Indian troubles inspired trepidation in most Virginia communities. The fact that Alice might—or might not—have borne the child outside of the marriage was no longer the central consideration.[36]

The case of Elizabeth Taylor vs. James Taylor is more typical of the pitched battles waged between spouses in the seventeenth century. Elizabeth Taylor's complaints against her adulterous, abusive husband, though brought in civil and not ecclesiastical court—as would have been the case in England—resonate with the passion of a wife whose expectations of a pious, decorous marriage in the sight of God have been quashed.

The wayward James Taylor, identified by court records as a "chyrurgeon," first appeared before the Surry County court in 1654 in a case brought by a household servant, Ursula Keetle, who claimed he had gotten her pregnant. The twenty-year-old Keetle alleged that her master had "often times urged to lye with him," requests that apparently became more urgent after Taylor married. Though Keetle "of a long time denyed him," she finally succumbed to his pleas. Several times, she claimed, he left his wife's bed to come to hers. Because "noe man ever lay with her but her . . . master," she knew the baby she had just delivered was his.

The beleaguered Taylor had not seen the end of his legal troubles. His wife Elizabeth soon lodged her own complaint. Not only had her husband "kept a whore in the house ever since he married her," but, to make matters worse, the slattern had the audacity to rub Elizabeth's nose in her husband's infidelity by treating her mistress in a "peremptory" manner. Elizabeth's complaint, however, was not against the servant Keetle, as offensive as her actions had been. Her adulterous husband was the true enemy. Moreover, his adultery apparently had not been shame enough; after he had got the servant with child and sent her away, he took his frustrations and anger out on Elizabeth by scandalizing her name in public. James Taylor had blasphemed when he brought dishonor upon his wife. Taylor, Elizabeth alleged, "did abuse her, Callinge her Whore, Jade, Bitch, and such like." He had threatened to "slitt yor Complaynants nose for a whore." That, it seemed, was the last straw. Not only had Taylor committed the sin of adultery, but he also brought shame upon an innocent woman, using language explicitly designed to impugn her purity. Elizabeth petitioned the court for a separation, expressed her desire to live with her mother, and made it clear to the court that she expected to have "a

Considerable maintenance allowed her from the Sd. Taylor." In Elizabeth's mind, not only did her husband's shameful, impious, and impenitent manner and actions bestow upon her the right to walk away from her marriage, but the terms of their contract guaranteed her the right to financial support whether she lived with him or not.[37]

Gender, Marriage, and Property in Colonial America

The financial implications of Elizabeth and James Taylor's case before the Virginia court run counter to the opinions of most scholars, who gage the relative strength of patriarchy in the colonies by the existence and enforcement of laws of couverture. A wife, "covered" under law by her husband, became in essence his property, and forfeited the right to control property of her own. English common law was not as restrictive in the American colonies as it was in England, however. Several mitigating factors, including the persistent influence of Roman-Dutch law in New York, the relative value of a wife in woman-deprived Virginia, and, as argued here, strong religious convictions that enhanced a woman's autonomy, all worked to benefit married women.[38]

As several of the above cases demonstrate, a married woman could juxtapose her own piety against her husband's impurity in ways that convinced the court to undermine laws of couverture. When a wife could prove that by his impious behavior a husband had violated the terms of the marriage contract, she could wrest control of property in the name of protecting and supporting herself and her children.

Rarely was a husband's lewd or adulterous behavior as widely broadcast as Daniel Parke's, whose scandalous affair with a woman he had brought with him to Virginia was denounced by Commissary James Blair from the pulpit of his church in Bruton Parish at the end of the seventeenth century.[39] Instead, evidence of the shifting balance of power between wives and their wayward husbands often lies buried in fragments of court cases.

The court in Surry County, Virginia seems to have been particularly sensitive to the plight of beleaguered wives who struggled to protect themselves and their property. The court responded to the barest hint of impropriety in 1670 when it subverted the law of couverture to insure that Elizabeth Warren, contracted to marry John Hunicut, retain control of all property she was bringing to the union. Though the circumstances prompting the order are not detailed in the court records, the tiny extant fragment serves as a window on gender relations in Virginia. Hunicut and Warren, it seems, had entered into the contract of marriage quite suddenly, with speed enough to cause some community speculation about the reason for such haste. In this case, however, it was a matter of property not pregnancy that encouraged the court to step in "for the better clearing of all doubts & Scruples that May arise as aspersions cast in the way to either of theire discreditts." Elizabeth Warren, listed by the court as "spinster," undoubtedly brought substantial property to the marriage. Had Hunicut pursued her for her money alone? Such thoughts clearly plagued the couple and consumed their neighbors, enough so that Hunicut, to "clear all doubts and Scruples" and protect his and his financé's honor, agreed to "make over unto the sd. Elizabeth Warren & to her heirs all such cattle Chattles & household goods as she stands possessed of." A woman of property in Virginia might well have been a valuable commodity, but women and men learned that neither court nor church would suffer the denigration of marriage by its reduction to merely property concerns.[40]

The Surry County court also stepped in to protect deserted wives from debts accrued by their husbands. In 1678, Samuall Mathews, "a Man of a strange Lewd Life & Conversation," departed the county leaving his wife with nothing to subsist on. At the wife's request, the court ordered "that what shee shall hereafter get bee & remaine for her owne Mainetaneance" until Mathews appeared in court and provided sufficient evidence that he would repeat neither his behavior nor his abandonment. Similarly, in 1672 Mary Hare, wife of the runaway William Hare, petitioned the court for protection of property given to her by her first husband, George Carter. The court ordered that profits from the land Carter had willed to Mary were not to be used to satisfy William Hare's debts, but were to be used solely for the maintenance of Mary and her child. Several months later Hare had apparently returned, for he filed a petition against Jonathan Kindred for "disorderly walking" with Mary. Kindred was ordered to keep his distance from Mary "unless at the Church or som othr. meeting." In spite of Mary's own suspect behavior, however, when Hare disappeared again in 1674, the court once more honored her petition that the land she brought to the marriage be returned to her and that any income she thereafter derived from her property be used for her maintenance and not to pay Hare's debts. Though Mary Hare relinquished her right to any part of William's estate should he be found dead, she had acted with authority to protect her welfare and that of her child. Their personal property would forever be protected from claims against her wayward husband's estate.[41]

THE Minister's Widow in seventeenth-century new york

Just as little attention has been paid to those instances in seventeenth-century Virginia when an abused wife used the courts to subvert couverture and lay claim to her own property, so too has little attention been paid to a special category of colonial widow, the minister's wife. Here the wife, by virtue of the honor accorded her as the spouse of a religious leader, gained certain property rights not usually guaranteed by colonial law. In Dutch New Netherland, widows of local ministers reaped the benefits of the Reformed Church's ecclesiastical hierarchy and its close ties to the mother country; according to Dutch ecclesiastical custom, replicated locally, the widow received the full salary of the quarter in which her husband died, together with the salary of the entire half-year following. In Flatbush, the articles of agreement with the minister in 1680 stated that, in the event of his decease, his widow would be paid "one hundred and twenty shepels of good wheat or fifty pieces of eight in money, and that yearly, in addition to the salary of one entire year . . . which is called the year of grace." She was also allowed to occupy the house until the arrival of the new minister. In the event of her remarriage, the widow would lose her year-ly support, though she maintained her right to the year of grace.[42]

Minister's widows were well aware of their due, and took in upon themselves to make sure they received the full benefits of widowhood. When parishioners fell behind in their payments (as they frequently did with respect to both a living min-ister's salary and his widow's benefits), widows petitioned the court for redress. Samuel Drisius' widow petitioned the court for her arrears in 1671; the court ordered that they be paid promptly, within fourteen days. In 1674 the widow and son of Domine Samuel Megapolensis enlisted the help of Cornelis van Ruyven in their petition to collect on the payment of the arrears of the minister's salary. The Reverend Caspar van Zuuren, minister of Flatbush, had to contend with the wrath of an especially contentious widow. Long before her husband's death, Catherine Polhemus had staked claim to her due as a minister's wife. In 1654, as she waited in Holland to be called to New Netherland by her husband, pending his official approval as minister to Flatbush, Catherine Polhemus wrote to the Amsterdam Classis requesting money she believed her husband had earned as a minister in Brazil. The Classis turned to the Directors of the West India Company for assistance in meeting the debt. The directors of the company procured for Catherine 100 guilders, not in payment of arrears—which apparently they did not believe she was due—but as a loan. Almost three decades later, the widow Polhemus continued to press a multitude of claims and suits against her neighbors and the Rev. van Zuuren in Flatbush. So upset was the widow over the disposition of one particular property that she absented herself from Communion until she was satisfied her claim was settled in her favor.[43]

* * *

Only a few colonial women could stake any claims—spiritual, economic, or social—based on their marriage to a minister of the Lord. But all Protestant women could aspire to become brides of Christ. Their faith, and the fortitude to pursue sal-vation with or without the aid of their earthly husbands, would lead them to that most sacred of unions. Moreover, as a woman made the transition from wife to mother, her pious authority and righteous independence assumed added weight. Protestant mothers, like John Bunyan's Christiana, took it upon themselves to insure that the salvation they had earned would be open to their children as well.

NOTES

[1] Thomas Hooker, *The Soul'd Exaltation* (London, 1638), found in *Salvation in New England: Selections From the Sermons of the First Preachers* eds. Phillis M. and Nicholas R. Jones (Austin, 1977), 114.

[2] John Calvin, *Institutes of Christian Religion* [1559], John Allen, ed. and trans. (2 vols., New York, 1936), II, 524–525.

[3] M. Halsey Thomas, ed., *The Diary of Samuel Sewall* (2 vols., New York, 1973), I, 349; "The Public Diary of John Hull," in *Puritan Personal Writings: Diaries* (New York, 1983), 167–168;

Thomas Shepard, "The Soul's Invitation to Christ," quoted in Charles Hambrick-Stowe, *The Practice of Piety: Puritan Devotional Disciplines in Seventeenth-Century New England* (Chapel Hill, 1982), 121–122. See also Shepard's own description of his acceptance of Christ as husband while attending a sermon as a young man in England in the 1620s: Michael McGiffert, ed., *God's Plot: The Paradoxes of Puritan Piety, Being the Autobiography and Journal of Thomas Shepard* (Amherst, Ma., 1972), 45; George Selement and Bruce C. Wooley, eds., *Thomas Shepard's Confessions*, Colonial Society of Massachusetts, *Publications*, 58 (Boston, 1981), 120; Mary Rhinelander McCarl, "Thomas Shepard's Record of Relations of Religious Experience, 1648–1649," *WMQ*, 3d, ser., 48 (July, 1991): 464. On marriage imagery in New England sermons, see Laurel Thatcher Ulrich, *Good Wives: Image and Reality in the Lives of Women in Northern New England, 1650–1750* (New York, 1983), 108. See also Elizabeth Dale, "The Marriage Metaphor in Seventeenth-Century Massachusetts," in Larry D. Eldridge, ed., *Women and Freedom in Early America* (New York, 1997), published after the completion of this study.

4 Edward T. Corwin, ed., *Ecclesiastical Records of the State of New York* (7 vols., Albany, 1901–1916), I, 535; William Powell to Edwin Sandys, April, 1621, Ferrar Papers, Virginia Colonial Records Project, Reel 573; Petition of Grace Grey to Governor William Berkeley, August, 1665, Charles City County Deeds, Wills, Orders, Etc. 1655–1665, Reel 1. For a more complete description of Grace Grey's case against her husband see below.

5 John Cotton, *A Conference...held at Boston with the elders of New-England...* (Boston, 1646). On the seductiveness for women of the Puritan concept of Christ as the "magnificent Bridegroom" see Amanda Porterfield, "Women's Attraction to Puritanism," *Church History* 60 (June, 1991): 198–199; on the relationship between gender, submissiveness, and religious conviction, see Gerald Moran, *Religion, Family and the Life Course: Explorations in the Social History of Early America* (Ann Arbor, 1992), 97–98. Also see Richard Godbeer, "'Love Raptures': Marital, Romantic, and Erotic Images of Jesus Christ in Puritan New England, 1670–1730," *New England Quarterly* 68 (Sept. 1995): 355–385. Godbeer traces the transformation at the end of the seventeenth century of images of Christ as a wronged husband to that of a supporting husband and lover. Preachers increasingly employed earthy language in their description, reinforcing emphasis on human marriage. I would place this shift even earlier in the century than Godbeer does.

6 Thomas and Virginia L. Davis, eds., *Edward Taylor's "Church Records" and Related Sermons* (Boston, 1981), 152.

7 John Calvin, *Institutes*[1559 edition], I, 339–340; William J. Bouwsma, *John Calvin: A Sixteenth-Century Portrait* (New York, 1988), 138, 270n. For a discussion of the Reformation rejection of virginity as a standard for piety, and the related denigration of the cloister, see Steven Ozment, *Protestants: The Birth of a Revolution* (New York, 1992), 152–153. On that point, see above, chapter 1, note 3.

8 John Calvin, *Commentary on the Epistles of Paul the Apostle to the Corinthians*, John Pringle, trans. (2 vols., Edinburgh, 1848), I, 225–229.

9 John Cotton, *A Meet Help, Or a Wedding Sermon* (Boston, 1699); Thomas Hooker, *The Soules Humiliation* (London, 1638); Benjamin Wadsworth, *The Well-Ordered Family* (Boston, 1712).

10 Michael McGiffert, *God's Plot: The Paradoxes of Puritan Piety, Being the Autobiography and Journal of Thomas Shepard* (Amherst, 1972), 50, 53; York County Deeds, Orders, Wills, etc. 1633–1657. Thomas Shepard described his second wife as a woman "of great prudence to take

care for and order my family affairs." McGiffert, ed., 70; Samuel Sewall, *The Diary of Samuell Sewall*, ed. M. Halsey Thomas (2 Vols., New York, 1973), I, 396. Dod's prayer for a "hard-favored" wife is particularly telling: according to seventeenth-century usage, the phrase meant an appearance lacking in grace or beauty. Perhaps Dod believed that a wife of particular beauty would be more likely to stray. In an entry written in Latin (translated by the editor), Sewall recorded a dream he had in which his wife died. Clearly troubled by some recent event in his relationship, Sewall dreamed that his four-year-old daughter Elizabeth whispered to him that his wife had died "in part because of my neglect and want of love." When he awoke from the nightmare, Sewall embraced his wife "as if I had newly married." *Ibid.*, 65.

[11] *Ecclesiastical Records*, II, 762–763, 764; Dina Versteeg, trans., and Peter Christoph, Kenneth Scott, and Kenn Stryker-Rodda, eds., *Kingston Papers* (2 vols., Baltimore, 1976), II, 478. Francis Howard to Philadelphia Pelham Howard, Warren Billings, ed., *The Papers of Francis Howard Baron Howard of Effingham, 1643–1695* (Richmond, 1989), 68. A classic account of the complexity of the relationship between a Puritan husband and wife, and the role of love in that relationship is found in Edmund S. Morgan, *The Puritan Family: Religion and Domestic Relations in Seventeenth-Century New England* (New York, 1944, revised edition, 1966), chapter 2.

[12] For accounts of the prescribed submission of wife to husband see, for instance, Laurel Thatcher Ulrich, *Good Wives*, 106–107; Richard Gildrie, *The Profane, the Civil, and the Godly: The Reformation of Manners in Orthodox New England, 1679–1749*, (University Park, PA, 1994), 90–91, 97–99; Carol Karlsen, *The Devil in the Shape of a Woman: Witchcraft in Colonial New England* (New York, 1987), 162–168, 171–172; Edmund Morgan, *The Puritan Family*, 43–44. Even Amanda Porterfield, one of the few historians to acknowledge the degree of power and authority afforded to women in the marriage bond, categorizes that authority as at best "indirect"—first, because a husband's authority in fact rested on a wife's willingness to accept and submit to it, and second, because wifely submission, affection, and obedience served as models for Christian piety: Porterfield, "Women's Attraction to Puritanism," 199–200, 202, 205. For visual representations of the conflict between the Reformed image of the companionate marriage and the negative characterizations of the unruly wife, see the illustrations that accompany Natalie Zemon Davis, *Society and Culture in Early Modern France* (Stanford, 1975), esp. plates 7, 8, 9, 10, and 11.

[13] Cornelia Dayton writes that in Connecticut, women were three or four times more likely to petition for divorce than their husbands, and that a majority of those petitions were accepted: Cornelia Hughes Dayton, *Women Before the Bar: Gender, Law, and Society in Connecticut, 1639–1789* (Chapel Hill and London, 1995), 109–110. Also see Nancy F. Cott, "Divorce and the Changing Status of Women in Eighteenth-Century Massachusetts," *WMQ*, 3d ser., 33 (1976): 586–614; Cott, "Eighteenth-Century Family and Social Life Revealed in the Massachusetts Divorce Records," *Journal of Social History*, X (1976–1977), 20–43; D. Kelly Weisberg, "'Under Greet Temptations Heer': Women and Divorce in Puritan Massachusetts," *Feminist Studies*, II (1975): 183–193.

[14] Cotton Mather, *Ornaments for the Daughters of Zion* (Boston, 1694); Hooker, *The Soul's Exaultation*; Calvin, *Commentary on Corinthians*, I, 240, 244–245; Michael Wigglesworth, *The Day of Doom*, in *The Puritans: A Sourcebook of Their Writings*, eds., Perry Miller and Thomas H. Johnson (2 vols., New York, 1938, revised 1963), II, 601.

[15] Katherine Chidley, *Justification of the Independent Churches of Christ...Briefly Declaring that the Congregation of Saints ought not to have Dependence in Government upon any other; or direction*

in worship from any other than Christ their Head and LAW-GIVER (London, 1641); *c.f.* Keith Thomas, "Women in the Civil War Sects," in *Crisis in Europe, 1560–1660* (New York, 1965), 333–336. Though Thomas acknowledges that Protestant women wielded spiritual authority in relation to their husbands, he is quick to deny that such authority did anything to mitigate the impact of patriarchy. See below for examples in each colony of wives who challenged the authority of their husbands. See also relevant sections in chapter five.

[16] On the gap between prescribed marital hierarchy and the realities of every-day life, see Martin Ingram, "The Reform of Popular Culture? Sex and Marriage in Early Modern England," in *Popular Culture in Seventeenth-Century England* ed. Barry Reay (London and Sydney, 1985), 133–134, 137. See below for a discussion of the contractual and legal obligations of husband and wife to one another in each of the three colonies.

[17] Richard Pierce, ed., *Records of the First Church in Salem, 1629–1736* (Salem, 1974), 247.

[18] Selement and Woolley, eds., *Thomas Shepard's Confessions*, 44–5; Mary McManus Ramsbottom, "Religion, Society, and the Family in Charlestown, Massachusetts, 1630–1740" (Ph.D. diss., Yale University, 1987), 39, 45, 67–68, 68n, 105–106, 111, 119. Ramsbottom's study adds welcome evidence to the case for the feminization of the church in New England. She lacks evidence, however, to support her statement that women more often understood their covenanting in terms of family relations than their relationship to God (p. 87). Though women indeed joined the church to insure that their children would gain the right to baptism (see below, chapter four), they also joined to insure their own salvation, to take responsibility for their own spiritual development. For a more detailed discussion of the feminization of the church in the American colonies, see below, chapter five. Though the suggestion that the feminization of the church is related to the increasing professionalization of the clergy is compelling, I would add that women sought membership in the church as an institution within which they were free to exercise autonomy and no small degree of authority, professional clergy notwithstanding.

[19] Robert G. Pope, ed., *The Notebook of the Reverend John Fiske*, Colonial Society of Massachusetts *Publications*, vol. 17 (1974), 180. See below, chapter five, for discussion of spiritual liberty and the sacrament of Communion.

[20] Hamilton Andrew Hill, *History of the Old South Church, Boston, 1669–1884* (2 vols., Boston, 1890), I, 168, 165. For a more complete discussion of the First Church schism, and the role women played in church politics, see chapter six, below.

[21] Thomas E. Burke notes that in some New York communities, the English played a smaller role in religious life than in others. In Schenectady, for instance, 1697 household census records reveal only seven individuals of English descent, five of them men married to Dutch women, all widows, a sixth married to a Mohawk woman (widow of a Dutch man): *Mohawk Frontier: The Dutch Community of Schenectady, New York, 1661–1710* (Ithaca, 1991), 119.

[22] Corwin, ed., *Ecclesiastical Records*, I, 387.

[23] Joyce Goodfriend offers exhaustive evidence of the role Dutch wives played in maintaining their religious culture and ethnicity in the face of diversity: Goodfriend, *Before the Melting Pot: Society and Culture in Colonial New York City, 1664–1730* (Princeton, 1992); "Recovering the Religious History of Dutch Reformed Women in Colonial New York," *de Halve Maen* 64 (Winter, 1991); "The Social Dimensions of Congregational Life in Colonial New York City," *WMQ* 3d ser., 46 (1989): 252–278.

[24] Goodfriend, *Before the Melting Pot*, 86–90; "The Social Dimensions of Congregational Life," 257–258. In both works Goodfriend provides substantial evidence for the feminization of the Dutch Church in the seventeenth century: in 1686 62% of members were women, with women predominating 2:1 over men from 1690–1730: *Before the Melting Pot*, 90; "Social Dimensions of Congregational Life," 257–258. See also "Recovering the Religious History of Dutch Reformed Women," 58. While Goodfriend supplies invaluable evidence for both the role women played in maintaining their family's ethnic ties and for the feminization of the Dutch church, her conclusions about the reasons for feminization seem less compelling: she maintains that women took the lead in family worship because men, "preoccupied with business and civic affairs," and "not inclined to strong feelings about religious issues, allowed their spouses to define family religious choices." "Social Dimensions," 275, 276; *Melting Pot*, 210. Her conclusions lead the reader to believe that those decisions fell to Dutch wives by default.

[25] Bartlett Burleigh James and J. Franklin Jameson, eds., *The Journal of Jasper Danckaerts* (New York, 1913, reprinted 1959), 146, 170, 202–205, 214.

[26] On Puritan jurisprudence, and the opportunities for women to appear in court, see Cornelia Hughes Dayton, *Women Before the Bar: Gender, Law and Society in Connecticut, 1639–1789* (Chapel Hill and London, 1995), 10, 31–32. Even in Massachusetts, where laws of couverture ruled, women could, under certain circumstances, gain access to the courts without being accompanied by their husbands. On the legal and property implications of *feme sole* in New York, see below.

[27] Berthold Fernow, ed., *Records of New Amsterdam* (7 vols., New York, 1897), VII, 60, 83, 107.

[28] Fernow, ed., *Records of New Amsterdam*, V, 206–207, 262, 263, 264–265, 271, 272; VI, 65, 193, 340; VII, 27.

[29] Terri L. Snyder, "'Rich Widows are the Best Commodity This Country Affords': Gender Relations and the Rehabilitation of Patriarchy in Virginia, 1660–1700," (Ph.D. diss., University of Iowa, 1992), 254–255, 259–268. See also my own chapter one, note 18. As the title of Snyder's dissertation indicates, she posits that while Virginia's demographic conditions for a time mitigated the impact of patriarchy, by mid-century male leaders in the colony and England saw female authority as a threat to patriarchal political control and social order and reined in on women who were perceived of and represented as undeferential and unruly: Snyder, 3, 61–64, 255, 287–299, 303. James Horn similarly rejects the notion that Virginia's demographic conditions restricted the entrenchment of patriarchy: *Adapting to a New World: English Society in the Seventeenth-Century Chesapeake* (Chapel Hill, 1994), 218–219. On the marriagability of widows, see also Edmund S. Morgan, *American Slavery, American Freedom: The Ordeal of Colonial Virginia* (New York and London, 1975), 164–168.

[30] H. R. McIlwaine, ed., *Minutes of the Council and General Court of Colonial Virginia* (Richmond, 1924, reprint 1979), 15. For an example of the laws that governed marriage—the procedure for granting and obtaining licenses, and the ministerial role in the posting of banns and sanctifying marriage, see C.G. Chamberlayne, ed., *The Vestry Book of Christ Church Parish* (Richmond, 1927), 41–42.

[31] Bishop Meade, *Old Churches, Ministers, and Families of Virginia* (2 vols., Philadelphia, 1878), I, 196–197. I have been unable to locate the records in which Bishop Meade found the text of the eulogy. Though Meade's work is rightfully criticized by scholars as the product of a non-historian driven by his desire to romanticize the slave south, it nonetheless includes within

its pages enticing bits from sources that unfortunately have long since disappeared from Virginia archives.

[32] Louis B. Wright and Marion Tinling, eds., *The Secret Diary of William Byrd of Westover, 1709–1712* (Richmond, 1941), 29, 110, 272, 273. For a contrasting interpretation of William Byrd, one which, I believe, undermines the complexity of Byrd's relationship with his wife and other women, see Kenneth A. Lockridge, *On the Sources of Patriarchal Rage: The Commonplace Books of William Byrd and Thomas Jefferson and the Gendering of Power in the Eighteenth Century* (New York, 1992). See also Lockridge, *The Diary, and Life, of William Byrd II, 1675–1744* (Chapel Hill, 1987).

[33] Warren Billings, ed., *The Papers of Francis Howard, Barron of Effingham, 163–1695* (Richmond, 1989), 48, 68. See also *ibid.*, 59, 73.

[34] Charles City County Deeds, Wills, Orders, Etc., 1655–1665, Reel 1, 569, 576–578.

[35] As a result of the petition, Grace Grey's case was in fact presented before Governor Berkely, who ordered an investigation and demanded that the husband pay the wife's maintenance until a decision had been reached. I have found no evidence of a resolution in the case.

[36] Quoted in James Perry, *The Formation of Society on Virginia's Eastern Shore* (Chapel Hill, 1990), 104 105.

[37] Wynette Parks Haun, transcr., *Surry County, Virginia Court Records, 1652–1663* (Durham, N.C., 1986), 19.

[38] Much work has been done on gender, property, and inheritance laws in the American colonies. Scholars uniformly acknowledge that Dutch wives, who according to Dutch-Roman law were considered *feme sole*, fared relatively well by comparison to women in England or in English colonies where common law deemed them *feme couvert*. Until the English conquest— and beyond—a Dutch woman could convey property, make a contract, sue or be sued, and execute a deed or a will, all of which were legal rights not accorded women in Massachusetts or Virginia: Linda Briggs Biemer, *Women and Property in Colonial New York: The Transition from Dutch to English Law, 1643–1727* (Ann Arbor, 1983), x-xi, 1–7; David E. Narrett, *Inheritance and Family Life in Colonial New York City* (Ithaca, 1992), 6–8, 17, 42–44; Joan R. Gunderson and Gwen Victor Gampel, "Married Women's Legal Status in Eighteenth-Century New York and Virginia," *WMQ*, 3d ser., 39 (1982): 114–134. Gunderson and Gampel make the valid point that even in common law colonies, women "were active participants in the legal system, both because the English Common law was not as restrictive as has been imagined and because certain practices...deviated from those in England in ways that benefited married women." (pp. 114–115). Both Biemer and Narrett conclude that the English conquest resulted in a resurgence of patriarchal control over women and property, though Narrett acknowledges that the persistence of Dutch customs did mitigate the impact of common law (p.71) and that "the respect for female property rights in Dutch law undoubtedly strengthened some women's loyalty to their own ethnic community and church." (p.203). In neither book does religion play a substantial role, nor does either scholar carefully consider the gap between law and experience that existed in all colonies.

[39] See Billings, ed., *Papers of Effingham*, 115n-116n; Helen Hill Miller, *Colonel Parke of Virginia: "The Greatest Hector in the Town"* (Chapel Hill, 1989), 83–85

[40] Haun, ed., *Surry County, Virginia Court Records*, II, 87.

[41] *Ibid.*, 11, 27, 29–30. Husbands too used the court to protect their assets from wives they deemed wayward. In Norfolk County in the 1680s George Turner issued a notice through the court that he refused to honor any debts accrued or bargains made by or with his absent wife, Elizabeth, who refused to cohabit with him. Anthony Lopus, whose wife Jane "absented his house and doth...so behave her selfe that hee much Doubteth that by her evill Carriage towards him intends his Ruine by Contracting of debt," warned the community that he had no intention of honoring her debts. Norfolk County Court Records, Reel 1.

[42] Corwin, ed., *Ecclesiastical Records*, II, 798; *Records of the Reformed Dutch Church of Flatbush* Vol. 1 A, Consistory Minutes, 21. See also Joel Munsell, ed., *Annals of Albany*, I, 91, for directions regarding the financial support of Johannes Megapolensis' widow, as detailed by the Albany patroon, Killaen van Rensselaer.

[43] Fernow, ed,, *Records of New Amsterdam*, VI, 300, 104; Corwin, *Ecclesiastical Records*, II, 771–773.

Chapter Four
PIETY, POWER AND THE FAMILY: THE MOTHER/CHILD RELATIONSHIP

Yea not only his Father, but his Mother also taught him the fear of the Lord, Prov.31.1,2 The words of King Lemuel, the Prophesy that his Mother taught him, what my Son, and what the Son of my womb! and what the son of my vows![1]

I NCREASE MATHER, IN HIS 1679 JEREMIAD "A CALL FROM HEAVEN TO THE PRESENT AND Succeeding Generations," articulated what many Puritan ministers had come to believe by the last quarter of the seventeenth century: if pious men and women hoped to maintain the purity of their churches and their communities in the face of increasing evil, both mothers and fathers had to play an active role in the Christian education of their children. The omnipresent threat of epidemic disease, Indian unrest, French Catholicism, and weather foul enough to ruin an entire year's crops encouraged the renewed vigor with which ministers across the American colonies exhorted their parishioners—male and female—to imbue their children with both fear and love of the Lord.

The expectation that mothers and fathers would share equally the responsibility and authority to educate their children in the Christian religion certainly predated the jeremiads of the seventeenth century. To any faithful Protestant who shared in God's Word, the Bible revealed countless positive images of the Christian mother. Reformers from Augustine to Calvin emphasized the complex meaning of the Fifth Commandment and the duty of children to honor both parents. And in the American colonies, where wives could expect to outlive their husbands, the woman of the household often became the prime purveyor of her family's spiritual inheritance. While there is little question that a "well-ordered family" depended upon the willing submission of wife to husband, a husband's authority in the home was tempered—or even on occasion undercut—by the autonomy a woman owned as a Christian mother. A mother could exercise direct power over her children. She took her place alongside the minister to insure that her children followed the path of the righteous.[2]

PIETY AND CHILDBIRTH IN COLONIAL AMERICA

The responsibility a woman bore for Christian nurture began with childbirth. Among married women in the seventeenth century, childbirth was one of the pivotal life experiences, one which inspired profound joy and fear, comfort and pain. So intense were the anguish and exaltation women experienced during birth that the language seventeenth-century Protestants used to describe their conversion experiences reflected the language of childbirth. The faithful, like a pregnant woman, felt a quickening within. According to John Cotton, just as "a woman that is breeding a child feels such qualmes and distempers, that shee knows thereby shee is with Child; so they that have the breeding of the Spirit in their hearts, and have perceived his motions, they know more clearly than any other." Blessed by God with the ability to bear children, women approached their own salvation with experience, knowledge, and sensitivity unavailable to men.[3]

Protestant theologians also acknowledged that the pain and suffering women endured during childbirth brought them closer to God; their suffering reflected Christ's agony on the cross—the pain of the righteous. Christ himself had compared his own death and resurrection to a woman's travail: "When a woman is in labor, she has pain, because her hour has come. But when her child is born, she no longer remembers the anguish." [John 16:21] Thomas Shepard seemed almost to covet his wife Joanna's anguish as she labored with the birth of their fourth child, for her delivery was also a *deliverance* toward salvation. "The last sacrament before her lying-in," he wrote in his journal in the 1630s, "seemed to be full of Christ and thereby fitted for heaven. . . . The night before she died . . . when she knew none else so as to speak to them, yet she knew Jesus Christ and could speak to him." Maria Van Rensselaer, who probably suffered a mild stroke during childbirth (she "became lame or weak in both of her sides, so that she had to walk with two canes or crutches") came closer to God as well. According to Jasper Danckaerts, "In all these trials, she had borne herself well, and God left not Himself without witness in her." Cotton Mather recognized that the pain women suffered during childbirth provided them with opportunities for redemption—from Eve's sin in Genesis, from their own sin— and repentance. The "Curse in the difficulties of subjection & Childbirth" was a blessing; the pain and vulnerability of childbirth prepared a woman for subjection to Christ. So great was a woman's capacity for suffering and humility that she was chosen to deliver Christ to the world: "a Woman had the Glory of bringing into the World that *Second Adam*, who is the *Father* of all or Happiness." On the evening of his own wife's labor with their child, he led his family in prayer from John 16:21. He appealed in his prayers on that night to the "Savior who was *Born of a woman*."[4]

In addition to the suffering that accompanied labor and delivery, with every pregnancy colonial women faced death. While there is some evidence to suggest that women and men practiced natural forms of birth control—the prolonging of lactation or *coitus interuptus*—in general, every twenty to thirty months a healthy woman of childbearing age gave birth, and thus confronted her own mortality. The joy of childbirth was tempered for both mother and father by the sobering reality of death; "All things within this fading world hath end,/Adversity doth still our joys attend," wrote Anne Bradstreet in a poem entitled "Before the Birth of One of My Children." Bradstreet, ever reflective, took the opportunity to bid farewell to her beloved husband and to prepare him for that time "when that knot's unty'd that made us one." A woman's lying-in was marked with the opportunity for reflection, penitence, and preparation for what might be her final pilgrimage.[5]

The prospect of that final passage was cause for anxiety, especially among members of Massachusetts' Puritan communities. Questions about salvation loomed large for women who faced an uncertain future. Some, like minister Thomas Shepard's wife, prayed and sought comfort in God. Joanna Shepard, gravely ill after the birth of her fourth child, awoke out of a restless sleep and broke "into a most heavenly, heartbreaking prayer after Christ, her dear redeemer . . . and so continued praying until the last hour of her death." Other birthing mothers like Sarah Goodhue of Ipswich and Anne Bradstreet of Boston used the opportunity to provide counsel to those they might leave behind. Goodhue, in *A Valedictory and Monitory Writing*, published in 1681, left instructions for both her husband and her children. Should her husband upon her death decide to place their children in other homes, she intended to make her wishes in the matter known. Thus, the new baby (in fact, Goodhue gave birth to twins) was to go to her parents, her son John to her cousin Symond Stacy, daughter Susanna to cousin Catherine Whipple. She implored her husband to "answer my desire" in the matter, as long as all parties were willing. Her instructions to her children reflected her role as family educator; their Christian upbringing was her concern, and she was bound by duty to them and to God to guide them. "I do not only counsel you," she wrote, " but in the fear of the Lord *I charge you all*, to read God's word, and pray unto the Lord." In addition, she instructed them to obey their father, cautioning that "the scripture holdeth forth many blessings to such children that obey their parents in the Lord, but there are curses threatened to the disobedient." Even in death, Sarah Goodhue meant to exert her influence as a Christian mother. Indeed, three days following the birth of her twins, Sarah Goodhue died.[6]

Elizabeth White, on the other hand, survived the birth that inspired her narrative, and used the experience to articulate the relationship between both the delivery of her child, and of her self to God. For White, pregnancy and childbirth were part of the long and arduous process of conversion, filled with continual doubt and fear. Like other Puritans, she sought some evidence of her own salvation, some assurance that she would be forgiven for her sins when she faced God at the end of her pilgrimage. "When I was with Child," she wrote in her 1669 narrative, "I was much dejected, having a sense of my approaching Danger, and wanting an Assurance of my everlasting Happiness." She sought comfort in the Psalms, most particularly in Psal. 53:15, "Call upon me in the Day of Trouble, and I will deliver thee, and thou shalt glorify me." Her prayers were answered, for her delivery went exceedingly smoothly, "beyond my expectation, which filled my Heart and my Mouth with Praises to the Lord." Soon after the birth, however, she was once again filled with doubt. This time she turned to Mr. Bolton, "in his Book of Instructions for right comforting of afflicted Conscience." There White learned that penitent Christians, plagued with doubt and temptation, would find strength in "some honest Imployment." Confined to her childbed, Elizabeth White wondered what work she could engage in; at last she turned her attention to her new baby, who was anxious to suckle. She fed her child, and thus found herself "pretty well freed from that Temptation."[7]

In the hours and days after the birth of her child, however, White was riddled with doubt, tempted, she believed, by Satan, who taunted her about her assurance. Her narrative, though self-consciously pious, is worth quoting at length. In it we see clear evidence not only of the process of conversion, but of the relationship between travail and the quest for justification and salvation. Confronted with Satan, and consumed with thoughts of her own mortality, White acknowledged

> It is true, I have no Assurance, but I have cast my self wholly upon the Lord Christ...and if I perish, I perish, but sure I am such shall not perish, for Christ hath promised them eternal Life. Thus being assisted by the Lord, I... dreamed there was a Ladder set upon the Earth, whose top reached to Heaven, and I thought I was to go up that Ladder into Heaven, and as that fast as I got up, I was pulled down again . . . but at last I thought I was in Heaven, where...I was filled with Rejoycing, but . . . I thought I was to go back again to Earth, and this thought very much troubled me: But then I thought I heard a voice saying, it would be but for a while, and that I should die in Child-bed, and that the night before I died, I should have full Assurance . . . (and I was very desirous to know of what Child I should die) but that was denied me . . . because I should always be prepared.

White's image of her ascent up a ladder to heaven aptly describes the psychic and emotional ups and downs all regenerate Christians experienced in their quest for salvation. That White dreamed she would survive one birth only to die during another, and in the process find assurance, is typical of the reaction most women had to giving birth. One successful birth did not diminish the chances of death during another, just as brief moments of assurance did not mean that doubts about salvation would not return. Elizabeth White did die in childbirth, about twelve years after her marriage.[8]

So compelling was the relationship between birth, death and the search for salvation that it permeated Dame Walker's dreams in the hours before her death in Boston in the winter of 1695. Samuel Sewall, who visited Dame Walker at her deathbed, recorded in his diary that the old woman prayed to God for the patience and fortitude to bear the suffering he inflicted upon her. Walker's granddaughter, Mehetable Thurston, told Sewall that she heard her grandmother cry out "How long

Lord, how long? Come Lord Jesus." Dame Walker, Sewall reported, "had an odd Concept all the last night of her life, that she was in Travail; and though she ceas'd groaning and gave attention to me when at prayer; yet one of the last words I heard her say was, My child is dead within me." Fears of maternal death, of stillbirth, and of God's harsh judgment continued to pervade Dame Walker's emotions in her final hours—in spite of the fact that she was years removed from her own birthing experience. The hallucination that she carried a dead child within her reflected the dual emotions of elation and the terror with which many nonconformists approached death: fear for their salvation plagued them, but only with death could there be rebirth. And though ministers used the language of travail to express the painful though joyous processes of conversion and death, only women could draw on their experience as childbearers.[9]

For a childbearing woman, the rituals attendant on the event were especially female centered: fathers, other male relations, and male neighbors were relegated to the periphery, leaving the birthing mother surrounded by female friends and family members. Present at the birth, they would share in and bear witness to the most intense test of faith any woman would experience in the course of a lifetime.[10]

So vital did the city of New Amsterdam deem the services of a midwife that in 1655 the city Council ordered that a woman be appointed to the position "in order to offer and appropriate service and assistance to the needy and those who might seek and require help." According to city officials, the midwife's experience as a birthing coach should be available to all women, even those who could ill-afford to pay her on their own. The Council examined the issue, and "as a result of reports and information given to us about Hillegont Joris, the present midwife here . . . nominated and appointed the same . . . to midwife of this city, which position she promises to acquit diligently and faithfully."[11]

The birth of a child was not without celebration, often among the women attending the birthing mother. In February of 1677, two months before his wife was due to give birth, Samuel Sewall brewed his wife's "groaning beer," drink provided for both attendants and visitors during the time of a woman's "groaning," or lying-in. A quarter of a century later, at the birth of Judith, his thirteenth child, Sewall recorded in his diary an account of a substantial birthing celebration. "My wife Treats her Midwife and Women," Sewall noted in the winter of 1702. "Had a good Dinner, Boil'd Pork, Beef, Fowls; very good Rost-Beef, Turkey-Pye, Tarts. Madam Usher carv'd." From soup to nuts, women (Sewall lists the names of nine) dominated the celebration.[12]

Celebration notwithstanding, the birth of a child was occasion for more somber reflection among the mother and her female friends. In keeping with the gravity of the circumstances of birth, female attendants took the opportunity to counsel a birthing mother, as Anne Hutchinson had a reputation for doing in Boston early in the 1630s. Hutchinson's ally, John Cotton, testified at her trial that "Shee did much good . . . in . . . Childbirth-Travells," where she "readily fell into good discourse with the women about their spiritual estates." Such discussions between a birthing mother and her attendants reinforced the bond between the community's women; during a period of profound spiritual doubt and joy, a Christian mother drew some satisfaction from the knowledge that while she needed no minister to mediate between her and God, she might well benefit from the experience and faith of another woman.[13]

PIETY AND THE PROTESTANT MOTHER: CHILDREN, NURTURE, AND SPIRITUAL GUIDANCE

From the moment a Protestant mother was delivered of a child, she commenced her role as nurturer and moral guide. Her first duty as a new mother was to bring her child to her breast to suckle. Though wet-nursing—the practice of sending an infant outside the home to receive its earliest care—remained popular among the landed classes in England in the seventeenth century, American colonial mothers of all classes routinely nursed their own babies.[14]

However trying the first hours of succor were—nursing did not always proceed smoothly—few women could deny the profound joy they also experienced, enhanced no doubt by their awareness of the equation of breastfeeding with God's spiritual nurture. A woman who daily witnessed contentment in her baby's eyes came closer to understanding the joy that Christians experienced feeding at God's and Christ's breast. God created in women the special drive to nurture her young. "Can a woman forget her nursing child, or show no compassion for the child of her womb," God exclaimed (Isa. 49:15). Protestant women who read or heard biblical passages daily were inundated with such images. According to Isaiah, God *delivered* the promised land to his people, a land through which they might find succor: "as soon as Zion was in labor she delivered her children," who were instructed to seek nourishment there: "Rejoice with Jerusalem, and be glad for her; rejoice in her joy . . . that you may nurse and be satisfied from her consoling breast; that you may drink deeply with delight from her glorious bosom" (Isa. 66:10–11).[15] Lewis Bayly's *The Practice of Piety*, immensely popular throughout the American colonies, recommended that congregations sing Psalm 22, which explicitly included maternal nurture as a step along the path toward God's grace. In the psalm, David uses as evidence of God's mercy and deliverance the familiar image of female nurture: "Yet it was you who took me from the womb;/ you kept me safe on my mother's breast./ On you I was cast from my birth,/ and since my mother bore me you have been my God." God chose the mother's womb and breast as a Christian's first sign of love and assurance.

In keeping with their fears of becoming too sure of God's blessings, however, Puritans warned against the dangers of spiritual complacency. Again, maternal imagery proved a useful illustration of thorny religious issues. Anne Bradstreet, in her "Meditations Divine and morall," compared spiritual complacency with the tendency of infants to resist being weaned. The nurturing mother, like God, some-times had to withhold her comfort, lest the recipient take it for granted:

> Some Children are hardly weaned although the teat be rubbed with wormwood
> or mustard, they will wipe it off, or else suck down sweet and bitter together; so
> it is with some Christians; let God embitter all the sweets of this life, that so
> they might feed upon more substantial food, yet they are so childishly sottish
> that they are still hugging and sucking these empty breasts . . . .

Written for her children in 1664, Bradstreet's "Meditations" are stylistically and in their content similar to the biblical Proverbs. Bradstreet, like the best of lay or clerical teachers, used the language of daily life, in this case imbued with profoundly feminine imagery, to express her spiritual concerns.[16]

One of a mother's foremost spiritual goals was the religious education of her children. Every child belonged to God, and it was the responsibility of both parents to set their child on the path toward salvation. Though the father was deemed the head of the household and bore the primary responsibility for the entire family's spiritual health, he shared with his wife the duty and authority to nurture faith in the children. In an epitaph written for her mother on her death in 1643, Anne Bradstreet acknowledged the role that she had played in the family's spiritual education; she was "A true Innstructer of her Family,/ The which she ordered with dexterity." And while most communities viewed with suspicion any women who dared to don the mantle of teacher in a church or other public settings, a mother who spoke with authority about faith in her own home was lauded as an example to others.[17]

John Calvin endorsed women teaching in the home, using as his example Pricilla, wife of Aquila, who gave shelter to the apostle Paul on his journeys. Left by Paul in Ephesus, Pricilla and Aquila maintained the faith there and promoted news of Jesus. When the Greek traveler Apollos arrived, "instructed in the Way of the Lord . . . he began to speak boldly in the synagogue; but when Pricilla and Aquila heard him, they took him aside and explained the Way of God to him more accurately." (Acts 18:25–27) According to Calvin, Apollos "doth suffer himself to be taught and instructed not only [by] a handy-craftsman, but also by a woman . . . as touching the accomplishment of the kingdom of Christ, those do polish and trim him who might seem to be fit minister." Calvin concluded that women "were not so ignorant of the word of God as the Papists will have them; forasmuch as we see that one of the chief teachers of the Church [Apollos] was instructed by a woman." Calvin was quick to point out, however, that Pricilla carried out her instruction within the privacy of her own home.[18]

John Bunyan's Christiana, whose story was shared throughout the American colonies, acknowledged that, in the absence of their father, Christian, she was her sons' primary teacher. She conducted them on their journey toward the Celestial City and salvation; her righteousness, courage, and faith stood as an example to her sons. Tempted several times to abandon their journey, fraught as it was with temptation and danger, Christiana persevered, proclaiming *Now I am risen a mother in Israel*.[19]

During the course of Bunyan's parable, several women in addition to Christiana assume the authoritative role of spiritual guide. Among them are Prudence, Piety, and Charity, occupants of the Porter's Lodge, where Christiana and her brood rest for a time. Women of "very comely and sober countenances," the three maids also prove able teachers. Prudence, "who would see how Christiana had brought up her children," asks her permission to catechize the three boys. Granted permission, Prudence conducts a catechism similar not only to those that mothers and fathers would have conducted in their homes, but those that ministers or teachers conducted with children in church. None of the three boys object to a woman examining them; when Prudence asks Joseph, the middle son, if he will allow her to catechize him, her responds "With all my heart." All three perform admirably, prompting Prudence to exclaim to Christiana "You are to be commended for thus bringing up your children." Prudence concludes the catechism with an admonition to "hearken to your mother, for she can learn you more." Though Christiana expressed doubts about her own ability to complete the journey with her children, most other characters in Bunyan's allegorical world exhibited clear confidence in her competence as a guide and teacher to her children.[20]

In all three colonies, mothers daily assumed the mantle of spiritual teacher to their young, leading them in prayer, teaching from the Bible, conducting them in song. They derived their authority to do so from the Scriptures, and in some cases from ecclesiastical or civil laws that acknowledged a mother's duty to participate in spiritual education. The first covenant made by the earliest members of the church in Salem asked men and women to vow "to our best abilitie to teach our children and servants, the knowledge of God and his will, that they may serve him alsoe." As Salem minister Joseph Green noted in his commonplace book at the end of the seventeenth century, nothing less than the fifth commandment demanded that children attend to both their parents: "If your father or mother bid you do any thing, I charge you to do it if you can without sin; and if they bid you abstain from any thing that is evil be sure you obey them O, have a care of telling your fathers or mothers that you *wont* least God strike you dead in the place." Indeed, Massachusetts children needed only to turn to the case of Benjamin Gourd for evidence of God's wrath against disobedient children: when Gourd, a seventeen-year-old from Roxbury, was executed in 1674 for "committing Bestiality with a Mare," he confessed that one of the causes of his sin could be traced to "not obeying his parents." Many children, however, heeded the Reverend Green's advice, not only in Salem, but in towns and villages across the colonies; maternal influence left clear marks, in conversion narratives, in court records, in wills, and in private correspondence.[21]

Gender and Moral Guidance in Massachusetts

Puritan ministers took special care to counsel parents about their spiritual duties toward their children. A community's covenant with God depended upon the pious participation of all of its members; it was never too soon to begin to teach children about their responsibility toward God, their family, and their town. Increase

Mather, in a jeremiad to his Boston congregation in the wake of King Philip's War and a smallpox epidemic, cautioned parents to beware of complacency; to neglect their children's spiritual welfare was to risk bringing the wrath of God down upon the entire community. The best actions any Christian parent could take to insure the perpetuity of God's covenant was to nurture their children, to envelop them in God's greatness and goodness.

Church leaders acknowledged that the earliest such spiritual nurture was often the province of mothers, whose physical attachment to and responsibility for their children made them especially sensitive toward their need for comfort and guidance. Richard Mather's *Farewel-Exhortations*, delivered to his congregation at Dorchester in 1657, offered special advice for mothers, who

> are more with your children whilest they are little ones, then their Fathers are, therefore be still teaching them as soon as ever they are capable of learning. You are at much paines with the bodyes of your children, and suffer not a little while you bear them in your wombs & when you bring them into the world, and will you not be at some paines for the saving of their soules? You are naturally of tender and dear affection for your children, and God mistakes it not that it be so.

God bestowed upon mothers—"naturally of tender and dear affection"—the authority to raise their children in the covenant, and the special ability to do so.[22]

Much of the evidence for the role Calvinist mothers took in the spiritual training of their children can be gleaned from conversion narratives, where each hopeful saint recounted his or her path toward faith. In many narratives, the narrator indicated simply the influence of "parents," making no distinction between mother and father. Thus Lt. John Mawdsley, a member of Edward Taylor's Westfield church, acknowledged "to the praise, and glory of, God, that he hath not onely given me life, and many outward mercies; as many Sweet Instructions from my Parents." Ensign Samuel Loomis, also of the Westfield congregation, confessed that "it pleased God to bestow upon me the Instruction of Religious Parents, who discovered unto me the bad Condition of every one by nature," and Josiah Dewey noted that "the Counsels of parents, and Christian friends to get an Interest in Christ took som hold upon me." Westfield's John Ingerson credited his faith to "Godly Parents, who tooke great pains & Care to bring me out of a State of Nature into a State of Grace." Mary Angier Sparrowhawk, a confessing member of Thomas Shepard's Cambridge congregation in the 1630s "had parents that kept her from gross sins," as did Sizar Mitchell, whose parents were "both godly saints." Sarah Smith of Cambridge confessed with simplicity and directness that "the first time I took notice of anything was when I was instructed by my parents."[23]

Hopeful saints also singled out their mothers as their moral and spiritual guides. In a relation made before his prospective congregation in Westfield, Edward Taylor credited his mother with "Sharp Correction," and noted that she frequently chided him about his intransigence by "giving acount of the Stubborn Son,

Deut.21:18—& that the eye that despise [the] father, & that despiseth to obey the mother the Ravens of the [valley] shall pick out, & the young Eagles shall eat it, Prov.[30:17.]" Taylor's mother also lectured him about the dangers of lying, extracting her warning, "what shall be given the lyer but brimstone & fire," from Rev.21:8. In his confession before Thomas Shepard's Cambridge congregation in 1639, Nathaniel Sparrowhawk related that in his childhood "his mother took much pain with him." In her own relation, Sparrowhawk's wife, Mary, cited her duties as a Christian mother as the impetus for her migration from England to Massachusetts: "Thinking that [my] children might get good it would be worth my journey," Mary explained. John Shepard, of the same congregation, "put on to the[e] duty by mother . . . sought after God." John Mawdsley's mother, impressed by the relation of a young man admitted to the Dorchester church who had engaged in secret prayer twice a day since the age of ten, advised her own son "that it was high time for me to pr[ay] unto God, for I was more than ten years old." Mawdsley, "in Obedience to my Parents, & in fear of Gods wrath . . . set upon secret prayer."[24] Thus did the dutiful Protestant mother devote herself to the task of setting her children on a path toward faith.

Foremost among the duties that inspired faith was prayer. To that end, mothers were expected to serve as examples to their children. They took special care to foster spirituality in the domestic sphere, and the exercise of private and family prayer. The covenant to which the earliest members of the First Church in Salem adhered included the demand that all men and women promise "to our best abilitie to taech our children and servants, the knowledge of God and his will, that they may serve him alsoe." Sarah Goodhue spoke with consummate authority when she advised her children to pursue their spiritual exercises. "I do not only counsel you," she wrote, "but in the fear of the Lord *I charge you all*, to read God's word, and pray unto the Lord." She instructed them more specifically to continue to listen to, read, and write God's word, tasks in which she had clearly guided them throughout their childhood. Displaying a similar concern for spiritual transmission, Salem minister Joseph Green, in a letter to his sister Bethiah Green Hicks, instructed her to "Live in the constant exercise of secret prayer; do not neglect it one day for a world; be not ashamed to let your husband or your family know that you make conscience of praying in secret dayly; but let your conversation be such as may win many to be Christians." The thought that a woman might be the family's prime spiritual guide was not foreign to Joseph Green; his grandmother, Ellin Green, "was continually instructing [my father] and giving him good councell so that he sought God when he was young." From an early age, the children of faithful parents learned that their mothers, like their fathers, were a source of scriptural knowledge and often the best example of a pious life.[25]

Among seventeenth-century families, which often included resident grandparents, maternal guidance might come from grandmothers as well. Samuel Sewall honored his mother-in-law, Judith Hull, as the best example of a pious life he could envision for his children. When he brought his ninth child, a daughter, to church to be baptized in 1690, he made special note in his diary that she was named for her grandmother, Judith Hull. He prayed that his daughter "may follow her Grandmother Hull, as she follows Christ, being not slothfull in Business, fervent in Spirit, serving the Lord." Sewall made no secret of Judith Hull's influence in his children's spiritual development, stating that "her Prayers and Painstaking for all my Children are incessant, voluntary, with condescension to the meanest Services night and day." So crucial was her contribution to the spiritual health of his family that Sewall "judged I could in justice doe no less than endeavor her remembrance by putting her Name on one of her Grand-Daughters."[26]

Among the most important legacies a mother could leave her children was membership in the church covenant, which she accomplished not only by teaching them scripture and conveying the importance of the Word as a path toward faith, but by providing for their baptism. For New England Calvinists, baptism was a seal of God's promise to his faithful, available only to infant children of believing parents. Though the conditions under which a parent might bring a baby forward to be baptized changed with the acceptance of the half-way covenant by some congregations, the principle remained the same: baptism was a child's spiritual inheritance, no less than the bequest of a family estate was a financial one.[27]

Minister William Hooke, in a sermon preached and published in London in the 1670s, established a clear link between temporal and spiritual inheritance and cautioned parents to pay heed to their children's needs on both counts. Parents with any means at all were careful to provide for their offspring's continued economic well-being; in their wills they left behind land, houses, money, furnishings, and businesses. Shall those same careful parents, Hooke demanded, "be *less* mindful to leave behind them and faithful transmit *Pure* Gospel?" God, he warned, "requireth, that Parents do not only give up themselves, but their *seed* also unto God . . . Will you love their *bodies* and neglect their *souls*?" Hooke's words echoed Richard Mather's exhortation to Dorchester mothers to match the pain they had suffered on behalf of their children during pregnancy and birth with "paines for the saving of their soules." Their own faith would act as a beacon for their children, Mather promised, for "who knows but the prayers and teares of a faithful Mother may be the salvation of the childs soule." By most accounts, New England's Protestant mothers heeded those words and took action to insure their children held a place in God's covenant.[28]

Richard Mather's exhortations to the mothers in his Dorchester congregation resonated in congregations throughout Massachusetts. One half or more of the women who became members of the Congregational church in the seventeenth and early eighteenth centuries—either through covenant renewal or the relation of a conversion experience—did so immediately before or upon the birth of their first or second child. In the Charlestown congregation, 60% of the women who joined the church in the 1630s did so to open the way for their children's baptism. In John Fiske's Wenham congregation, Hannah Blake brought her two children forward for baptism the same day she was received into full communion in 1669. In July of 1673

Lydia Perham joined the Wenham church and the same day brought forth her children Mary, John, Joseph, and Anna for baptism. Later the same year the church received Hannah Farwel into full communion; her children Hannah, Joseph, and Elizabeth were baptized the same afternoon. In the Dorchester church in 1660, the "wife of James Minot . . . desiring baptism for her children says she will own the covenant." Mary Grey, widow of Benjamin Grey of Salem, so desired to bestow upon her children the right to the sacrament that she "made a Publick Confession of her repeated Scandalous violations of the Seventh Commandment, with one person and Another, in Order to her Entering into Covenant with God in this Church...that Baptism might be Administered to her Self and Children." Women frequently understood their own covenanting in terms of their maternal responsibility as well as their personal salvation. While colonial laws restricted a woman's ability to insure a temporal legacy for her children, it was well within her authority to bequeath them a spiritual inheritance.[29]

MOTHERHOOD AND RELIGION IN NEW YORK

In New York, where until the English conquest (and often beyond) Roman-Dutch law granted women the right to dispose of their own property, evidence for a mother's concern for her child's spiritual growth appears not only in church and personal records, but in wills and other temporal forms of bequest. Throughout the seventeenth century, Dutch Reformed women prepared for the day when they would no longer be around to counsel their children by arranging for their care, bequeathing them Bibles and other religious books, and taking steps to insure that their spiritual education would continue.

Obedience to God was required of Dutch Reformed children and adults alike, and the wills of Dutch men and women—and those filed jointly by husband and wife—reflected parental concern with spiritual compliance. In a codicil to his will, filed jointly with his wife Elizabeth, Sybrant Van Schaick insisted that his children should be "exercised in the fear of the Lord, and instructed in reading, writing, and Arithmetic." In their "joint, respective and reciprocal last will and testament" Philip Schyler and Margaret Van Slichtenhorst stipulated that "the longest live of the two stands obliged honestly to maintain, bring up and keep until they come of age their four underage children." The joint will specified that the surviving parent vow to raise the children "in all piety" and to take care that they were taught to read, write, and perform a handicraft. [30]

Widows who prepared for death had special cause for concern: they left behind no parent to take responsibility for their children's spiritual health. Though by the middle of the seventeenth century Dutch New Netherlanders had created an institution to supervise the care of orphans, including their religious education, some mothers chose to take matters into their own hands. In at least two cases widows arranged for their orphans to be cared for by the minister and deacon, whose responsibility it would thus be to supervise the distribution of the estate and oversee the children's continued education. On her deathbed in Brooklyn in 1662,

Teuntie Strautsmans "urgently requested that Henricus Selyns and Teunis Jannssen, minister and deacon, take care of and look after her orphans left behind." Several days after her death, Reverend Selyns and the entire consistory, "in accordance with our duty and promises," arrived at Teutie Straetsmans' house to begin the task of caring for the children and their estate. Twenty-three years later, this time in Manhattan, Sarah Weber drafted a will and "therein Nominated and appointed Dominicus Henricus Selyns . . . and Mr. Pieter Jacob Marius to be Tutors or Overseers for the Children." Perhaps because the widows' concern for their children's spiritual estate matched their concern for the temporal one, they used their authority as faithful Christians to assign care to the one member of the community sure to adhere to their wishes: the minister.[31]

Even in those instances when the orphanmasters stepped in to supervise the estate, care, and education of minor children, they had the option to assign the mother that responsibility. And though the institution had been established to protect children's estates from the greedy hands of some future step-father, there were times when the court could find no better custodian for the children than their mother. In 1657, the Orphan Masters court appointed Truyntie Hendricks, widow of Cors Pietersen, guardian of her children's estate and welfare, this in spite of the fact that she was preparing to remarry. The "virtuous Truyntie Hendricks," as she was referred to by the court, promised "to bring up the said three children...as well as she can, to have them taught reading, writing and a good trade or occupation...further to instruct them in the fear of the Lord and in religious exercises and to do all, a good mother is bound to do."[32]

In their own wills Dutch men acknowledged that their widows could ably attend to the children's pious upbringing. Under Dutch custom and law, a widowed mother could control her family's resources only so long as she led a pious life and saw to both the practical and spiritual education of her children. Certainly a few husbands took the occasion of their will to issue curt instructions to their wives, as Teunis Dey did when he commanded his wife "to bring up the children to learn an art or trade to live by, and as a pious mother, for God's sake is bound to do." Others used their wills to articulate the full force of their conviction that their spouses held the authority and duty to oversee the lives of their children. Isaac Van Vlecq, after bequeathing a "new Testament tipped with silver" to his daughter Hester and another to his daughter Magdalena, warned that they were forbidden to "say or do anything against their mother, all being left to her discretion, and she is to bring them up as a pious mother ought to do." According to their grandfather's will, Hester Erwyn and Maria Gerrittsen, raised by both grandparents in New York, were to receive twenty florins each when they came of age or married. Grandfather James Mattews' will stipulated, however, that neither girl was to marry without the consent their Grandmother.[33]

Female caretakers in New York—mothers, grandmothers, and aunts—derived the authority to direct their children's spiritual growth from sources similar to those in Calvinist Massachusetts. Images of Eve notwithstanding, both civil and ecclesiastical law reinforced the notion that moral guidance was the responsibility of both parents. If Dutch New Yorkers were to survive Indian unrest, plagues, and challenges from the English to perpetuate their covenant with God, mothers and fathers alike had to take responsibility for training the succeeding generation. As Pieter Hillebrants and Aeltje Wygerts prepared their marriage contract in Kingston in 1665, "in accordance with the canons of the reformed religion," they agreed to combine their real and personal estate "to be used by them in community, according to the customs of Holland." There was to be one exception, however. Aeltje, who had four children (from two prior marriages), demanded that fifty guilders be set aside for each of her children "that the aforesaid bride shall have her children instructed in reading and writing." When the consistory of the Dutch church in Flatbush sought to import a number of religious books "necessary with other things for the instruction of old and young, that the weekly sermons may be listened to with profit and greater edification," it was with the expectation that "individuals also could by this opportunity purchase their own store." Conscientious parents, the consistory assumed, would strive to provide their children with the resources necessary to learn to lead a pious life. Similarly, parents—with no distinction between mother and father—were admonished to keep control of their children and teach them respect for the Sabbath. In the midst of a particularly trying time in New Amsterdam, blamed in part on the actions of those residents who continually desecrated the Sabbath, the court passed an ordinance that, among other things, warned "if any children be caught on the streets playing, racing and shouting, previous to the termination of the last preaching," their parents were to be fined two guilders.[34]

Dutch mothers took seriously their responsibility to educate their children at home, apart from the catechetical training both boys and girls would receive under the tutelage of a schoolmaster. Arising from the dual goals of maintaining Dutch cultural traditions and sustaining their pious mission, Dutch mothers were the prime purveyors of both religion and the Dutch language in their homes. Despite the threat of assimilation posed by the English conquest of the colony, Dutch mothers remained loyal to the church, even as their husbands began to stray from it. In their effort to preserve Dutch culture and traditions, mothers bequeathed that loyalty to the church and the Reformed religion to their children; even Dutch women married to Anglican men took their children to be baptized in the Dutch Reformed Church. And in spite of the drive to educate Dutch children in English schools, mothers continued as "guardians of the Dutch tongue in their homes."[35]

As their children grew to adulthood, pious Dutch mothers continued to tender advice and admonitions. In 1691, three months after her son Jacob Jr. had fled New York for Boston, Elsie Leisler wrote to him there to apprise him of the deplorable circumstances of their life among hostile rulers. In addition to reminding him of his promise to leave a will, "that by happening death, your sisters be no Sufferers," the widow Leisler counseled her son to "Serve the Lord and fear God, for it is but a little while that we shall be in this world, Carry it quioutly, and Use your Endeavour to set forth to the world your father, and brothers innocensy." [36]

During the seventeenth century, when the vagaries of death often deprived children of their mother's counsel, others stepped in to fill the void. Aunts and uncles, godparents, and neighbors shouldered the responsibility of guiding their wards toward faith. Moreover, the missionary zeal with which Catholics and Protestants alike tried to convert the native population left some young Indians bereft of Christian instruction once missionaries had departed, leading them to abandon their biological families in search of further learning. One girl, known only as Illetie, fled her allegedly abusive Indian mother (her father was Christian) to join a Dutch settlement in Schenectady. There she lived with a pious Dutch woman who taught her to read and to write. Illetie in turn instructed her nephew, a Mohawk named Wouter, who abandoned his Indian family to live with his converted Christian aunt and her brother. "He is endeavoring," wrote Jasper Danckaerts in his journal in 1680, "to learn the Dutch language, so as to be instructed in Christianity, and to be among good Christians who live like Christians." To that end, the young Wouter turned to Illetie, who like all pious Protestant mothers "assisted and instructed him as much as she could, and always with love, with which God much blessed her." Against great odds—including the objections of her covetous brother—Illetie struggled to teach her nephew to worship with the Dutch Bible, taking great pains to instruct him "how he must pray, which she recommended to him to do every time he returned home, morning or evening." At last, she arranged for him to accompany Danckaerts, who agreed to tutor the young man and encourage his faith in the Christian God. "I must shame myself for the honor and happiness He causes me in enabling me to speak with you about these things," Illetie exclaimed to Danckaerts, with words befitting any pious, proud, and grateful mother.[37]

PIETY AND MOTHERHOOD IN COLONIAL VIRGINIA

Perhaps more than any other colony in the seventeenth century, Virginia families comprised all manner of members; mothers took responsibility for the pious upbringing not only of their own children, but of servants, slaves, and neighbors. Similarly, orphaned children, deprived of their parents' counsel, turned to godparents, relatives, or other legal guardians for care and education. Women and men shared the duty and authority to see that the colony's children were educated in the Protestant religion.

In Anglican Virginia as in Puritan Massachusetts and Dutch Reformed New York, religious authorities expressed concern with the progress in education among colonists. Parents and colonial leaders recognized that the seedbed of faith was found at home, and that parents had to be the primary cultivators. In a colony where it took several decades for some counties to establish permanent churches, much less catechetical schools, parents or guardians by necessity had to assume the roles of purveyors of faith.

Parents were responsible for their wards' most basic education. All minors in the family were expected at the very least to learn to read in the Bible. And though some scholars have expressed skepticism about the ability of women in particular to monitor the religious training of their wards, mothers and fathers each played a role in the transmission of Anglican liturgy and scripture.

Few husbands were as effusive in their admiration for their wives' abilities as spiritual caretakers as Francis Howard, Baron of Effingham was about Philadelphia Pelham Howard. Early in 1684 her wrote to his wife concerning his gratefulness to God, who "blessed me with so virtuous, so prudent a wife, with whom (if God should be pleased to take me) I do with so much confidence and assurance beleeve my Dear Children will be carefully educated in their duties to God, and Man." Later that summer he reiterated his pride and confidence in his pious wife. "Nothing can augment my happinesse," he wrote, "but to live to see those dear children that came from thy dearest selfe Imitate your Goodnesse and vertue which I trust in God they will by the assistance of God's grace and the advantage of the Carefull Education, and good example." Effingham acknowledged that even in his absence his children would receive the best of pious educations.[38]

Many of Virginia's children were not as fortunate as the Howard's, who had two living parents, both concerned about their pious upbringing. A startling number of children could expect to be deprived of parental guidance early in their lives. Darrett and Anita Rutman estimate that in Middlesex County almost 25% of children had lost one or both parents by their fifth birthday, over 50% by their thirteenth birthday, and 73% by age twenty-one. In this environment, it was increasingly important to insure that the surviving spouse, man or woman, understood the duties required to raise pious and faithful children.[39]

Directions for the children and the remaining spouse were frequently left in a last will and testament, prepared when the testator was gravely ill or faced other potential causes of death. When John Moon, a sometime-burgess from Isle of Wight County, made his will, he instructed his children "before God & the Lord Jesus Christ who shall judge the Quick & the Dead, to demean yourselves loving, obedient, comfortable unto your Mother." He cautioned his wife to "provoke not your Children to Wrath lest they be discouraged, but bring them up in nurture & Admonition of the Lord & live peaceably and lovingly together." Perhaps his wife was a bit too harsh with the children. No matter; Moon maintained faith enough that even in his absence his wife would lead his children toward salvation. Similarly, Christopher Kirke of Accomack-Northhampton County specified that his entire estate, including cattle, be left to his wife, Alice, "towards bringeinge [the children] upp with Learninge and the feare of God." George Travellor stipulated in his will in 1642 that his daughter, when she neared marriage age, "take the Councell of her Mother in her Match, if shee bee then Living." He asked his "deare and Loveing wife," Alice, to take "an Especiall care of the good Education of my tender Children That they may bee well brought up in the Feare of God." When William Byrd I left home in England to come to Virginia, he came to stay with his Uncle Thomas Stegg, his mother's brother, who took him in and treated him like a son, a sentiment illustrated by his will and testament. Stegg's will expressed his love for his nephew, to whom he intended to leave his business and 3000 acres of land. He did so, however, only under the condition that Byrd, who was but a boy at the time, agree to defer in all matters to his Aunt Sarah Stegg. Sarah was to continue managing the estate for her nephew, "not so experienced in the transactions of the world." Thomas Stegg warned William "not to be led away by the evil instructions he shall receive from others, but to be governed by the prudent and provident advice of his aunt." Guardians sought to ensure proper care for all of their charges, sons or daughters, nephews or nieces; often the best spiritual guidance available came from a woman.[40]

So prevalent was the risk of parental death in seventeenth-century Virginia that the custom of naming godparents (a ritual practiced most frequently among the Catholics of southern Maryland during this period) took on added significance among Anglican families in Virginia. The godparent promised to oversee the religious education of their godchild in the absence of both biological parents.[41] Orphaned children without godparents or other relatives to turn to, and children of poor parents unable to support them were bound out to apprenticeship by the church vestry or the county court. Even under those circumstances, the county and church sought to guarantee certain levels of religious education for the wards, education often supervised by women. As early as 1642, the general court passed a law mandating that every orphan or apprentice be taught to read and write, and be instructed "in the Christian religion and the rudiments of learning." So it was in Lancaster County that Jonathan, "the base child of Thomas Mannen, borne of Eliza: Tomlin, shall *according to the will of the mother*, bee kept by Roger Harris and his wife," where he was to be taught to write and read. In Elizabeth City County in 1698, the court ordered that Ann Chandler, orphan of Daniel Chandler, bound out to Phyllemon Miller, "be taught to read a chapter in the Bible, the Lord's prayer, and ten commandments, and seamstress work." Similarly, Arnold and Deborah Jefford were to bear the responsibility of teaching the same skills to their apprentice, five-year-old Robert Craddock. Churches and courts made no distinction between the religious educational requirements for male or female apprentices. Similarly, mistresses were expected to participate in the education process, either with their husbands or, if they were single or widowed, on their own.[42]

If the parents of an apprenticed child were still living at the time of the contract, they had the right to monitor their child's progress and to object if they felt the master or mistress fell short of the required goals, or if the circumstances of the apprenticeship changed. When Thomas Andrews of Southwarke Parish in Surry County put his daughter Ann out to apprentice with Robert and Mary Staunton in 1658, he set specific constraints on the arrangement. First, Staunton and his wife were to employ Ann in duties "as fitt for a woman and no other." In addition, Andrews stipulated that if Mary Staunton died before her husband, he reserved the right to remove his daughter from Robert's service. On the other hand, if Robert Staunton died before his wife, Ann would remain to serve out her full time. Mrs. Staunton would then be solely responsible for Ann's education, which included instruction in the Christian religion, sewing, "and other things as a woman should know." Was the removal of his daughter from a home where only a man resided

Thomas Andrews' way of protecting his daughter from any impropriety? Or did he simply believe that the mistress of the household was better suited to the role of educating a girl? Whatever his motivation, Andrews made it clear that he trusted the ability of a woman to see that his daughter was properly educated.[43]

* * *

In all three colonies in the seventeenth century, Protestant women participated in the pious upbringing of their community's children—their own or others. As child bearers, they came closer to understanding the pain of Jesus; as nurturers, they excelled at inspiring in their children the desire to learn from the Bible and to strive for salvation. As pious Christians in their own right, they expected to serve as an example to their children in prayer, in study, and in their dedication to the church. And to further insure that their children recognized the signs of a life lived piously, Christian mothers knew that they had a duty to demonstrate their piety and their authority outside of the home as well. Where better to illustrate the tenets of soul equality to their daughters and sons than in their churches?

NOTES

[1] Increase Mather, "A Call from Heaven to the Present and Succeeding Generations..." (Boston, 1679).

[2] See Phyllis Bird, "Images of Women in the Old Testament," in *Religion and Sexism*, ed. Rosemary Radford Ruether (New York, 1974), 60–63 for a description of the positive roles Biblical women played in the protection and education of their children. On the humanist roots of mutual parenting in early New England see Gerald F. Moran, "'The Hidden Ones': Women and Religion in Puritan New England," in Richard Greaves, ed., *Triumph Over Silence: Women in Protestant History* (Westport, Ct., and London, 1985), 137–139. For a discussion on the dangers of marginalizing or ghettoizing women's lives by examining them only within the context of the family, by imposing strict lines between public and private spheres, or by leaving men out of family history see Merry Weisner, "Beyond Women and the Family: Towards a Gender Analysis of the Reformation," *Sixteenth-Century Journal* 18 (1987): 316.

[3] John Cotton, "A practical commentary, or an exposition with observances, reasons, and uses upon the First epistle generall of John" (London, 1656). Patricia Caldwell also has noted the peculiarly female language used to express personal religious awakening: Caldwell, *The Puritan Conversion Narrative: The Beginning of American Expression* (Cambridge, England, 1983), 8.

[4] Michael McGiffert, ed., *God's Plot: The Paradoxes of Puritan Piety Being the Autobiography and Journal of Thomas Shepard* (Amherst, 1972), 71; Bartlett Burleigh James and J. Franklin Jameson, eds., *The Journal of Jasper Danckaerts* (New York, 1913, 1959 reprint), 214; Cotton Mather, *Ornaments for the Daughters of Zion Or the Character and Happiness of a Vertuous Woman* (first pub.1691, England, 1694); *Diary of Cotton Mather*, 307, Mather's emphasis. See also *The Sermon Notebook of Samuel Parris, 1689–1694*, eds., James F. Cooper, Jr. And Kenneth P. Minkema (Boston, 1993), 108. In the fall of 1690, Parris delivered a series of sermons on Christ's wounding and death on the cross, primarily out of Isa. 53:5. Amanda Porterfield

notes the relationship between suffering in birth and piety: *Female Piety in Puritan New England: The Emergence of Religious Humanism* (New York, 1992), 129–130.

[5] *The Poems of Anne Bradstreet*, ed. Robert Hutchinson (New York, 1969), 45. Bradstreet goes on to ask her husband to take special care of her children, including the warning that he must "protect from step Dames injury." Anne Bradstreet's poetry—including "Before the Birth of One of My Children"—and prose appears in numerous published collection. See for instance Adelaide P. Amore, ed., *A Woman's Inner World: Selected Poetry and Prose of Anne Bradstreet* (Washington, D.C., 1982). For a rich description of birthing rituals and reality in seventeenth-century northern New England see Laurel Thatcher Ulrich, *Good Wives: Image and Reality in the Lives of Women in Northern New England, 1650–1750* (New York, 1983), chapter seven. On maternal death in the early Plymouth colony, see John Demos, *A Little Commonwealth: Family Life in Plymouth Colony* (New York and London, 1970), 66, 131–132; On maternal death in the Chesapeake see Lois Green Carr and Lorena S. Walsh, "The Planter's Wife: The Experience of White Women in Seventeenth-Century Maryland," *WMQ*, 3d ser., 34 (October 1977): 542–571; Darrett B. and Anita H. Rutman, "'Now-Wives and Sons-in-Law': Parental Death in a Seventeenth-Century Virginia County," in *The Chesapeake in the Seventeenth Century: Essays in Angle-American Society* eds. Thad W. Tate and David L. Ammerman (Chapel Hill, 1979). For a discussion of the life expectancy of birthing mothers in early modern England, see Keith Wrightson, *English Society, 1580–1680* (New Brunswick, N.J., 1986), 104–105; Ralph A. Houlbrooke, *The English Family, 1450–1700* ((London and New York, 1984), 129.

[6] McGiffert, ed., *God's Plot*, 71; Goodhue's monitory writing, the original of which has disappeared, is reprinted in Thomas Walters, *Ipswich in the Massachusetts Bay Colony*, (2 vols., Ipswich, 1905), I, 519–524, esp. 519,521. See also Ulrich, *Good Wives*, 129. On childbirth as a pilgrimage in preparation for death and salvation, see Charles Hambrick-Stowe, *The Practice of Piety: Puritan Devotional Disciplines in Seventeenth-Century New England* (Chapel Hill, 1982), 219–241, *passim*.

[7] Mrs. Elizabeth White, *The Experiences of God's Gracious Dealing with Mrs. Elizabeth White*[1669] (Boston, 1741). Robert Bolton's works, which included "Instructions for a right comforting afflicted consciences," were published in London in 1641.

[8] Elizabeth White, *The Experiences of God's Gracious Dealing*, 12–13. Though many historians have been drawn to and fascinated by Elizabeth White's narrative, some scholars, Patricia Caldwell included, have cast some doubt on the authenticity of the piece. What can be proved is that the narrative was discovered early in the eighteenth century, published, and that it became exceedingly popular. Whether it was written by Elizabeth White is not important for the purposes of my argument, which emphasizes the relationship between birth and conversion and salvation, and a woman's ability to take responsibility for her own pilgrimage.

[9] M. Halsey Thomas, ed., *The Diary of Samuel Sewall, 1674–1729* (2 vols., New York, 1973), 342–343.

[10] Not only did neighboring women—most especially midwives—share in the birthing mother's joy and pain, and bear witness to her moments of faith and doubt, they were not infrequently called upon to testify in trials held to determine paternity. The court recognized that the childbirth experience was transforming enough to inspire woman to confess profound secrets, and that if she did so it was other women who were most likely privy to those confessions.

Samuel Sewall's diary is filled with references to the network of women who attended family members during their travail. See, for instance, *Diary*, 12–13, 41. The most recent— and most exciting—analysis of the role of the midwife in the lives of birthing women is Laurel Thatcher Ulrich, *A Midwife's Tale: The Life of Martha Ballard, Based on her Diary, 1785–1812* (New York, 1991). Though Ulrich deals primarily with midwife culture in the eighteenth century, much of her analysis, I believe, is equally applicable to the seventeenth century. On the relationship between midwifery and female authority, see Porterfield, *Female Piety*, 96.

[11] Charles T. Gehring, trans. and ed., *Council Minutes, 1655–1656* (Syracuse, 1995), 35–36. Thomas Burke points out that midwives were sworn in as civic officials in Albany as well as New Amsterdam. He assumes that this practice held true for Schenectady as well: Thomas E. Burke, *Mohawk Frontier: The Dutch Community of Schenectady, New York, 1661–1710* (Ithaca, 1991), 209n.

[12] Sewall, *Diary*, 36, 460.

[13] David D. Hall, *The Antinomian Controversy, 1636–1638: A Documentary History* (Middletown, Ct., 1968), 412. Hutchinson's role as an attendant to some of Boston's first birthing mothers is rendered more poignant by the fact that shortly after her excommunication from the church she gave birth prematurely to a deformed fetus. Like the birth of her friend Mary Dyer's "monstrous" child not long before, Hutchinson's misfortune was directly attributed by John Winthrop and local church leaders to her blasphemous actions and speech. While healthy births were a sign of God's blessing, births that resulted in a deformed baby could be interpreted as a sign of God's disfavor, a punishment for sin. For a description of the reaction to both "monstrous" births see Hall, *Worlds of Wonder*, 100–101. In his diary, John Hull used Mary Dyer as an example of the ways God worked through birth. Dyer, he recounted, "brought forth a hideous monster, part like a man, part like a fish, part like a bird, part like a beast, and had no neck. . . ." By the same token, God's providence resulted in a healthy birth for Constance Madock, who miscarried several times before she embraced the church: n.e., *Puritan Personal Writings: Diaries* (New York, 1983), 188–189.

[14] On wet-nursing in England see Roger Thompson, *Women in Stuart England and America* (London, 1974), 154–155; on nursing as the norm in New England, see Ulrich, *Good Wives*, 188–189.

[15] Catholic culture too reveled in images of breastfeeding as equated with spiritual nurture. See Carolyn Walker Bynam, *Jesus as Mother* (Berkeley, 1982), esp. 110–169. On Puritan culture's respect for maternal love and nurture, see Porterfield, *Female Piety*, 94–96.

[16] Bradstreet's "Meditations" in Amore, ed., *Woman's Inner World*, 71.

[17] *Poems of Anne Bradstreet*, 54. In at least one colony, Dutch New York, women were permitted to catechize children outside of their homes, though the circumstances under which that was permissible were admittedly limited: see below, chapter five.

[18] Jean Calvin, *Commentary Upon the Acts of the Apostles*, ed., Henry Beveridge, for the Calvin Translation Society (Edinburgh, 1844), II, 202–203.

[19] John Bunyan, *Pilgrim's Progress*, ed., Roger Sharrock (New York, 1978), 268.

[20] Bunyan, *Pilgrim's Progress*, 274–277. Though a female leader was by no means the norm, there were occasions when a woman might serve as church teacher. See below, chapter five, for a discussion of church catechizing of boys and girls.

21 Richard Pierce, ed., *Records of the First Church in Salem, 1629–1736* (Salem, 1974), 5; "Commonplace Book of Joseph Green," in *Puritan Personal Writing: Autobiographies and Other Writings* (New York, 1983), 217.

22 Richard Mather, *A Farewel-Exhortation to the church and people of Dorchester in New-England* (Cambridge, Massachusetts, 1657).

23 Relation of John Mawdsley, in *Edward Taylor's "Church Records" and Related Sermons*, Thomas and Virginia L. Davis, eds. (Boston, 1981), 104; Relation of Samuel Loomis in *Taylor's Records*, 107; Relation of Josiah Dewey in *Taylor's Records*, 109; Relation of John Ingerson in *Taylor's Records*, 109; Mary Angier's Confession in *Thomas Shepard's Confessions*, 65; Sizar Mitchel's and Mistress Smith's Confessions in "Shepard's Record of Relations," 455, 463.

24 *Taylor's Records*, 100, 105; *Thomas Shepard's Confessions*, 62, 66; "Shepard's Record," 443–444.

25 Richard Pierce, ed., *Records of the First Church in Salem, 1629–1736* (Salem, 1974), 3–5; Sarah Goodhue, "Valedictory and Monitiory Writing," 521; "Commonplace Book of Joseph Green," 226–227, 234. In the absence of a mother—or father—saints might turn to other female relatives as well: Katherine, a maid to Mrs. Elizabeth Russell, credited her aunt with her conversion in a narrative before Shepard's congregation. Elizabeth Luxford of the same congregation had her first exposure to the means to grace from her sister, as did Edward Taylor. *Thomas Shepard's Confessions*, 99, 39–41; *Taylor's Records*, 98.

26 Sewall, *Diary*, I, 264–265.

27 On the role of baptism in Calvinist churches, see E. Brooks Holifield, *The Covenant Sealed: The Development of Puritan Sacramental Theology in Old and New England, 1570–1720* (New Haven, 1974), chapter three, esp. pp. 64–76. On the impact of the half-way covenant on baptism and church membership see Robert G. Pope, *The Half-Way Covenant* (New Haven, 1969). See also below, chapter five.

28 William Hooke, *The Privilege of the Saints on Earth beyond those in Heaven...* (London, 1673). In addition to this sermon, Hooke, an English nonconformist minister who preached in Taunton, Massachusetts, in the 1640s, published several that addressed New England's relationship to Old England.

29 Anne S. Brown and David D. Hall, "Family Strategies and Religious Practices in Early New England: An Essay in the History of Lived Religion," Unpublished paper prepared for a Conference at the Harvard Divinity School, 1994, 28–30; see also 6, 24, 25. On the Charlestown church, see Mary McManus Ramsbattom, "Religion, Society, and the Family in Charlestown, Massachusetts, 1630–1740" (Ph.D. diss., Yale University, 1987), 43, 87, 268–269; Robert Pope, ed., *The Notebook of the Reverend John Fiske* (Boston, 1974), 218, 230, 231; Pope, *The Half-Way Covenant*, 34–35; *Records of the First Church in Salem*, 276. Though Ramsbottom's Charlestown evidence is persuasive, she overstates the primacy of the role maternal responsibility played in encouraging women to seek church membership. On p. 87 she claims that women more often understood their covenanting in terms of gender and family relations than their relation to God; not only do I question how she can be sure of this, but I would suggest that those two relationships need not be considered separately. A woman's relationship with God was shaped by a multiplicity of roles—as hopeful saint, wife, mother, and neighbor. See also Robert Pope, *The Half-Way Covenant*, 217–218.

30 *Abstract of Wills, 1665–1707*, New-York Historical Society *Collections*, vol.25 (1892), 132–133; George W. Schyler, *Philip Schuyler and His Family* (2 vols., New York, 1885), I, 162–163. See

David E. Narrett, *Inheritance and Family Life in Colonial New York City* (Ithaca, 1992), 166–167 for a discussion of the link between inheritance and the religious adherence of children.

[31] A.P.G. Van der Linde, ed., *Old First Dutch Reformed Church of Brooklyn* (Baltimore, 1983), 51–53; P. Christoph and Florence Christoph, eds., *Books of General Entries of the Colony of New York, 1674–1688* (Baltimore, 1982), 368. In their joint will Philip Schuyler and Margaret Van Slichtenhorst "with all due respect" dismissed the potential attention of Albany's orphan-master; the survivor was to act as the children's sole guardian. Similarly, in New York in 1685, Jacob Sanders' will directed "that his wife be not troubled by the orphan masters, Trustees, Constables, the Court of the Town, or any other power...that they shall not...intermeddle with the children or estate: *Abstract of Wills* , 132. On the Dutch use of orphanmasters to care for the colony's children, see Adriana E. van Zwietan, "The Orphan Chamber of New Amsterdam," *WMQ*, 3d. ser., 53 (April, 1996): 319–340.

[32] Berthold Fernow, ed., *The Minutes of the Orphanmasters of New Amsterdam, 1655–1663* (New York, 1902), 39–40.

[33] *Abstract of Wills, 1665–1707*, 217, 253, 167. On a widow's obligation to oversee her children's spiritual education, see Narrett, *Inheritance and Family Life*, 87.

[34] Dina Versteg, trans., Peter R. Christoph, Kenneth Scott, and Kenn Stryker-Rodda, eds., *Kingston Papers* (2 vols., Baltimore, 1976), II, 557; Records of the Reformed Protestant Dutch Church of Flatbush, vol. 1a, Consistory Minutes, 10; Edward T. Corwin, ed., *Ecclesiastical Records of the State of New York* (7 vols., Albany, 1901–1916), II, 633.

[35] On the role mothers played in the transmission of Dutch culture—especially language, and thus religion, see Joyce Goodfriend, *Before the Melting Pot: Society and Culture in Colonial New York City, 1664–1730* (Princeton, 1992), 94,196–199, 209–210; Goodfriend, "The Social Dimensions of Congregational Life: Church Life in Colonial New York City," *WMQ*, 3d ser., 46 (1989): 265; Goodfriend, "Recovering the Religious History of Dutch Reformed Women in Colonial New York," *de Halve Maen*, vol. 64 (Winter, 1991): 57. On the catechizing of Dutch girls and boys, see below, chapter five.

[36] Elsie Leisler to Jacob Leisler, Jr., August 8, 1691, Leisler Papers, Doc.5, New York University. Earlier that year, Jacob Leisler Sr. and his aide and son-in-law Jacob Milborne, had been executed as traitors in the aftermath of Leisler's Rebellion.

[37] *The Journal of Jasper Danckaerts*, Bartlett Burleigh James and J. Franklin Jameson, eds. (New York, 1913, 1959 reprint), 202–210.

[38] Warren Billings, ed., *The Papers of Francis Howard, Baron of Effingham, 1643–1695* (Richmond, Va., 1989), 47, 133.

[39] Darrett and Anita Rutman, "'Now-Wives and Sons-in-Law': Parental Death in a Seventeenth-Century Virginia County," in *The Chesapeake in the Seventeenth Century*, eds., Tate and Ammerman (New York, 1979), 174.

[40] *VMHB*, VI (1899): 34; James R. Perry, *The Formation of a Society on Virginia's Eastern Shore, 1615–1655* (Chapel Hill, 1990), 79–80; Ames, ed., *County Court Records of Accomack-Northhampton*, 247; on William Byrd I's early years in Virginia, see Terri L. Snyder, "Rich Widows are the Best Commodity: Women in Virginia, 1660–1700" (Ph.D. diss., University of Iowa, 1992), 255–266.

[41] On godparenthood in the Chesapeake in the seventeenth century see Lorena Walsh, "'Till Death Us Do Part': Marriage and Family in Seventeenth-Century Maryland," in *The Chesapeake in the Seventeenth Century*, 147, 149.

[42] Rutmans, "Now Wives and Sons-in Law," 161; William Hening, ed., *Statutes at Large; Being a Collection of All the Laws of Virginia* (New York, 1823), I, 260, 416; *WMQ*, 1st ser., 5 (1889): 220–222; Rosemary Corley Neal, comp., *Deeds, Wills, Court Orders, Etc. Elizabeth City County, Virginia, 1634, 1659, 1688–1701* (Bowie, Md., 1986), 86. For similar examples of the orphans/apprentices educated in religion and the Bible, see *ibid.*, 88, 89, 128, 131, 131–132; C. G. Chamberlayne, trans., *The Vestry Book of Petsworth Parish, Gloucester County, Virginia, 1677–1793* (Richmond, 1979), 67, 92, 113; Susie M. Ames, ed., *County Court Records of Accomack-Northhampton, Virginia, 1640–1645* (Charlottesville, 1973), 368. Some distinctions were made between male and female apprentices when it came to learning a craft or a trade: girls were instructed in domestic arts—weaving, housekeeping, cooking, sewing—while boys were more likely to be instructed in farming, smithing, or whatever other trades the master engaged in.

[43] Elizabeth Timberlake Davis, comp., *Surry County Records, 1652–1684* (Baltimore), 38.

Part III

CHURCH: GENDER AND PUBLIC WORSHIP

Chapter Five

SABBATH AND SACRAMENT— WOMEN AND WORSHIP IN THE PROTESTANT CHURCH

O N AN APRIL MORNING IN 1698 A "NEGRO WOMAN, FORMERLY THE SERVANT WOMAN OF Lieutenant Thomas Gardiner," professed her faith, made a public confession, and was baptized a member of the First Church in Salem, Massachusetts. Church records indicate that she answered questions during her examination "according to Mr. Cottons Catechise very exactly," and that she provided the requisite account of the work of God's spirit upon her, as evidence of "the efficacy and sovereignty of the grace of God." In addition, several church members testified to her "Christian conversation." For the most part, the account of her covenanting is similar to other public confessions, evidence enough that women participated vocally in certain church rituals. One detail in the record stands out, however, a compelling reminder that a woman possessed of God's spirit could recreate herself both in private and in public: though her name prior to her conversion was Venus, "she was at her Baptism at her desire named Hanna." She deemed Venus a name "unworthy of a Christian woman." In choosing a new name for herself, Hanna seized the opportunity to create and present a public face that reflected her private piety. The biblical Hannah, whose private and public prayers to the Lord were answered when she conceived and bore the mighty Samuel, might well have epitomized the liberty, hope and joy a free black woman experienced as she participated in the ritual rebirth associated with her conversion and baptism. "I am the woman who was standing here in your presence," the Bible's Hannah proclaimed, " . . . and the Lord has granted me the petition that I made to him." [1 Samuel 1][1]

As regenerate Christians, women were active participants in—and shapers of— the rituals that formed the religious anchor of their communities. Even as they grappled with private notions of faith and salvation, women included in their definitions of grace rituals that blurred the lines between the personal and the communal, the private and the public. Though Paul's decree concerning women's silence in church indeed shaped attitudes toward female worship in the seventeenth century, women, as heirs to Reformation-inspired freedom of conscience and a belief in the equality of the soul, refused to withdraw and allow men—ministers, husbands, fathers, or brothers—to determine the nature of their faith.

From the outset, the reformed tradition dramatically altered the relationship between church leaders and members of their congregations, just as it altered the relationship between the individual and God. Though all three Protestant denominations examined here acknowledged to a greater or lesser degree the power of the minister as teacher and translator of God's word, the Holy Spirit imbued each regenerate Christian with a sense of God's direct presence. The Church was an entity unto itself, with or without the presence of an ordained leader. It mattered only that Christians had access to God's house, for there, in God's bosom, "all of the church were a royal Priesthood, all of them Prophets, and taught of God's Spirit. . . ."[2]

Among women, the tremendously empowering symbolism embodied in the idea of a "royal priesthood" might well have been heightened by the gendered concept of a mother church. In numerous sermons and tracts representing all three reformed traditions the church was conceived of as feminine, "the Mother of All Pious." In language that reflected and reinforced images of female piety in the home—mother as nurturer and moral guide—the church was a place "to be nourished by her assistance and ministry during their infancy and childhood . . . to be governed by her maternal care . . . .there is no other way of entrance into life, unless we are conceived by her, born of her, nourished at her breast." The church, according to Puritan divine John Cotton, drawing on an allusion to worldly love in the Songs of Solomon, "is the fairest among women."[3]

The church—nurturing, uplifting, "the mother of us all" (Gal.4:26)—was a primary part of the foundation of each community settled in the seventeenth-century colonies. One of the first priorities in each new settlement was the establishment of the mother church and the construction of a place of worship. In each colony magistrates worked quickly to establish a body of laws that among other goals instituted regulations for worship and pious conduct.[4]

Laws pertaining to colonial worship addressed the need to establish a weekly, yearly, and seasonal Protestant calendar. At the center of that holy calendar was the Sabbath, the ritualistic key to the spiritual health and well-being of individuals and their communities. In keeping with their rejection of Anglican holy days as remnants of popish superstition, Puritan divines from the 1590s on emphasized the need for a regular day of worship, a day which honored the sacredness of *all* time and space. Sabbatarianism, suppressed by conservative Anglicans in England, flourished in the early years of the Puritan colony. It is a mark of the impact of both Calvinism and social and economic conditions peculiar to the American colonies that the Sabbath lay at the core of Protestant worship in both New Netherland and Virginia as well.[5]

Gender, Spiritual Equality, and Reformation Church Architecture

To accommodate the celebration of the Sabbath and sacraments, Protestant communities struggled to build a suitable house of worship as soon as economic circumstances allowed. And from the floor to the rafters, each church was a product of the Reformation attitude toward the relationship between congregants and their minister and between the individual and God. The Protestant emphasis on preaching and hearing the Word necessitated reform of church architecture as well as church liturgy. The result was the "auditory church," designed and constructed to allow worshippers the greatest exposure to the pulpit.[6]

In Calvinist churches especially, church exteriors and interiors reflected reordered relationships. Gone were Catholic monoliths, filled with "idolatrous" representations of the trinity. In their place, English and Dutch colonists erected structures free of the multiplicity of crosses and stained glass that had come to represent Catholic—and conservative Anglican—abuses. Gone was the chancel, which separated the laity from the priest and the choir. In their drive to undermine Catholicism's idolatry and the liturgical significance of the altar, Calvinist churches incorporated the communion table into the large main room central to Puritan worship. The Calvinist minister, though responsible for preaching the all-important Word, was no more or less potentially graced that any of his congregation, male or female; his physical position in the church, at a pulpit in full view of all of his worshipers, reflected that equality.[7]

Anglican church architecture reflected the reformed relationship between preacher and listener as well. Colonial churches especially were subject to a reordering of space that placed increased emphasis on preaching and hearing the Word. In both cruciform and north-south rectangular arrangements, examples of each of which were built in Virginia, the pulpit and reading desk were re-located to offer all parishioners an uninterrupted view of the minister or lay reader. The T-plan or cruciform arrangement, popular with Calvinists as well as Anglicans, focused attention specifically on the pulpit, acknowledged in all reformed churches to be the center of liturgical ritual. And as one historian has recently noted, it was not unusual to find Anglican churches that had even abandoned a stationary altar in favor of temporary tables around which communicants sat along side their church elders. Though Laudian Anglicans expressed discomfort with such an arrangement, the 1662 *Book of Common Prayer* did not forbid it, and churches on both sides of the Atlantic encouraged communicants to stand around the table, or even to receive communion at their pews. Thus in Virginia, as in Massachusetts and New York, the Word belonged to the people.[8]

Though much has been made of the fact that in reformed churches women sat separately from men, it is important to note that this in no way reflected poorly on the standing of female congregants in the church. In fact, as Amanda Porterfield points out, women were seated most often on the right side of the church, directly in front of the minister, while men sat to the left, behind the deacons.[9]

In their descriptions of their places of worship, reformed ministers often employed language infused with domestic allusions familiar to any settlers in the midst of constructing their own family dwellings. And because the home was a site of woman-centered activity and authority, such domestic allusions might well have carried additional meaning for female congregants. Using a complex mixture of metaphor and literal description, the Reverend Edward Taylor included in his Foundation Day Sermon of 1670 a description of "God's Building." Within the church dwelling lay "furniture," including both "Utensills" and "Officers." Among the "utensills," described as "household goods . . . most costly, precious, & Excellent that are brought into dayly use in his service," Taylor included candle sticks, the alter, the Lord's Table, the laver, and the "Bason or Ure of Soules." Was it mere coincidence, then, that these objects were among those most frequently donated to churches by women in all three colonies?[10]

SABBATH WORSHIP IN THE COLONIAL CHURCH

Though there were marked similarities in the ways all Protestant denominations responded architecturally to the reformed emphasis on the pulpit and the Word, there is no question that specific rituals attending Sabbath celebrations varied dramatically from colony to colony. Often, scholars have assumed that by comparison to the New England Sabbath, worship in Anglican Virginia was devoid of spiritual meaning, a pale reflection of the popish tendencies of the Church of England. Much has been written, for example, on the Nonconformist rejection of Anglican forms of worship, including the set liturgy, responsive prayer, kneeling at Communion and bowing at the name of Jesus, cross signing at baptisms, and the ministerial use of surplice and stole. At the heart of these liturgical innovations lay an increased emphasis on personal piety and a rejection of spiritual distinctions between ministers and lay worshippers. These innovations shaped Puritan attitudes toward the potential spiritual authority of both men and women, and infused worship in colonial Massachusetts.[11]

From this perspective, it would be easy to dismiss Anglican worship as a source of spiritual authority for any lay parishioner. On the surface, the use of the liturgical form of the *Book of Common Prayer* and of attire that set ministers apart from their lay worshipers seems more akin to Catholic traditions which maintained the distance between priest and parishioner and undermined individual piety. Once we examine the ways men and women actually experienced Anglican worship in Virginia, however, it becomes clear that Anglican rituals and traditions in their own way allowed for and encouraged lay people of both sexes to exercise spiritual independence and spiritual authority. Moreover, that independence—in doctrine and practice—was enhanced by Virginia's geographic distance from the church's hierarchy in England and by the demographic circumstances that shaped the church's evolution in the colony.[12]

The Sabbath, as the central ritual of all three Protestant denominations, was the prime attraction for congregants everywhere. Families—including children, servants, and in some Virginia parishes, slaves—traveled distances of up to thirty miles to perform their Christian duty, to socialize, and to obey the letter of the law. Though outliving among second generation colonists created the need for additional churches on the Massachusetts frontier, and settlers in the outlying New Netherland boroughs often complained of a dearth of ministers, churchgoers in those colonies worked quickly to insure that the distances from local churches were not prohibitive.[13]

In Virginia, where "neighborhood" assumed a somewhat different connotation than it did in either New or Old England, settlers endured journeys of the greatest distances. Though church attendance was mandated by law, and ministers, vestrymen, and legislative leaders urged colonists to settle within a central distance from church and town, settlement patterns reflected instead the lure of the land stretching west from the tidewater. Planters, guaranteed a "head right" of fifty acres for every indentured servant they brought with them from England, settled far from Jamestown and the few other population centers that existed in Virginia in the seventeenth century. And though Virginia's population increased steadily between 1630 and 1680, parishes, forced to expand geographically to encompass enough of a tithing base to support a minister, became unwieldy. Court and vestry records for the mid-seventeenth century are punctuated by appeals for new parish churches or chapels located closer to the ever-shifting population centers. As late as the turn of the eighteenth century, a Swiss traveler to the American colonies remarked that in Virginia, "going to church means at some places a trip of more than thirty miles." In 1700, in New Kent County, Virginia, the vestry declared that as "the Lower Church . . . Standeth very inconvenient for the most of the inhabitants of the Said parish . . . as Soon as Conveniently may be a new Church . . . to be built and erected." The inhabitants of St. Paul's Parish in Hanover County, "seated very remote from the upper Church," asked that the minister, Mr. Thomas Sharp, "preach on the Frontiers of this parish once a Month . . . for which he shall be paid accordingly." Petitioners also requested that the minister "give timely notice when he will preach, in order the parishioners may have timely notice." Far from simply discouraging parishioners from weekly attendance (though to be sure, church records offer many examples of individuals and families fined for nonattendance), the inconvenience seems to have inspired outliving neighbors to act in concert to demand change.[14]

Though descriptions of Congregational and Dutch Reformed divine services abound in contemporary accounts left by both ministers and lay people, the Anglican Sabbath service seems by comparison cloaked in shadows. In addition to sketchy references to Sabbath schedules in vestry books, historians must rely on sources generated by the Church of England, ecclesiastical laws and regulations to which the Church expected every parish to adhere. *The Book of Common Prayer* set the standard for Anglican liturgy; ministers—or in their absence lay readers—were expected to derive every aspect of the Sabbath service from its pages. Sabbath services began with the minister reading a series of set prayers and biblical passages, interspersed with responsive readings and psalm singing. A sermon followed, derived or read directly from *The Book of Common Prayer* or one of several authorized books of homilies. According to Virginia laws established by the Assembly in 1641, the afternoon was to be devoted to catechism.[15]

In both New Netherland and Massachusetts, a separate day of the week was set aside for catechizing children. Sabbath services were held in both the morning and the afternoon. The Sabbath celebration in Massachusetts began at 9 am with an opening prayer of thanksgiving or intercession, followed each week by the reading and exposition of another chapter of the Bible, presented in order from beginning to end. The congregation next joined in psalm singing, and then settled in for the sermon, which ranged in length from one to three hours. Those members of the congregation who had prepared themselves for the sermon by reading and discussing the appropriate biblical chapters at home might experience the thrill of revelation; the Word was more accessible to the heart and mind prepared to receive it. After the sermon, the congregation sang one or two more psalms, and the service ended with another prayer and a blessing. The Sabbath schedule was modified in the morning on those days the Lord's Supper was offered—monthly or bi-monthly depending upon the congregation—and in the afternoon when there were children who awaited baptism.[16]

Anglican Set Liturgy and Spiritual Equality

While there were similarities between the elements of Anglican and radical Protestant Sabbath services—psalm singing, sermons, and prayers—one of the most profound points of liturgical contention was over the Anglican use of a set liturgy. Criticized by Puritan divines for encouraging laziness and stifling individual piety and the personal exercise of God's gift of prayer, the Anglican liturgy remained intact throughout the seventeenth century in England and, less explicitly, in Virginia. As interpreted by separating Nonconformists and, more recently, colonial historians of an evangelical bent, the set Anglican liturgy appears stripped of any spiritual meaning, devoid of piety, merely a tool to promote and maintain the cultural hegemony of the elite in Virginia.[17]

Though there is little question that the Anglican defense of and adherence to Prayer Book ceremonies in part lay in obedience to the King and to ecclesiastical hierarchy, there were theological justifications as well, justifications that go to the heart of Anglican worship and at the same time speak to the potentially liberating and "democratic" nature of the Anglican experience in Virginia.

Prayer Book liturgy was the key to Anglican security, a security grounded in the constant, familiar opportunities to know Christ. Knowledge held the key to Christian duty toward God and man, which in turn lay at the heart of salvation. Those things that were essential to salvation should be easily comprehensible and few in number, further insurance that God's saving grace be accessible to all pious Christians, regardless of gender or age. Moreover, according to Anglican tenets, profound familiarity with a set liturgy of a manageable size protected the pious against the whims of "mere men"; ministers or church leaders who were tempted to manipulate their congregations were forced to acknowledge that their parishioners were as capable of assimilating the liturgy as they were, and were thus less likely to fall prey to clerical manipulation.[18]

The liturgical controversy surrounding the set liturgy arrived with Puritans on the first boats. At a conference of church elders held in Boston in 1645, John Cotton presented his pamphlet *"Twelve Reasons* Laid down against prescribed and stinted formes of Prayers . . . so hindering the spiritual petitions and phrases that otherwise would be, if God's good gifts were used." In spite of such criticism, however, there was something inherently "democratic" in set forms of worship, where everyone, regardless of the level of their inspiration, prayed in the same way week after week. Those worshippers not yet visited by the spirit, or, more practically, those unable to read, were thereby also privy to the word of God.[19]

Moreover, though use of the Prayer Book was mandated in Anglican Virginia, this did not mean that all parishioners or ministers complied. Referring to the religious experiences of some Virginia settlers early in the seventeenth century one correspondent reported "there is an unhappy dissension fallen out amongst them, by reason of their minister, who being . . . somewhat a puritan the most part refused to go to his service to hear his sermons, though by the other part he was supposed favored." In 1645, two churchwardens from Elizabeth River Parish brought suit against their puritan-leaning parson, Thomas Harrison, for refusing to read from the Prayer Book.[20]

Though churchwardens or vestries might object to a leader's refusal to abide by the Sabbath rituals prescribed by the Prayer Book, parishioners could prove to be a source of support for nonconforming ministers. Early in 1649, in the midst of the Civil War and Cromwell's ascension to power, the minister of a parish in Nansemond, Virginia was banished for refusing to use the *Book of Common Prayer* in his services. The congregation, clearly more non-conforming than conservative, appealed for help in a petition sent directly to Cromwell, prompting Cromwell's council to write to Governor Berkeley demanding an account of the minister's banishment. Common prayer, the colonial government responded, was central to worship in the Church of England, regardless of the hue and cry of the worshippers themselves or the winds of change in the mother country. For all of their bluster, however, the colony's leaders must have been aware that the bookshelves of ministers and lay people throughout the colony were lined with the writings of many of England's most ardent Puritans.[21]

SPIRITUAL EQUALITY AND THE PROTESTANT SERMON

Regardless of whether they performed services that complied with a set liturgy or offered an ever-changing array of sermons and homilies, ministers of the Word struggled to employ language that was as accessible to common lay people as it was to the learned members of their congregations. Reformed theologians cautioned ministers to "accommodate" themselves to their entire congregation, lest those weakest members be obstructed from conversion. In his sermon on Job, John Calvin proclaimed that God "wants not only to instruct learned clergy and people who are very subtle and have been trained in school, but wishes to accommodate to even the roughest common people." Increase Mather, in a eulogy for his father Richard, acknowledged the elder's God-given skill in ministering the Word:

> His way of preaching was plain, aiming to shoot his Arrows not over people's heads, but into their hearts and consciences. . . . The Lord gave him and excellent faculty in making abstruse things plain, that in handling the deepest mysteries he would accommodate himself to Vulgar Capacities, that even the meanest might learn something.

So it was that all congregants—men, women, and children—became, as one historian states, "fluent in the language of spiritual experience." Each shared in the potential for God's grace through equal access to his most cherished tool, the sermon.[22]

As the prime purveyors of spiritual experience, ministers frequently were described in gendered language similar to that applied to the Church. Graced by God with the ability to preach the Word, ministers were regarded as feminine nurturers, the bearers of fruit. Early in the eighteenth century Joseph and Anna Gerrish, in-laws of the Reverend Joseph Green of Salem, Massachusetts, wrote that at his death he had been taken from them, "his breast full of milk and his bone full of marrow." Increase Mather remarked of the same untimely death that "sometimes Pious young ministers are nipt in the Floe, snatched away when much more fruit has been hoped for from them . . . when others that have been a long time barren and unfruitful are spared."[23]

"Fruitful" ministers used their sermons—whether structured in the evangelical style of Calvinists or the more rhetorical Aristotelian style popular among Anglicans—to strike deep in the hearts and consciences of their listeners. The principle ritual in the journey from sin toward salvation, sermons also served as the primary source of guidance on moral conduct, and more practically as a source of local news and information. In 1685 Samuel Sewall remarked that, according to a prayer offered by Reverend Willard in the morning service, he "understood that some Minister was dead..." It was not until the noon break, when he had the opportunity to ask his apparently better-informed wife, that he learned it was Nathaniel Chauncey of Hatfield who had died.[24]

Above all else, the Protestant sermon appealed to the "heart prepared," a recognizable and accessible key to the rebirth of the soul. Through the sermon, Protestant men and women found the strength to do battle with Satan, a battle they were likely to wage several times over the course of their lives. Calvinist and moderate Anglican men and women in the seventeenth century were vocal participants in the struggle to be reborn, and the most likely to stress the relationship between the sermon and their regeneracy.[25]

Ministers and lay auditors alike understood and referred to the regenerate heart and soul in explicitly feminine terms. References to meekness, humility, patience, and nurturing, most often acknowledged as womanly qualities, peppered sermons delivered by ministers in all Protestant denominations. Puritan ministers especially relied on images of female piety in their descriptions of the workings of grace on the human soul. As Thomas Shepard explained, "God doth shew his powere by the much ado of our weakness to do anything . . . .The more weak I, the more fit I to be used . . . ." Roger Clap, describing his family in his autobiography written in the 1670s, noted that Mr. Hopestill Clap was "endowed with a great Measure of Meekness and Patience . . . "26

Feminine imagery was not new to Christian preaching in the seventeenth century; much of it was rooted in early Catholic images of Jesus as Mother, "who, like a hen, collects her chickens under her wings." The heart and feelings, according to Calvin, must stand alongside reason in a soul prepared to accept God's grace. To that end, Calvin was decidedly cool toward Stoicism, "that requires men to be utterly without feeling if they are deemed wise." Ministers of the Word, though they were cautioned to maintain decorum, were expected by their parishioners to communicate their emotional devotion to Scripture and its teaching. 27

And to the prepared heart, Christ appeared not only as mother, but also as husband. In Catholic and Protestant sermons alike, ministers exhorted their auditors, male and female, to receive Christ as a bride would receive her spouse, with overwhelming love, humility, and meekness. So Edward Taylor preached in his 1678 Foundation Day sermon, "Consider, Soule that thou art called to enter here, if Prepared.Christ Speakes unto thee in his language to his Spouse, Cant. 2:10,11,12,13, arise my Love, my fair one, & come a way." Thomas Shepard, in his *Parable of the Ten Virgins*, published in 1659, and in his sermon "The Soul's Invitation unto Jesus Christ," frequently employed images of Christ as a bridegroom preparing to take his bride. Drawn from the Song of Songs and numerous other books of the Bible, Shepard's sermons on the coming of Christ are filled with parochial references to contemporary courting traditions that illustrate the rituals necessary to prepare a bride for marriage to Christ. In his explanation of the role of the Holy Supper in the preparation for heavenly union, Shepard wrote

> Then there shall be a personal meeting between his spouse and himself, as there is in marriage; before the marriage is consummated, there are the friends of the bridegroom and spokesmen, and he sends letters and tokens, but then he comes himself; so here Christ sends his spokesmen . . . and his word and spiritual refreshings. . . .

Again, the image of the loving wife was used as the standard for piety to which regenerate Christians of both sexes must try to adhere.28

The Word in itself was "fruitful," capable of providing motherly nourishment, especially when it worked on men and women prepared to receive its succor. Judith

Hull, the pious mother-in-law of Samuel Sewall, was so prepared. Her epitaph, written on her death in 1695, heralded her as a "Diligent, Constant, Fruitfull Reader and Hearer of the Word of GOD." In a letter to the Amsterdam Classis in 1680, the Consistory of the Flatbush Church prayed for "the supreme Shepard of Sheep . . . to grant His divine blessing to the growth and fruitfulness of the word of the Gospel." Using language even more explicitly linked to feminine characteristics, John Cotton entitled his popular 1646 pamphlet and catechism "Milk for Babes, Drawn out of the Breasts of Both Testaments. Chiefly for the Spirituall nourishment of Boston Babes in either England." In 1670, Thomas Thacher, the first minister of the Third Church of Boston, preached a sermon from Cant. IV.5, "Thy two breasts are as two young roes that are twins, which feed among the lilies." Thacher expounded on the text, in language that must have struck a chord with his female congregants, "These breasts are by some thought the old and new testament; by others, mildness, simplicity, purity of heart and life; by others doctrine in the church for exhortation, etc.; by others, for the ministry sent fourth of Christ by two and two, and appointed pastors and teachers." Protestant women, whose personal notions of faith, grace, and salvation were formed in part by reading biblical references to female fruitfulness, nurture, and strength, found powerful reinforcement for those private notions of female piety in weekly Sabbath services.[29]

In addition to making symbolic links between salvation, the Word, and motherhood, ministers relied on exempla and allegory drawn from domestic life to help their sermons ring true among their congregants. Puritan ministers drew on the image of a housewife who must wage a never-ending battle against "dung" and "scum." Without her constant attention, the foundation of her well-maintained household was likely to crumble. Like that housewife, tested by uncleanness at every step, so all godly men and women must maintain their vigilance against the evil that was sure to infect their lives and communities.[30]

Reformed ministers relied on the Bible for examples of humility, penitence, faith, and strength in adversity, qualities found frequently in stories where women played key roles. Sermons about penitence or humility often invoked the story of the woman of Nain, in Luke Chap. 7, who washed Christ's feet with ointment. Jael, who slew Sisera in Judges, Chap.5, served to illustrate the bravery and power with which God endowed women in times of adversity. Should any congregants doubt the wisdom or strength of women, they need only to have listened to a sermon on Matthew 27. Women attended Christ at the cross, and upon his death women were chosen to declare his power and grace to the world, for, when led by the spirit of God, "there is in them more audacity than in men, even those [apostles] who had been elected to publish the gospel in all the world . . . ." Judith Hull's epitaph included a litany of biblical women whose piety was matched by Hull's own:

> Great Sarah's Faith; joined with good Hannah's Prayer
> For hearing of the Word, glad Marie's Care;
> Aged Elizabeth's just walk; To dwell
> Nigh Prophets, a true Shunamitish Zeal. . . .
> All of these Expir'd at once! Array'd with them,
> Our Huldah's gone to God's Jerusalem. . . .[31]

In a sermon directed especially to his female congregants, Cotton Mather offered an equally impressive list of biblical women, apparently in an effort to reinforce the importance of reading Scripture. According to Mather, as a result of their faith in God, the Bible's holy women had been privy to numerous heavenly discoveries. Witness, he claimed, the Songs of Deborah and Hannah, Huldah's prophecies, and the instructions of Bathsheba to Solomon in the 31st Chapter of Proverbs. Female and male readers had much to learn from biblical women.[32]

Beyond mere reading of the Bible, Cotton Mather also noted that "though the Apostle . . . gives the prohibition . . . *that the woman may not Speak in the Church*, yet our God has Employ'd many *Women* to *Write* for the Church, and *Inspir'd* some of them for the Writing of the *Scriptures* . . . " Mather, like other Reformed ministers in the seventeenth century, tempered Paul's dictum forbidding women to speak with opportunities to express piety in other ways. Even in New England, women "to whom the common use of *Swords*, is neither Decent nor Lawful, have made a most Laudable use of *Pens*."[33]

women's words and "things indifferent": spiritual equality and protestant church ritual

For all of the resonance of Paul's decree, women did speak in church. Historians have been quick to assume that simply because ministers and magistrates reminded their female congregants of Paul's words, women remained silent. In fact, women's voices, while not nearly so loud or clear in seventeenth-century texts as those of men, nonetheless made themselves heard. Women's voices carried weight; women's words signaled both their piety and their influence within the walls of the church.

Even within the bounds of accepted religious practice, women spoke with some authority. According to English separatist minister John Robinson, who fled with his church to Amsterdam in 1609, women could

> make a profession of faith, a confession of sin, say Amen to the Church prayer,
> sing Psalms vocally, accuse a brother of sin, witness an accusation, or defend
> themselves being accused, yea in a case extraordinary, namely where no man
> will, I see not but a woman may reprove the Church, rather than suffer it to go
> on in apparent wickedness and communicate with in therein. . . .[34]

And while a woman's words infrequently upset or even challenged the patriarchal structure of the churches or communities to which they belonged, they did undermine the ability of male leaders to maintain rigid control over a woman's behavior in a public place.

If Protestant ministers seemed equivocal in matters of female silence in church, it may have been the result of Calvin's impact on their teachings. Calvin's *Institutes of Christian Religion* undermined the potency of Paul's decree by including women's speech among those things that were "indifferent," that is, not central to church doctrine. Like the covering of a woman's head, women's silence in church was neither commanded nor forbidden in scripture; it was, therefore, among those issues to be decided on practical grounds. In both the 1536 and the 1559 *Institutes*, Calvin took issue with Paul, classifying as historically conditioned his dicta on silence, head covering, long hair on men, and dancing. Within the bounds of contemporary notions of decorum (as "things indifferent" were classified in the 1536 *Institutes*) or order (according to the *Institutes* of 1559), women identified numerous opportunities to speak.[35]

Early in the eighteenth century, Amsterdam minister Wilhelmus a Brakel wrote in the preface to an edition of his late wife's work:

> For the building of his church God uses all kinds of people, pious, impious, young, old, not only men, but also women. . . . We know the hymn of Deborah, of Hannah, of Mary, women have fought with Paul in the Gospel. God would also fill women with his Holy Spirit, and they would prophesy, thus did the four daughters of Philip the Evangelist. . . .

It was expected that women who were filled with the Holy spirit would be unable to prevent themselves from expressing their joy; it was not uncommon, "under strong emotions, for the tongue to break forth into sounds, and the other members into gestures, without the least ostentation. Hence the uncertain muttering of Hannah . . . ." As long as the content of her expressions—whether of joy, fear, sorrow, or contrition—did not violate church doctrine, a woman might speak before the congregation.[36]

Though Sabbath day lay readers—called on to assist the minister by reading specific prayers before or after the sermon—were rarely drawn from the female church population, in at least one case in New York a girl was chosen by the Rev. Henricus Selyns to read before the congregation. Five-year old Marycken Popinga recited the "regular Sunday-prayer," delivered after the minister's address but before the sermon. Marycken "recited without any mistake, and with energy and manly confidence." As Selyns noted in his letter to the Classis soon after the event, the congregation was so moved by the child's performance that they repeated the prayer "not without tears." While a young girl's speech before the congregation would have been less threatening—and therefore more acceptable—than a grown woman's, girls learned at an early age that they were as capable as boys of contributing to the spiritual health of the church community. That realization was reinforced during Selyns' examination of his catechism students: in that public performance (held during the week and not on the Sabbath), not only did girls comprise a third of the catechists, they "learned and recited more, in proportion to the boys."[37]

song and spirituality

One of the easiest ways to express joy vocally, for both men and women, was in song. Protestant churches condoned the singing of psalms as a part of Sabbath services, for scripture itself included singing among the duties of the faithful. Though Paul admonished women to remain silent in church, he also instructed all Ephesians "to speak one to another in Psalms and Hymns and Spirituall Song." Romans 10:17 encouraged worshipers to "make a joyfull noyse unto the Lord," and to "come before his presence with singing." And in Judges 5:12, Deborah, "mother of Israel," sang the praises of the Lord, as did Miriam in Exodus 15. It was Miriam's example that John Cotton used specifically in support of women singing in his pamphlet "The Singing of Psalms."[38]

Song singing was no light matter among congregants. Singing was spiritually born, as profoundly meaningful as recitation of scripture without song. Calvin cautioned singers not to be more consumed with the "modulation of the Notes" than the spiritual meaning of the words. Anglican James Owen warned that while "the use of singing Psalms is very apt for the Edification of Churches . . . Musical Instruments . . . are more apt to change Religion into Fancies." Catholic worshippers ridiculed Protestant forms of psalm singing, for without an instrumental accompaniment or harmony, chaos prevailed. As one sixteenth-century French Catholic remarked, "No one is on the same verse . . . .The fine-voiced maidens let loose their hums and trills . . . so the young men will be sure to listen. How wrong of Calvin to let women sing in church." Protestant worshippers, however, recognized that the psalms were an outlet for both individual and communal spirituality.[39]

John Cotton explained that in the Nonconformist church songs could be sung by one spiritually motivated singer, to which the congregation would say "amen," or could be sung by the entire congregation. Instructions to Readers at the Flatbush Dutch Reformed Church in New Netherland were not so specific. Records indicate only that in the afternoon "the further service of God be begun with a Christian Song." Early in the eighteenth century, William Byrd of Virginia noted in his diary that he attended church one Sabbath afternoon to "hear the people sing Psalms." The singing master, apparently not one to allow passive participation, "gave me two books, one for me and one for my wife." Byrd recorded in his diary that later that afternoon he and his wife quarreled about learning to sing Psalms; his diary is silent on the exact reasons for the quarrel. Was it that Mrs. Byrd welcomed the opportunity to sing, while her husband preferred simply to listen? Byrd writes only that his wife "was wholly in the wrong." Though the Byrds attended Anglican services, the distribution of psalm books to both husband and wife reflected Puritan liturgical guidelines that recommended that all congregants, regardless of age or sex, participate in this part of the service. According to the *Reliquiae Liturgicae*, in order "that the whole congregation may join in, every one that can read is to have a Psalm book; and all others not disabled by age or otherwise, are to be exhorted to learn to read."40

Female speech and the conversion narrative

One category of women's public speech peculiar to the Puritan church was the narration of a conversion experience. While churches of all Protestant denominations required some sort of public profession of faith—a signature to a covenant, oral responses to a test of scriptural knowledge—only certain Nonconformist churches made public profession a requirement for visible sainthood. A point of contention between moderate Anglicans, Presbyterians, and Puritans in England, the conversion requirement was debated among New England churches as well.41

At its heart, however, the requirement of a conversion narration rose from a concept of faith and duty central to Reformed beliefs; in theory, public profession of a conversion experience would not have been at odds with religious practice in any Protestant denomination. Protestant worship emphasized the need for personal expression, a rejection of the popish tendency to promote slavish repetition of superstitious or idolatrous phrases. The public relation of a narrative reinforced the Reformed emphasis on a voluntary, verbal commitment to a covenant, a covenant subject to communal, not papal judgments.42

Though Puritans in general shared with other Christians the concept of visible sainthood, for some the approach to church admission went several steps beyond a simple profession of faith. In several Massachusetts churches in the seventeenth century, men and women alike were required to appear before the entire congregation to relate a conversion experience. For those Puritans, public profession was essential to heighten the assurance not only of the individual, but also of the entire congregation. For, as Patricia Caldwell has so astutely observed, "It is not profession . . . that makes the man a believer, but it is profession that makes a church a church."43

For both the speaker and the audience, the conversion experience and the related public profession were spiritual acts. Hearing the profession of a fellow member was almost as important as making one. In their quest to form the purest visible church, regenerate Christians expected to recognize the working of God's grace in others as well as in themselves. God, through the Holy Spirit, imbued all Christians with the ability to hear, understand, and speak of grace. This "skill," to recognize and articulate personal knowledge of grace, was not acquired at university. The Holy Spirit might work through any faithful Christian, regardless of their education, social standing, or gender. And once they acquired a personal knowledge of grace, regenerate Christians were obliged to share it with their congregation, and the congregation was obliged to listen. And as Cotton Mather preached in his sermon "Ornaments for the Daughters of Zion," the justification for public confession could be found in Scripture: "Having had her Soul purify'd by *Regeneration*," the church daughter willingly "brings her *Offerings* to the *Tabernacle. She presents unto the Church*...a sensible Account, like another *Lydia*, of some never to be forgotten Things which *God has done for her soul*; or at least she makes the Church to understand, like *Ruth* of old, *That she would come to rest under the Wings of the God of Israel.*"44

So it was that both male and female congregants obeyed the rule laid down in the Cambridge Platform of 1648 that called for "relations, confessions personally [made] with their own Mouth." According to the Platform, conversion was meant to be both "personall and Publick." Once again, reformed religious practice undermined Paul's decree, for women spoke before their congregations as both professors and judges. Of the total of sixty-four confessions recorded by Thomas Shepard at his church in Cambridge, almost half (31) were women; Shepard required all those seeking full membership in his church to make a public profession and to answer questions posed by him and other members, male and female. In Dedham in 1638, the wife of John Frayry "gave good satisfaction both in publike & private." The Reverend John Fiske, minister of the new church in Wenham in the 1640s noted that Mistress Farwel's relation "was brief, clear, and full as respecting the manner of God's drawing her soul unto Himself."45

That is not to say that the notion of female profession in public met with no objections, for many church leaders in Old and New England held fast to Paul's decree. At his church in Wenham, John Fiske contended with objections from some of his first members. Was not a public profession synonymous with the teaching of prophesy, forbidden to women in 1 Corinthians and 1 Timothy? Surely there was danger inherent in the public professions of women, for "such a speaking argues power." But Fiske and numerous other Puritan ministers persisted, and though women in Fiske's congregation had the option of having their narratives read for them by their minister, many chose to read them themselves. The First Church in Boston offered prospective members another option: there, a number of women chose to read or declare their professions before the church elders. Amy Evans, for instance, dismissed from Roxbury, was admitted to the Boston church "having declared hir spirituall Condition to the Elders" in 1644. Similarly, Elizabeth Wayte, dismissed from Newbury, "related her Condition to the Elders in their private meeting" in October 1645. 46

Though Fiske, Shepard, and other Puritan ministers denied the danger in female profession, declaring it unrelated to the teaching of prophesy and well within the bounds of Protestant interpretations of Paul's decree, public conversion in fact functioned as a means to edify the church body and glorify its holy covenant. There is little question that many women discovered through their narration an opportunity to share with their families and their community their own personal interpretation of the journey toward salvation. Their narratives, filled with references to scripture and the shared experience of migration, demanded the attention of not only church members, whose job it was to judge the quality of the experience, but of the entire congregation, including those who had yet to be visited by grace.

Women may even have been aware that such experiences might be published in one of the "guides to godliness" that were so popular in the seventeenth century.[47]

Puritan ministers recognized the stress that public relations put on the more reticent members of their congregations. While it was usually assumed that it would be women who had greater difficulty standing before the congregation, by the 1660s the Reverend John Fiske was reading men's relations as well as women's. In the 1680s Joseph Green recorded in his commonplace book that his relation was read to the congregation by a church deacon, "this being Read: Mr. W[alters] propounded me to the terms of the covenant." And while few men or women had a reaction to the requirement for public confession as dramatic as Goody Hinsdell in Dedham, who "not able to speake in Publicke but fainting away," the narration requirement surely produced anxiety in most prospective members. Some made their professions in the face of unusual conditions: in 1678, Mrs. Baldwin of the First Church in Salem, "a French Gentlewoman who came from the Isle of Jarsey and brought with her considerable Testimonialls from sundry French Ministers concerning her piety and good conversation" made her confession of faith before the entire congregation "in her owne way in the French Tongue."[48]

communion ritual in colonial america

One of the primary advantages to membership in the Protestant church was the invitation to join other visible saints in the rites of Holy Communion and Baptism. Like public profession, the sacraments constituted rituals of both individual and communal affirmation. In addition, participation in the sacraments affirmed the right of women to speak before their congregations in rituals that articulated the Reformed belief in the equality of the soul. According to Calvin, faith held the key to productive participation. To the heart prepared, the sacraments were the same as the word of God, "to offer and present Christ to us, and in him the treasures of heavenly grace."[49]

Of the three colonies, Puritan Massachusetts set the most rigid standards for admission to Communion. As noted above, throughout much of the seventeenth century Puritan churches required the relation—before the congregation or before the minister and elders—of a conversion experience as condition for admission to full membership, which brought with it the privilege of communion. And with a ready supply of ministers, Massachusetts churches consistently offered the sacrament on a more regular basis than either New Netherland or Virginia, usually once every month or six weeks. On sacrament days, after the sermon, prayer, and psalms, non-members were dismissed from church with a blessing from the minister while members remained in their pews. Ministers and elders took their place at a table usually set in the center of the chancel. Depending upon the custom of each particular church, communicants received the bread and wine seated in their pews or gathered around the table.[50]

Unlike the Puritan Church, the Dutch church required only a profession of faith as a condition of admission to communion, and that to be performed in a semi-private ceremony, not before the entire congregation. In 1660, for instance, the Dutch church in Brooklyn resolved that "those who wanted to be admitted to the Lord's Table and accepted in the Christian community" would be required to "confess their true and sanctifying faith in the presence of the consistory and witnesses." But an initial shortage of professing members, and a persistent dearth of appropriately ordained ministers, meant that the Sacrament was offered less frequently there than in the well-supplied towns of Massachusetts. In 1628 New Netherland's first minister, Jonas Michaelmas, noted that the Lord's Supper was to be administered only once in four months "until a larger number of people shall otherwise require." The first administration in the new colony "was observed not without great joy and comfort to many, we had fully fifty communicants." As late as 1664, New Amsterdam's Rev. Samuel Drisius reported to the Classis in Amsterdam that he offered communion to the French on Staten Island every two months, as they were too few in number and too poor to support their own minister. In Brooklyn in 1660, Henricus Selyns suggested that the sacrament be offered four times a year, on Christmas, Easter, Whitsuntide, and in September. Flatbush, Brooklyn, and Midwoud often shared a minister, who offered communion to each community in turn.[51]

Virginia, like New Netherland, had to contend with a dearth of ministers throughout the seventeenth century, thus diminishing opportunities to receive the sacrament. Though some parishes strove to administer communion monthly, that was a standard to which few could adhere on a regular basis. Technically, only those ministers ordained in England were permitted to offer the sacrament, and they were few in Virginia's early history. So too, Anglican churches in Virginia and other colonies often lacked the appropriately railed-in altars and ritual accouterments—silver chalices and cups, and brocade altar cloths—that accompanied communion services in England. Those very absences, however, shaped the character of the church in Virginia and set it apart from the mother country.

As noted above, not all Anglican churches in Virginia railed in their altars; some offered communion in settings similar to the Calvinist church. In Virginia as in the more liberal Anglican parishes in England, churches abolished the use of a high altar in favor of a simple wooden communion table. Though some churches continued to fix the altar at the east end of the chancel, many favored a movable table, often set in the center of the chancel, to enhance parishioners' and communicants' visual and auditory experience. Where communicants would assemble to receive the sacrament also proved to be a point of great contention in the Anglican church. The 1662 Prayer Book did not forbid receiving communion seated in a pew, leaving that option open. Not bound by the same traditions as the more established, Laudian churches in England, Virginia's parishes might well have taken advantage of such liberalization.[52]

As early as 1617 settlers at Jamestown, for lack of a resident ordained minister, solicited the Archbishop in London to give the power to administer the Lord's Supper to "Mr. Wickham . . . being no other Parson." And Anglicans in early eighteenth-century Rhode Island expressed the opinions of their fellows in Virginia when they chose "to partake of that holy Sacrament without those necessary conveniences that the Tables in England are furnished with, (well-knowing that they add not to the worthiness of the Guests) rather than be without it."53

In all three Protestant churches, preparatory sermons and personal reflection preceded the sacrament of communion. According to Calvin, communion went hand-in-hand with the administration of the Word of God. "The office of the sacraments is precisely the same as that of the word of God," Calvin wrote. Communion should "offer and present Christ to us, and in him the treasures of heavenly grace...there is no true administration of the sacraments without the word." Communion thus meant little without scriptural knowledge and preparation, through study at home and through the ministrations of church leaders. Protestant mothers and fathers were instructed to devote the evening or morning hours before communion to preparatory lessons. In 1637, at one of the first meetings of the Dedham Church in Massachusetts "it was thought meete & agreed upon that all the inhabitants that affected church communion...should meete e'ry 5th day of the weeke [Thursday] at severall houses in order, lovingly to discourse & consult together such questions as might...prepare for spirituall communion in a church." Similarly, at Christ Church in Middlesex County, Virginia, the minister was instructed to offer special preparatory sessions on the Saturday afternoon preceding the sacrament, "not Doubting but that all Parents . . . who Tender the Everlasting welfare of the Souls Committed to theire Charge would Readily Comply and allow Convenient Liberty to theire Children and Servants to Repaire to Church at Such Times." Francis Howard, Baron of Effingham, Governor of the Virginia colony from 1683 to 1692, wrote frequently to his wife, Philadelphia, who remained in England, to remind her of her duty to tend to the spiritual health of their children as she took the time to ready herself for communion. During his Saturday evening preparation for Sabbath-day communion, Effingham wrote "too morrow I intend to receive the Blessed sacrament and so I beleeve do you. God Almighty heare us for each other, and J.C. for us all so Constantly prayeth." Faithful men and women took care to reflect on their blessings and pray for inner grace in preparation for communion. 54

Neither the Word nor the Sacrament would bear true fruit without the presence of faith. And faith, the door to grace and salvation, might burgeon in any soul, regardless of sex. When confronted with a seeming contradiction in his forbidding women the powers of baptism according to the rules of silence while allowing them to speak during communion, Calvin responded, "Here we are content with the rule of faith. For when we weigh what the institution of the Supper implies, it is also easy to judge from this to whom the use of it ought to be granted." The privilege of communion, Calvin claimed, must be offered as a measure of faith, not according to arbitrary rules regarding gender-appropriate behavior.55

In fact, the reformation of communion ritual in the Protestant church reflected changing attitudes toward the equality of the soul, regardless of gender or status. In their rejection of the Catholic belief in transubstantiation, Protestant reformers challenged not only what they perceived to be the perpetuation of a pagan ritual, but the ultimate power of the clerical establishment to control that ritual. Once the bread and wine were presented as symbols, rather than as true manifestations of the body and blood of Christ, their consecration by a priest or minister lost its meaning and necessity. According to Puritan minister Samuel Parris, who preached on the subject in Salem in 1693, communion bread was the bread of daily sustenance, "durable & abiding...the most common food." Only through faith could communicants find any meaning in bread and wine, for only the soul could "find the food in Christ."[56]

Gender and Communion Ritual

Laden with domestic allusions, the ritual of the Supper must have struck a special cord with female congregants. A celebration of domestic life, a sphere in which women were acknowledged by all to wield some authority, the Supper symbolized female generosity and hospitality. Those elements fundamental to corporeal sustenance, offered by women at their own tables to family and friends, took on added symbolic meaning accessible to all. As Thomas Shepard wrote in his journal in 1642,

> At the time of receiving [the Sacrament], I saw the Lord did seal up his love by
> such common things as bread and wine . . . because hereby . . . he made him-
> self more familiar with us . . . because we are so childish and such babes that he
> seals by things best known unto us, shows us his love not by strange and won-
> derous works but by common and ordinary things . . . [57]

Communion bread, no longer baked under the supervision of the priest, became the responsibility of lay parishioners or deacons, perhaps even baked by the woman of the household. According to Samuel Parris, communion bread bore little resemblance to the mystical Catholic host; it was, after all, simply "baked or dried in an oven," and could be handled by lay church members. Neither men nor women needed to receive communion bread from a cleric. Moreover, male and female communicants contributed equal sums specifically to maintain the elements of the Lord's Supper. Reverend Fiske of Wenham, Massachusetts, bemoaned the mounting expense of procuring wine, which frequently had to be fetched outside of town; in 1662 he was forced to raise the levy on all communicants two pence, no longer collected with the regular Sabbath contributions. In the Dutch Church at Flatbush, the lay reader was responsible for providing both the bread and wine. Vestry books in several Virginia parishes in the seventeenth and early eighteenth century included in their monthly accounts payments to both men *and* women who provided communion wine. Stripped of the otherworldliness inherent in transubstantiation, communion bread and wine might have been more easily perceived as a link between the Holy Spirit and the female-centered domestic world. [58]

Gender, communion, and spiritual autonomy

Just as the communion elements represented both spiritual and earthly nourishment, so too decisions about who might attend Communion were based on both spiritual health and earthly behavior. Because it was a potent symbol of community covenant and of visible sainthood, the institution of the Lord's Supper in any congregation demanded that special attention be paid to the behavior of those eligible to receive it. In the Congregational churches of Massachusetts, full members—a majority of whom were women throughout the seventeenth century—sat with their ministers in judgment of those who hoped to partake of communion. In all Protestant churches lapses in behavior could result in suspension from the Lord's Table, though only the notoriously evil were routinely excluded in the Anglican church. Hopeful communicants were cautioned to "take care to attend the preaching of the sanctifying Word," to "cause no offense" in their daily carriage, and to avoid an "inconsistent walk." Willem Juriaensen Bakker, restored to full communion after being banished from his Albany congregation in 1644 for murder, lost that privilege when he insulted a group of women preparing to participate in the sacrament. According to "trustworthy persons," Bakker offended the women when he taunted, "Is it a bit of bread you want? Come to my house and I'll give you a whole loaf." Bakker was barred from communion for his blasphemy—particularly odious given the time and place of his insult—and was eventually banished from the town.59

Hopeful communicants weighed outward signs of piety alongside their inner sense of grace to determine their worthiness to partake of the Lord's Supper. Church members were asked to examine their own hearts and evaluate the depth of their faith to determine whether they were suitably prepared to receive the sacrament. In the end, all communicants knew that while pious behavior and adherence to human laws served as outward signs of grace, only God could sit in final judgment on their right to attend the sacraments. The result of this seemingly contradictory combination of faith and free will was a ritual process that afforded members and aspirants alike, regardless of gender, a surprising degree of freedom to publicly express self-confidence or contrition in their decision to receive or abstain from communion. According to Cotton Mather, a Christian woman "is not satisfied until she come to *eat* among the *Friends*, to *drink* among the *beloved*, of the Lord *Jesus Christ*. She will not make Part of that *Unworthy Croud*, which throng out of Doors, when the *Supper* of the Lord is going to be administered, as if they were frighted at it." In 1680 Jasper Danckaerts wrote admiringly in his journal of a Dutch women who refused to be "frighted" by the sacrament; she partook of communion as a sign of her faith, in the face of clerical apathy and bad-hearted naysayers. The woman had experienced a joyous conversion. She heard a voice that compelled her to "make this glory known," and approached her minister, Domine Nieuwenhausen, for advise. He told her "he did not know what to say." She then was advised by a man "who played the part of a wise man, but who was not a good man" to abstain from the Lord's Supper, but confessed to Dankaerts that "not to go to church, and to leave the Lord's Supper, she could not in her heart consent." God had entered her heart and provided her with the authority to proclaim her faith through participation in the sacrament. 60

While the decision to receive the sacrament depended in part on the approval of the minister or church membership, the decision to abstain was a private one. Though laws governed church attendance, no minister or elder could force a man or a woman riddled with self-doubt to partake of the Lord's Supper. In the fall of 1651, Ann Burden was excommunicated from Boston's First Church for "withdrawing from the fellowship of the church at the Lord's table." When asked by the brethren why she chose to thus absent herself, "shee would Give no Reason of it, save only shee was Commanded silence from the lord." Early in the eighteenth century, Margaret Skerry, a member of the First Church in Salem, Massachusetts chose to absent herself from the table "by reason of a Melancholy and Doubting Spirit which prevailed upon her." In 1670, Mrs. Taylor, a member of the Old South Church in Boston, abstained, for "she did not judge herself worthy or as yet fit for the Lord's Supper." Though certain of the most orthodox Puritans considered feelings of unworthiness an "unwarrantable excuse" for not attending the sacrament, Samual Sewall was wracked with continual doubts about his worthiness and "unsuitable deportment." He prayed for the ability "to give my self to thy Son as to my most endeared Lord and Husband," and hoped that his wife and children would also feel so prepared, "not as Umbra's, but on their own account." No mere shadows of their husbands, Protestant women decided for themselves when they might in good conscience partake of communion.61

Protestant women and men based their decision to abstain from the sacrament on moral grounds as well as on personal doubt or feelings of inadequacy. At the First Church of Boston in the months leading up to a major schism in 1668, dissenters who objected to a matter of church polity refused to celebrate communion with the minister and elders, for fear that in so doing they would "demonstrate our acknowledgment and consent to the teaching officers which the Church hath chosen, as much as if we had consented to their Election from the beginning." Salem church members, steadfast in their belief that communion represented a ritual affirmation of church teaching and preparation as well as of personal grace, used their abstention to demonstrate their dissatisfaction with church leadership.62

The decision to receive or abstain from communion reflected local social circumstances as well. In June of 1681, the formidable widow of the Rev. Polhemus of Flatbush, New York, in the midst of a land dispute with certain of her neighbors, voiced her intent to abstain from the Lord's Supper "because she had been injured by every one." Once the courts had vindicated her land claim, however, Mrs. Polhemus blithely asserted her intention to rejoin communion "because her case was decided in her favor, and the other side had their mouth stopped." As interpreted by Mrs. Polhemus, communion was a symbol of an individual's and a community's covenant with God *and one another*. Discontented with the behavior of her fellow church members, Mrs. Polhemus used her abstention from communion to make a statement about her neighbors' comportment and worthiness. In a similar case in Albany in 1681, a group of women in Gideon Schaets's congregation so objected to the moral comportment of Schaets's daughter that they refused to take communion with her. Her father in turn refused to attend to the needs of his congregation, and Anneke willingly absented herself from the sacrament "as it was her duty, so as to prevent as much as possible all scandals in Christ's flock."[63]

Once they asserted their intention to take communion on a particular Sabbath, women and men had to be prepared to justify their choices and actions, and to counter those accusations from their ministers or fellow church members that might bar them from the sacrament. When Janneken Pieters was questioned in 1661 by the minister of the Dutch Church in Brooklyn about her desire to join the church in spite of attestations that she had only infrequently attended ordinary Sabbath services, she apologized and explained that her former church was too far from her home. She promised the membership that if she was admitted to communion in Brooklyn she would "come and hear the sanctifying Word of God more diligently." The church accepted her apologies, and she was admitted to the sacrament.[64]

* * *

In the 1559 edition of his *Institutes of the Christian Religion*, John Calvin acknowledged that "it is very common, under strong emotions, for the tongue to break forth into sounds, and the other members into gestures, without the least ostentation." As his example, he chose "the uncertain muttering of Hannah (1 Sam. 1:3), somewhat similar to which is experienced by the saints in all ages."[65] Given that he elected to use Hannah's prayers to illustrate the compulsion worshipers might feel to express their faith vocally, clearly Calvin included women among "the saints of all ages" whose voices would not be silenced in church. One hundred and thirty years later, in Salem, Massachusetts, a free black woman on the brink of rebirth chose Hannah as her example as well; in name and action, she proclaimed her faith before the assembled church, firm in her belief that both God and congregation would listen.

NOTES

1 Richard Pierce, ed., *Records of the First Church in Salem, 1629–1736* (Salem, 1974), 181, italics mine.

2 M. Halsey Thomas, ed., *The Diary of Samuel Sewall* (New York, 1973), I,36–7. Sewall was recounting a conversation he had with one Mr. Norton, whose words he paraphrased in this quote. Norton went on to become minister at the church in Hingham, Massachusetts.

3 John Calvin, *Institutes of the Christian Religion* [1559] trans. and ed. John Allen (New York, 1936), II, 270, 273; John Cotton, "The Bloody Tene[n]t Washed and Made White in the Blood of the Lambe" (London, 1647).

4 For examples of books which include narrative accounts of the establishment of the church in each colony see John Frederick Woolverton, *Colonial Anglicanism in North America* (Detroit, 1984); Sydney E. Ahlstrom, *A Religious History of the American People* (New Haven, 1972); Winton U. Solberg, *Redeem the Time: The Puritan Sabbath in Early America* (Cambridge, 1977);

George Maclaren Brydon, *Virginia's Mother Church and the Political Conditions Under Which it Grew* (Richmond, 1947); Gerald F. De Jong, *The Dutch Reformed Church in the American Colonies* (Grand Rapids, 1978); and Francis J. Bremer, *The Puritan Experiment: New England Society from Bradford to Edwards* (New York, 1976). Also see above, chapter one.

5 For a thorough description of the origin of Sabbatarianism and its place in American colonial religious history, see Solberg, *Redeem the Time*. See also Richard P. Gildrie, *The Profane, The Civil, and the Godly: The Reformation of Manners in Orthodox New England, 1679–1749* (University Park, PA., 1994), 114–124. On the role of the Sabbath in New Netherland, see Solberg, Chap.9. Solberg acknowledges the role of the Sabbath in Virginia, which he describes in the period before the Stuart Restoration as "the product of the interaction between an imported ideal, largely Puritan, and local religious, economic, and social conditions." Solberg, 89–93. He is quick to point out, however, that as colonists in Virginia moved further away from central settlements the Sabbath was more difficult to supervise and enforce. Here his book, I think, suffers from a lack of evidence, and fails, particularly with regard to southern history, to plumb the depths of religious *experience*.

6 Carl Lounsbury, "Churches and Meetinghouses in Early America" (unpublished paper), 5–7.

7 Horton Davies, *The Worship of the American Puritans, 1629–1730* (New York, 1990), 13–14.

8 Nigel Yates, *Buildings, Faith, and Worship: Liturgical Arrangement of Anglican Churches, 1600–1900* (Oxford, 1991), 93–103. See also Lounsbury, "Churches and Meeting Houses in Early America," 5–8. For a discussion of the adaptation of pre-Reformation English church interiors to accommodate the vernacular liturgy of the Reformation, see G.W.O. Addleshaw and Frederick Etchells, *The Architectural Setting of Anglican Worship* (London, 1948), 15–19, 45, 108–109. On the importance of auditory clarity in the Anglican Church see Addleshaw, 24, 45, 52 54. Because Anglicans in Virginia were not confined by the need to adapt older Catholic structures to Protestant worship—as they were quite frequently in England—churches there could more easily reflect Calvinist sympathies. For a more complete description of the evolution of Anglican church architecture and a description of the four plans most prevalent in England and Virginia, see Yates, *Buildings, Faith and Worship*, 77–103; cf. Dell Upton, *Holy Things and Profane: Anglican Parish Churches in Colonial Virginia* (Cambridge, 1986). Also see Joan Gunderson's review of Upton, in *WMQ*, 3rd ser., 46 (1989): 379–382. For a rich description of a more settled example of Anglican church architecture in Virginia in the eighteenth century, see Rhys Isaac, *The Transformation of Virginia, 1740–1790* (New York, 1982), 58–65.

9 Amanda Porterfield, "Women's Attraction to Puritanism," *Church History*, 60 (June, 1991), 197. Even Joyce Goodfriend, the champion of Dutch women in colonial New York, lists separate seating as evidence of temporal inequality (vs. spiritual equality) without exploring the physical relationship between women's pews and the church leaders. See Goodfriend, "Recovering the History of Dutch Reformed Women in Colonial New York," *de Halve Maen*, 44 (Winter, 1991), 58. See also Lounsbury, "Churches and Meetinghouses in Early America," 53–54.

10 Edward Taylor, *"Church Records" and Related Sermons* eds. Edward Thomas and Virginia L. Davis (Boston, 1981), 121–124. For a discussion of the importance of female donations to colonial churches, see below, chapter six.

11 Davies, *The Worship of the American Puritans*, 12–13, 39. On the Sabbath as ritual in Massachusetts churches, see Richard P. Guildrie, *The Profane, the Civil, and the Godly*, 114–124.

12 See *ibid.*, 117, 121–22, for a comparison of the Massachusetts and Virginia Sabbath.

13 For a discussion of the impact of outliving on community consensus, and its relationship to religious declension, see Richard L. Bushman, *From Puritan to Yankee*, chapter four.

14 Francis Louis Michel, "Report of the Journey of Francis Louis Michel," *Virginia Magazine of History and Biography* 24 (1916): 21–22. Michel reported in the same document that as far as he could determine, Virginia services were "held according to the principles of the reformation, as in our [Swiss] churches . . . ."; C.G. Chamberlayne, *The Vestry Book and Register of St. Peter's Parish*, 68–69; C. G. Chamberlayne, *The Vestry Book of St. Paul's Parish* (Richmond, 1940). For a discussion of the impact of settlement patterns on the formation of Virginia parishes see Warren Billings, John E. Selby, and Thad Tate, *Colonial Virginia* (White Plains, NY, 1986), 65; Brydon, *Virginia's Mother Church*, 80–82. For examples of works which chart the stability of community networks in spite of settlement patterns see Darrett B. Rutman and Anita H. Rutman, *A Place in Time: Middlesex County, Virginia, 1650–1750* (New York, 1984); and James R. Perry, *Formation of a Society on Virginia's Eastern Shore, 1615–1655* (Chapel Hill, 1990). Perry, alas, devotes only four pages to religion: 183–186.

Historians have consistently pointed to Virginia's reputed dearth of ministers as evidence of the colony's poor religious state. In addition to the fact that I question the validity of using the existence of a professional clergy as a measure of popular piety, it seems that even with regard to professional preaching, the state of formal religion was not as bad as some have assumed. By 1680, Virginia's 48 parishes were served by 35 ministers, several of whom did serve more than one parish, two of whom served parishes in more than one county. Estimates range from 1.5 to 4 parishes that were served only by lay readers. Brydon, 187–190; *Colonial Records of Virginia* (Baltimore, 1964), 103–104; Woolverton, *Colonial Anglicanism*, 37–38. Also see above, chapter one.

15 *Virginia Magazine of History and Biography* 9 (1902): 51; Upton, *Holy Things and Profane*, 9. For a detailed bibliographic history of *The Book of Common Prayer* see Rev. Leighton Pullan, *The History of the Book of Common Prayer* (London, New York, and Bombay, 1900). The Rev. Pullan's apparently high church bent is evident throughout his book. On catechism classes in eighteenth-century Virginia see Patricia U. Bonomi, *Under the Cope of Heaven: Religion, Society, and Politics in Colonial America* (New York and Oxford, 1986), 115, 250n.

16 Horton Davies, *The Worship of the American Puritans*, 15; Charles E. Hambrick-Stowe, *Practice of Piety: Puritan Devotional Disciplines in Seventeenth-Century New England* (Chapel Hill, 1982), 103–104.

17 See for instance, Upton, *Holy Things and Profane*, and Joan Gunderson's review of that book in *WMQ*, 3rd ser., 46 (1989): 379–82.

18 English Nonconformist John Collinges ironically provided one of the most cogent explanations of the value of Prayer Book worship in his 1681 pamphlet attacking the practice: [Collinges], "The Vindication of Liturgies, Lately Published . . . proved NO VINDICATION . . ." (London, 1681). Also see J. Sears McGee, *The Godly Man in Stuart England: Anglican, Puritans, and the Two Tables, 1620–1670* (New Haven, 1976), 98–103.

19 John Cotton, "A Conference Mr. John Cotton held at Boston with the elders of New-England" (London, 1646).

20 [John?] Beaulieu to Mr. William Trumbull, undated, Virginia Colonial Records Project, Reel 554, Parish Records, IV:70, emphasis mine; Edward James, *Lower Norfolk Virginia Antiquary*, II, 2. The churchwardens also accused the parson of not administering baptism according to the rules laid down in the Cannons. Harrison seemingly deserted the church not long after the incident, according to church records, by 1648 the minister Robert Powis had been administering the sacraments for four years.

21 *VMHB* , 5 (1898), 229; Woolverton, *Colonial Anglicanism*, 45–47. For a description of the non-conforming literature available in Virginia in the seventeenth century see Woolverton, 41–48. For examples of Puritan books, including Lewis Bayly's *The Practice of Piety*, in private libraries in Virginia, see Inventory of the estate of John [ ]field, 1640, Norfolk County, Reel 1, Deed book A, 1637–46; Inventory of Thomas Deacon in Edward James, "Libraries," *WMQ*, 1st ser., 3: 181; Will of John Goslin in 1648 in Vincent Watkins, ed., *York County: Deeds, Orders, Wills, Book 3, 1657–1662* (Poquosan, VA., 1989), 36. Also see above, chapter two.

22 Bouwsma, *John Calvin: A Sixteenth-Century Portrait* (New York, 1988), 124; Phillis M. and Nicholas R. Jones, eds., *Salvation in New England*; David D. Hall, *Worlds of Wonder, Days of Judgment: Popular Religious Belief in Early New England* (Cambridge, 1989), 119. For a compre-hensive analysis of the Puritan "Plain Style" of preaching, see Perry Miller, *The New England Mind: The Seventeenth Century* (New York, 1939), Chap. 12. See also Harry Stout, *The New England Soul*; Babette Levy, *Preaching in the First Half Century of New England History* (Hartford, 1945); Plumstead, ed., *The Wall and the Garden*, 31–37; and Edward Thomas' and Virginia L. Davis' Introduction to *Edward Taylor's Church Records and Related Sermons* (Boston, 1981).

23 "The Diary of Joseph Green," in *Puritan Personal Writings: Diaries* (New York, 1983), 96, 165.

24 Perry Miller, *New England Mind*, 337–338, Chap. 12, passim, A. W. Plumstead, ed., *The Wall and the Garden: Selected Massachusetts Election Sermons, 1670–1775* (Minneapolis, 1968), 31–37; Charles Hambrick-Stowe, *The Practice of Piety: Puritan Devotional Disciplines in Seventeenth-Century New England* (Chapel Hill, 1982), 118; Patricia U. Bonomi, *Under the Cope of Heaven: Religion, Society, and Politics in Colonial America* (New York, 1986), 68–69, 100–101; Thomas, ed., *The Diary of Samuel Sewall*, 82.

25 For examples of the relationship between scripture, the sermon, and the renewal of faith, see above, chapter two, *passim*. See also the portion of this chapter devoted to public confes-sions of faith.

26 Porterfield, *Female Piety in Puritan New England*, 40; McGiffert, ed., *God's Plot*, 24, 117,139; "A Short Account of the Author [Roger Clap], *Puritan Personal Writings: Autobiographies*, 9.

27 Caroline Walker Bynam, *Jesus as Mother* (Berkeley, 1982), 114–116 and 110–169, *passim*; Bouwsma, *John Calvin*, 133–135.

28 Taylor, "Foundation Day Sermon," 152; Hambrick-Stowe, *Practice of Piety*, 121–122; Shepard, "Parable of the Ten Virgins," in *The Works of Thomas Shepard*, II, 514. See above, chapter four.

29 "Diary of John Hull," *Puritan Personal Writings*, 272; Flatbush Church Records, vol.1a, Consistory Minutes, 32; Cotton, *Milk for Babes*. On the popularity of Cotton's catechism, which appeared in several editions by the mid-seventeenth century and was often appended to *The New England Primer*, see James Axtell, *The School Upon a Hill: Education and Society in Colonial New England* (New York, 1976), 26, 36, 144; Hill, *A History of Old South Church*, 180.

30 Davies, *Worship of the American Puritans*, 90.

31 Calvin, Comm. on Luke 7.44, in Bousma, *John Calvin*, 200; Halsey, ed., *Diary of Samuel Sewall*, 116; Calvin, *Sermons de la passione*, quoted in Jane Douglass, *Women, Freedom, and Calvin* (Philadelphia, 1985), 58; "Diary of John Hull," 272.

32 Mather, Cotton, "Ornaments for the Daughters of Zion" (London, 1694), 4–5.

33 *Ibid.*, 3.

34 Quoted in Joyce Irwin, *Womanhood in Radical Protestantism* (New York, 1979), 163.

35 Douglass, *Women, Freedom, and Calvin*, 30–31, 45–47, 53, 106; on the difference in categorization of "things indifferent" between the 1536 and 1559 editions of the *Institutes*, see *ibid*, 31; on the impact of humanism on Calvin's definition of "indifferent" church laws, see Bouwsma, *John Calvin*, 113–127, esp. 117 and 121. See also John Lee Thompson, *John Calvin and the Daughters of Sarah* (Geneva, Switzerland, 1992), 29.

36 Miriam DeBaar, "'Let Your Women Keep Silence in the Churches': How Women in the Dutch Reformed Church Evaded Paul's Admonition, 1650–1700," in *Women in the Church*, W.T. Shiels and Diana Wood, eds. (London, 1990), 391; Allen, ed., Calvin's *Institutes*, I, 144.

37 *Ecclesiastical Records*, II, 1233–1240. For a more complete discussion of catechism practices in the colonies see above, chapter two.

38 John Cotton, "Singing of Psalmes, A Gospel-Ordinance" (London, 1650); Hambrick-Stowe, *Practice of Piety*, 113. Samuel Sewall noted in his diary that he and his family sang psalms at home as part of their preparation for the Sabbath service: *Diary of Samuel Sewall*, I, 95.

39 Allen, ed., Calvin's *Institutes*, II, 141–142; James Owen, "Church-pageantry displayed, or Organ-worship arraign'd and condemned" (London, 1700); Douglass, *Women, Freedom, and Calvin*, 87.

40 Cotton, "Singing of Psalms," 38–42; Flatbush Church Records, vol. 1a, Consistory Minutes, 1681,.40; *The Secret Diary of William Byrd of Westover, 1709–1712*, eds., Louis B, Wright and Marion Tinling (Richmond, 1941), 272; Davies, *Worship*, 126. In spite of weighty theological justifications for a woman's singing in church, any deviation from acceptable public behavior was perceived as a threat to the congregation's order and harmony. Sister Joan Hogg, a member of the First Church of Boston, was excommunicated in 1657 for, among other things, "disturbing the congregation by her disorderly singing." "Public Diary of John Hull," 191–192; *Records of the First Chruch in Boston*, 55, 56. Joan Hogg and her husband had been members of the church since 1639; *ibid.*, 24

41 I have chosen here to make a distinction between the public meaning of conversion narratives and the private. The conversion experience, it seems to me, functioned differently from one sphere to the other. Women who experienced conversion privately and also participated in their congregation's key ritual of affirmation—as speakers *and* listeners—had access to a source of both personal and public power. For a more thorough discussion of the relationship between gender and the private conversion experiences, see Chapter two. For a discussion of the controversy surrounding the narrative requirement, see Caldwell, *The Puritan Conversion Narrative*, chap. two.

42 Caldwell, *Puritan Conversion Narrative*, 50.

43 Robert Pope, ed., *The Notebook of the Reverend John Fiske* (Boston, 1974), xv-xvii; Caldwell, 85–86, 108. For a classic monograph on the puritan concept of visible sainthood, see Edmund Morgan, *Visible Saints* (New York, 1961).

44 Cotton Mather, "Ornaments for the Daughters of Zion" (Boston, 1692). Caldwell, *Conversion Narrative*, 91–92.

45 George Selement and Bruce C. Woolley, eds., "Thomas Shepard's *Confessions*," Colonial Society of Massachusetts *Publications*, vol. 58 (1981), 4–5; Hill, *Dedham Records*, 14; Pope, ed., *Notebook of Rev. John Fiske*, 146.

46 Caldwell, *Puritan Conversion Narrative*, 45–46; *Notebook of Rev. John Fiske*, 4, xvi-xvii; *Records of the First Church in Boston*, 40, 43. See also *ibid.*, 42, 50, 51.

47 Caldwell, *Puritan Conversion Narrative*, 26, 2.

48 *The Notebook of Rev. John Fiske*, xvi-xvii; "Commonplace Book of Joseph Green," 241 244; Hill, *Dedham Records*, 21; *Records of the First Church in Salem*, 145–146.

49 Allen, trans., *Institutes*, II, 571.

50 *Records of the First Church in Salem*, 87, 142; Hambrick-Stowe, *Practice of Piety*, 125. For a thoughtful and thorough discussion of the sacraments in New England, see E. Brooks Holifield, *The Covenant Sealed: The Development of Puritan Sacramental Theology in Old and New England, 1570–1720* (New Haven, 1974). Holifield points out that with regard to rules for admittance to the Lord's Supper, there was great variety among Massachusetts churches: *ibid.*, 159–163, esp. 162–163. On the controversy over the liberalization of standards for admission to the Lord's Supper that divided the Congregational church by the 1670s, see Thomas and Davis, eds., *Edward Taylor's 'Church Records'*, Introduction, especially xvii-xxix; Stout, *New England Soul*, 99, 339n.

51 A. P. G. Van der Linde, ed., *Old First Dutch Reformed Church of Brooklyn* (Baltimore, 1983), 15; Jameson, ed. "Letter of Rev. Jonas Michaelmas," 119–133, esp.125–125; Edwin T.Corwin, ed., *Ecclesiastical Records of the State of New York* (7 vols., Albany, 1901–16), I, 554–555; Jameson, ed., "Henricus Selyns to Classis," 407; Records of the Reformed Dutch Church of Flatbush, 7, 18, 86–87.

52 Addleshaw, *The Architectural Setting of Anglican Worship*, 25–27, 32–35, 108–109, 148–155; Nigel Yates, *Buildings, Faith, and Worship: Liturgical Arrangement of Anglican Churches, 1600–1900* (Oxford, 1991), 24, 31–32.

53 Chamberlayne, ed., *Vestry Book of Christ Church Parish*, 44; "Letter from Samuall Argall, Esq.," *VMHB* 4 (1897): 29; SPG Letterbooks, Series A, Letter 44. For a discussion of the relationship between church architecture and the administration of the Lord's Supper in England, see Yates, *Buildings, Faith, and Worship*, 24, 32.

54 John Calvin, *Institutes*, 571, 697; Don Gleason Hill, ed., *Dedham Records, 1638–1845* (Dedham, 1888), 1; C.G. Chamberlayne, ed., *The Vestry Book of Christ Church Parish* (Richmond, 1927), 44; Warren M. Billings, ed., *The Papers of Francis Howard, Baron Howard of Effingham, 1643–1695* (Richmond, 1989), 47, 76. On the degree of mysticism with which Calvin viewed the sacraments see Louis Bouyer, *Orthodox Spirituality and Protestant and Anglican Spirituality* (London, 1969), 89–91.

55 Douglass, *Women, Freedom, and Calvin*, 49; Calvin, *Institutes*, II, 571, 692, 697.

56 Calvin, *Institutes*, II, 650; James F. Cooper and Kenneth P. Minkema, eds., *The Sermon Notebook of Samuel Parris, 1689–1694* (Boston, 1993), 234–235.

57 Shepard, *God's Plot*, 172.

58 *Notebook of Rev. John Fiske*, 174–175; *Sermon Notebook of Samuel Parris*, 243–244; *Records of the First Church in Salem*, 87, 266; Flatbush Church Records, 40,47; Chamberlayne, ed., *The Vestry Book of Petsworth Parish*, 137, 141, 142; *The Vestry Book of Kingston Parish*, *The Vestry Book of Christ Church Parish*. For a compelling discussion of the Lord's Supper as a celebration of female piety in Puritan New England, see Porterfield, *Female Piety*, 117, 130–131.

59 Van der Linde, *Brooklyn Church Records*, 37; *Ecclesiastical Records*, I, 283; Joel Munsell, ed., *Annals of Albany* (10 vols., Albany, 1855–1869), I, 76–77. See Holifield, *The Covenant Sealed*, 55–56, for a comparison of Anglican and Puritan standards for admission to communion.

60 Cotton Mather, "Ornaments for the Daughters of Zion" (Boston, 1692); *Journal of Jasper Danckaerts*, 231–232.

61 *Records of the First Church in Boston*, 53; Pierce, ed., *Records of the First Church in Salem*, 280; Hill, ed., *A History of Old South Church*, 166; Thomas, ed., *Diary of Samual Sewall*, 33, 36, 349.

62 Hill, ed., *History of Old South Church*, 46–47.

63 *Ecclesiastical Records*, II, 771–772; *Ecclesiastical Records*, II, 764; Munsell, ed., *Annals of Albany*, I, 94; VI, 75. The conflict seems to have been resolved among the congregation when Anneke sought the help of the court to resolve her marital problems: see above, chapter 3.

64 Van der Linde, ed., *Brooklyn Church Records*, 21.

65 Allen, trans., *Institutes*, II, 144.

Chapter Six

"A PRIESTHOOD OF ALL BELIEVERS": WOMEN AND CHURCH POLITICS

T HROUGHOUT THE COLONIES, PROTESTANT WOMEN AND MEN JOINED TOGETHER IN rituals that reinforced the notion of equality of the soul. Most worshippers recognized, however, that equality of the soul did not necessarily mean equality of authority within church walls. Ministers were not likely to relinquish their power over their congregations, a power born of their calling, and rooted in their authority to offer affirmation to their members. At the same time, church leaders recognized that the relationship worked the other way as well. They too depended on the affirmation of their congregation to legitimize their power. In this context, women's opinions frequently carried as much weight as men's.[1]

Protestant teaching, and that of Calvinists in particular, emphasized the role of the laity in calling and judging the minister, just as they were instructed to judge one another. In his Commentary on Paul's Epistle to the Corinthians, Calvin proclaimed "All who discharge the office of the ministry, are *ours*, from the highest to the lowest, so that we are at liberty to withhold our assent to their doctrine, until they show that it is from Christ." Ministers in the Protestant church were human; they were as likely to experience a lapse of judgment, or to fall short of their pious aspirations as lay parishioners, and all church members had an obligation to measure a minister's aptitude, and to monitor his performance. Whether ministers were appointed and ordained by a central governing body, as they were in Virginia and in New Netherland, or called by individual congregations as they were in the Puritan churches of Massachusetts and the more pietistic Dutch churches, parishioners, including women, were free to make their demands and dissatisfactions known.[2]

women, the establishment of local churches, and the call to ministers

The call for ministers was frequently heard in the early and middle years of the seventeenth century, as congregations settled in and their populations grew, as settlers formed new congregations farther afield, or as parishes sought to replace absent clerics. Women offered their opinions on the need for new churches and were among the founding members of new congregations. In 1683, on the death of their minister, the vestry of Christ Church Parish in Middlesex County, Virginia, instructed two of its members to write to the Lady Agatha Chichley and Robert Smith, both lately returned to London from Virginia, "to request them or Either of them that they will please to take the Trouble to procure a fitt minister in England to Come over and Supply the place of Mr Sheppard." Though the all-male vestry in Virginia held the ultimate responsibility for bringing a minister to their fold, they were not averse to enlisting the help of a woman to make their decision. In Virginia, where early in the seventeenth century the civil government wrested control of church law from the ecclesiastical courts, parishioners petitioned the county court for a minister to serve them. Parishioners in Norfolk County in 1640 "being this day convented for the providing of themselves an able minister to instruct them . . . Mr. Thomas Harrison hath tendered his faith to God and the said inhabitants." Upon the inhabitants' attestations of "zeale and willingness to [pursue] God's service" the court ordered the establishment of the parish at Elizabeth River.[3]

In New York, five women were listed among the eleven founders of the Dutch church in Tappan in 1694. And in a number of instances, women used their authority as members of the Dutch church to secure a minister for their congregations. In the Hudson River town of Kingston in 1680, the death of a minister prompted his wife to take action on behalf of the bereft congregation "anxious to have another minister." In a letter written directly to the Classis in Amsterdam, the widow Gaasbeeck informed them that her brother-in-law was available to come to the colony. "I take the liberty to say, at the request of our Consistory . . . that I wish that he may be delegated in preference to anybody else." On the widow Gaasbeeck's advice, the Classis called her brother-in-law within the year. Richard van Rensselaer, appointed by the court in 1682 to find a second minister to serve the church at Albany, wrote to his sister-in-law Maria to ask her to introduce Reverend Dellius to the Albany consistory, court, and congregation. As a devout member of the Dutch church, well connected politically and socially in the Dutch community, Maria van Rensselaer was an appropriate person from whom to enlist aid.[4]

In the Congregational churches of Puritan Massachusetts, church law demanded that the church membership call a minister, without interference from a governing body or requirements for ordination in mother England (though inhabitants interested in establishing a new church were required to petition the town where their church currently existed). The minister derived his authority from his congregation.[5]

Though gender was not explicit in any parish request for a minister or a new church, it would be reasonable to assume that women, who constituted a majority of church membership, exerted no small influence in the initial appeals. Mothers, saddled with babies and young children in need of attention, food, and care, found that once they and their families had moved farther from the town church it was increasingly difficult to make the journey. Indeed, women often proved a motivating force in the decision to gather a church closer to shifting population centers. In 1672, Hannah Gallop, niece of Massachusetts governor John Winthrop, Jr., wrote to him for support in her efforts to establish a church at Mystick. The distance that congregants were forced to travel to their current meeting posed an undue hardship, especially on mothers "that have young children sucking, manie times are brought exeding faint, and mutch weakened, and divers are not able to goe al winter." In an effort to establish a more convenient congregation, Hannah Gallop explained, "the people of the west side Mistick River are joyning with us in a petition to the Court." In addition, she wrote, "I make bold to wright my mind to yow, hoping that yow will be pleased to tak pittie on us." [6]

The process of gathering a church and enlisting a minister was not always smooth. Here too women were often at the center of conflicts surrounding community decisions. In 1677, when the town of Ipswich, Massachusetts refused to hear the petition of the residents of neighboring Chebacco who sought liberty to call a minister, it was Chebacco's women who persisted in applying pressure on town leaders. The women eventually took matters into their own hands:

> while . . . all things seemed to act against us [,] some women without the knowledge of theire husbands and with the advise of some few men went to the other towns and got help and raised the house that we intend for a meeting house if we could get the liberty.[7]

Though Chebacco's renegade women were fined for contempt of authority, within a few months the town obtained permission to call a minister.

When a new church was gathered in Suffield, Massachusetts, a number of men and women in full communion at Edward Taylor's Westfield church "desired not their Recommendations to the Work from us but only their Liberty, which if they saw meet not to use, their state might abide firm with us." In spite of Taylor's objections to the minister the Suffield church had chosen—an admitted Presbyterian—he noted in the church records that members of his church were granted liberty to proceed.[8]

Women comprised a majority of the petitioners in the community of Billingsgate, on outer Cape Cod, early in the eighteenth century when residents there attempted to block the ordination of the Reverend Mr. Osborn in neighboring Eastham. Intent on gathering a church closer to their own settlement, Billingsgaters schemed that they would be granted liberty to proceed if they created a lengthy disruption to Osborn's ordination by proving him unworthy of the post. Even after

Osborn's ordination, four female signers of the petition—including one Hannah
Doane, who with her husband had led the battle to discredit the minister—refused
to recant. All four women were admonished by the church for "disorderly Walking,"
and were barred from the sacraments. Though three of the women eventually
recanted, Hannah Doane refused; she then demanded a meeting of Billingsgate's
ecclesiastical society to decide her fate. Doane was exonerated by the society on the
grounds of freedom of conscience, thereafter receiving at her request non-
prejudicial dismission from the Eastham church. Clearly, women, like men, had the
right to object to a minister on moral or doctrinal grounds.[9]

In a case against Thomas Cheever, the minister at Malden, Massachusetts, the
testimony of four women and one man resulted in Cheever's suspension from service and his barring from the Communion Table for six weeks. In this case, witnesses, among them Eliza Wade, Abigail Russell, and Thomas, Esther, and Eliza Newhall
presented their charges against Cheever before the accused and a group of clerical
leaders representing the three Boston churches. The council recommended, in
light of the accusations, that the town of Malden also set aside a day "solemnly to
humble themselves by Fasting and Prayer."[10]

CLErICaL AUTHOrITY In VIrGINIa

Members of the clergy were equally as likely to face opposition in colonial Virginia.
Moreover, in Virginia ministers fought their battles against two major (sometimes
overlapping) forces: their parishioners, and their church vestries. Over the course
of the seventeenth century, even as Virginia's Anglican clergy gained increasing
prominence and visibility, church vestries gained greater control amidst increasing
laicization. Ministers' complaints about their parishioners and vestries, often cited
by historians as evidence of pervasive irreligion, may have had as much to do with
their frustration over an increasing lack of influence as with their disgust over an
unregenerate population.[11]

As a result of the high degree of lay control in Virginia's parishes, ministers
were forced to respond to pressure from male and female parishioners and vestry
alike. And though women are rarely singled out in challenges to a minister's authority, it would be reasonable to assume that, as active and tithing members of their
parishes, their concerns and complaints resonated in their communities. In 1640,
the inhabitants of a remote section of a parish in Norfolk County refused to pay the
lion's share of their minister's salary "unless the said minister teach and instruct
them as often as he shall teach at the Parish church." The parish inhabitants decided among themselves that the minister would preach alternately at the parish
church and, until a chapel could be constructed, at a private residence in the remote
Elizabeth River section of the parish, home to the "greatest number of tithable persons." Early in the eighteenth century the parishioners of St. Peter's Church
instructed the church wardens and the vestry to inform a Reverend Forbes that they
were not satisfied with his performance; they were "[n]ot willing to Entertain him,
his voice being so Low that the [ ] people cannot edifie."[12]

Gender and the challenge to clerical authority in New Netherland

Parishioners rejected ministers in not only in Massachusetts and Virginia but in New Netherland as well. In 1657 the "burghers and inhabitants of Breucklelen generally and the neighbors" challenged the tax assessed them for the Reverend Polhemus' support. In a letter to Director General Stuyvesant, the Brooklyn magistrates complained on behalf of their inhabitants that

> for such meager and unsatisfactory service as they have had hitherto, even if they could, they would not resolve to contribute anything, for during the two weeks he comes here only for a quarter of an hour on Sunday afternoon, gives us only a prayer instead of a sermon, from which we learn and understand little, . . . On the Sunday before Chriotmas . . . in the place of a sermon, which we had expected to have, we had to listen to a prayer so short, that it was over before we had collected our thoughts.

Though Stuyvesant ultimately ordered the Brooklyn residents to comply with the assessment, they had exercised their right to criticize a minister's performance, ending their letter with one final barb: they might, they wrote, "enjoy the same, if not more edification by appointing one of our midst to read a sermon from a book of homilies."[13]

In 1698, when the New Amsterdam consistory called Reverend Hieronymous Verdieren to assist the aging Henricus Selyns, one of the church elders joined members of the congregation in their objection to the call. While objections to the minister were probably politically motivated (Verdieren was a known anti-Leislerian), church members stated for the public record that they objected on the grounds that too few members of the congregation had been consulted. In the face of tremendous community strife, Verdieren refused the call.[14]

Ministers were sometimes the victims of personal attacks grave enough to gain the attention of public officials or threatening enough to the ministers to prompt them to complain to civic authorities. In a letter written by the Reverend Caspar Van Zuuren of Flatbush, New York, to the Classis in Amsterdam in 1681, the minister complained that his predecessor's widow, Mrs. Polhemus, was making his life miserable. According to Van Zuuren, the Widow Polhemus had enlisted the support of his own church elders against him; the elders had served as her messengers, bearing word of the widow's intention to abstain from Communion, and her vow to enter a complaint against him before the ministers and elders of New York. Her charge, that the minister had sided unfairly with the opposition in a land dispute, carried weight in the community. When news of their confrontation leaked out, Van Zuuren "was accused by great and small, by English and Dutch, by the Lieutenant-Governor . . . as well as by the Rev. Consistory of New York of having . . . therefore made out her late husband a thief, and her children rogues." A powerful parishioner, regardless of sex, could shape public opinion and bring shame upon even the most powerful cleric in the community.[15]

Women with less influence than the widow Polemus also challenged ministers' authority. Marretie, wife of Cornelis Teunissen Bosch, absented herself from the Albany church in 1657 to protest the behavior of its minister, Gideon Schaets. Though the precise details of her complaint do not appear in the records—it is likely that the conflict had nothing to do with theological or spiritual issues—Marretie framed her dissatisfaction in language that challenged Rev. Schaets's piety. "Those who are willing to revel and feast with the Domine are his friends," Marretie claimed, "and because I do not want to do it, I am a Child of the devil. If only I could sit in church with a book before me, like hypocritical devils, I would be a child of God, but because I refuse to do it, I am a child of the devil; but let me be a child of the devil." In this case, Marretie's complaints carried little weight; Schaets in fact charged her with slander.[16]

In 1682, however, a group of Dutch Reformed women took the lead in a case that again disrupted the community and resulted in the dismissal of a clerical leader. This time, the target of their ire and determination for a dismissal was not their minister, but the Flatbush Church's school master, Jan Thibaud.

Schoolmasters played a central role in the daily operations of the Dutch Reformed Church. They served as regular readers, led psalm singing, rang the church bells, and appointed members of the congregation to read or sing in their stead should they be absent on a particular Sunday. Above all, the schoolmaster was charged with catechizing the community's children, to teach them "from their earliest childhood the fear of the Lord, set a good example, begin classes with the prayers and end with the psalms . . . ." Most often, a schoolmaster's appointment had to be approved by the Director General and Councillors of New Netherland. It seemed, however, that no amount of careful examination nor an arduous approval process could prevent bad seeds from gaining the office of schoolmaster. In addition to the charges brought against Jan Thibaud in Flatbush, church and court records reveal at least two other cases against wayward schoolmasters. In each, women played a central role.[17]

The consistory minutes of the Flatbush Church reveal in rich detail a case that surely disrupted the entire town over the course of several months. In June of 1682 the Flatbush consistory took action initially "to ascertain the truth in regard to the rumors that have been spread abroad for some time past." To that end, the consistory summoned two of an undisclosed total number of women to testify to schoolmaster Thibaud's "unseemly" behavior. Lysbeth Van Ravenstein testified that Thibaud had "used certain vile words and speeches against her," and had "resorted to dishonorable feeling and touching of her, which took place in her own house." Gerritje Spiegelaar's testimony was similar to Lysbeth Van Ravenstein's. Although according to the consistory minutes there were more women prepared to make charges, the consistory chose at this point to stop the investigation to allow Thibaud the opportunity to clear himself of the charges. During the twelve-day period

Thibaud was granted to prepare his defense, he was suspended from service and barred from the Lord's Supper. The consistory considered the women's accusations serious enough to suspend the accused from one of the church's most public sacraments, an action that would not have gone unnoticed by the congregation.

Town magistrates were invited to join the second hearing, held two weeks later. Van Ravenstein and Spiegelaar reasserted their charges against Thibaud, this time adding that they had each struck the schoolmaster in self-defense. The testimony of Jannetije Roemers, similar to the others, was added to the record. To each charge Thibaud had the opportunity to respond. Yes, he admitted, he had called two of the women "pissers," and had slapped each of them on the behind. While he claimed that these did not constitute "dishonorable deeds," Thibaud did admit that "he noticed [Spieglaar] was angry about it, as she gave him a slap in the face."

After several opportunities to air charges and counter-charges, and the admission of affidavits on behalf of Thibaud, Jannetje Roemers "accused him to his face, that he had touched her dishonorably, that he also showed his rod, near or in the back door, in a very scandalous manner." Though Thibaud denied the charges in her presence, he later admitted that he couldn't be sure what he had done, since he was "wholly intoxicated" at the time.

Seemingly eager to give Thibaud the benefit of the doubt—or hesitant to accept out-of-hand the testimony of a group of women—the Consistory and magistrates voted unanimously to suspend the schoolmaster for one month, during which time he might "search his heart to arrive at the truth." At the end of that time, if he could provide no suitable excuse or explanation for his behavior, Thibaud was to be banished from church service. One month later the Consistory removed Thibaud from his school and church service, stating "we could not continue him . . . without greatly offending and disturbing our community." In a contest between a small group of women and one of the community's ranking church leaders, the women for a time prevailed. While they alone had been willing to bring charges against Thibaud, the consistory recognized that Thibaud, by behaving so impiously, threatened the fabric of the community.[18]

Gender and the Case for Church Dismission

Lay dissatisfaction with a school master's or minister's performance rarely resulted in his dismissal. According to church law, however, grievances against a minister that resulted in an irreparable schism did constitute grounds for dissent and ultimately for dismission from church membership. Men and women alike had the right—the duty—to leave a congregation and a minister they believed was not serving them well. As Puritan divine John Cotton wrote in 1654:

> We doe generally allow every servant so much liberty for his outward comfort and advantage, as to choose his own Master, in whose Family, and under whose Government and inspection he is to live, and why should not Christians also

> (being made free-men by Christ) have as much liberty for their spiritual com-
> fort and edification.

When congregants found themselves under the ministry of a preacher "which they
cannot find so suitable to their spirits . . . as some others," they were at liberty to
seek a letter of dismission to another church and minister "whom [they] can more
freely and comfortably close in his spirits withall." Though Cotton employed mas-
culine language throughout his tract, women were as free to seek dismission as
men.[19]

One of the most divisive instances of church schism in the seventeenth century, and one in which women played an active and well-documented role, occurred
in the late 1660s and early 1670s when dissenting members of First Church of
Boston sought to break away and establish their own church, the Third Church of
Boston, later known as Old South Church.

Claiming that on a number of occasions they had been deprived of their liberty to manage church affairs by their minister and his church elders, dissenting
brethren of the First Church sought an "honorable" dismissal to form another congregation. When their requests failed to win them dismissal, the dissenters
appealed to a council of elders from neighboring churches and to the Governor and
Council of Massachusetts, asserting they had been "wholly shutt upp and deprived
(as we conceive) of that Christian Liberty, which Christ hath purchased for his people in church estate." Finally, early in 1669, a new church—the Third Church in
Boston—gathered in Charlestown.[20]

In language that reflected, as one historian recently noted, the prominence of
women among them, the dissenters compared the difficulties they had experienced
during the dismission process to birth pains: "this work of God after sore pangs and
throws of many prayers and sore labours and conflicts very hardly escaped stran-
gling in its birth, notwithstanding all the midwively care that the good Lord sent in."
Just as the rigors of childbirth prepared women especially for the struggle to find
faith and face death, so too their birthing experiences steeled them for other godly
battles.[21]

And if the process of gathering a new church was arduous for the male dissenters in Boston, it was even worse for the women. Even as women from outside of
Boston applied to and were granted admission to the new church, the wives and
other female members of Boston's First Church were denied dismission to it. A
substantial group of women thus embarked on a journey that would ultimately take
three and a half years to complete.[22]

Presumably in response to actions taken by women whose husbands had been
dismissed, late in 1669 the Reverend Mr. Davenport of the First Church delivered a
pointed sermon to his congregation warning that it would be considered a grave
breach of covenant for any members to hear the word preached or partake of the
Sacraments at any other church. Shortly after the sermon, at least two women
approached Davenport with the request that they be allowed to take Communion

with their husbands. When their request was denied, a group of twenty women together drafted a petition to the Reverend Davenport, the Elders, and church members requesting regular and complete dismission from the First Church. Their words in this and subsequent petitions reveal the sanctity with which they viewed the right and spiritual liberty to worship where they pleased. Citing scripture which taught "the Comeliness and sweet order when whole familyes worship together, On the contrary the confusion, disorder, and disturbance . . . when husbands goe to one place and wives to another," the twenty petitioners sought freedom to join the Third Church. Church elder Bracket refused to read their petition to the church, demanding instead that each of the petitioners submit her own individual statement. They did so in January of 1670, "subscribing the same petition only altering the term we to me."[23]

This action too proved to be insufficient for the First Church elders. Perhaps in an attempt to force the women to perform yet another time-consuming task, they suggested that each of the women draft an individual petition requesting indefinite as opposed to full dismission. The women, prepared this time to respond immediately, submitted their requests in writing within days of the elder's demands. This time, their appeal rested not so much on their need to join their husbands, but on the desire to "have liberty so to provide for our own peace and Spirituall comfort as may in our own consciences be most suitable to our duety for our oedification in the Lord." They acknowledged they had already taken Communion with the Third Church, and had judged the experience wholly beneficial.[24]

So vocally discontent were the First Church's dissenting women, that the new minister of the First Church, the Reverend Mr. Oxenbridge, indicated he preferred that they not attend his ordination. The situation continued to deteriorate, with the women punished periodically by being barred from the Communion table. Finally, in 1674, after three and a half years of trying to reconcile their differences, First Church declared itself "discharged from any Covenant duty" toward the dissenting women. The women in turn declared that they no longer stood "in any memberly relation" to the church. "Wee have," they wrote, "upon our own irregular choyce, gone out from them and away from any further Authority of their church." On June 27, "hopeless of help" from the First Church elders, the dissenting women "made a Secession from them upon their refusing a dismission unto us," and applied for admission to the Third Church. On October 16, 1674, twenty-six women from the old congregation were admitted as full members to the new one.[25]

There is evidence, however, that even a year after the success of the dissenting group of women the First Church continued to make the process of securing dismission arduous. One woman, Anna Search, inspired the wrath of the church elders when she "put her selffe into fellowshipe with the 3d church in boston without dismission or demandinge any thither." Labeled a "disorderly walker" and a "Covenant-breaker," Anna Search was barred from communion with the First Church. Faithful women, like men, were prepared to risk their reputations among their neighbors to follow their hearts and souls to a new congregation.[26]

Throughout the long and painful process, the women of Boston demonstrated time and again their strength, conviction, and ultimately their power. Mary Norton, the widow of John Norton—minister at the First Church for a time after John Cotton's death—was one of the most vocal and active sympathizers with the dissenters. Her influence, however, ranged beyond the spiritual and social powers reflected in the very nature of dissent. A widow of comfortable circumstances, she chose "of her own free mind and pious desire to promote the blessed work of the Gospell," by providing for the Third Church in her will. On her death, the church received a deed of land suitable for their meetinghouse. The actions of "that pious and worthy Matron" insured that her influence would extend long beyond her life.[27]

Gender, Power, and Church Bequests

While not all bequests were as magnanimous as Mary Norton's, it was not unusual for women of all three denominations under consideration here to remember their churches in their wills, or to make outright donations while they lived. Though the gifts were often small, they carried profound symbolic meaning, especially when they included objects of great spiritual import: sacramental silver, communion cloths, and communion tables. The bequest of such items, used in the Protestant church's holiest rituals, guaranteed that donors' names would forever be associated with the spiritual life of the entire congregation.[28]

Some donations were more ephemeral than others. A widow in Brooklyn gave a gift of a bull-calf to two newly appointed deacons of the Dutch Church there. Madam Mary Smith of Petsworth Parish in Virginia left five pounds in her will to be distributed amongst the poor, according to the directions of the church vestry. In 1713, Madam Elizabeth Churchill donated to Christ Church Parish in Virginia 100 pounds for the purchase of a new version of the psalms. Several times she donated to her church bottles of communion wine. In her will drafted in 1718, Mrs. Churchill bequeathed twenty-five pounds "towards buying Ornaments for the Midle Church." The following year in St. Peter's parish, Madam Francis Littlepage offered a bell to her church, "out of her generous inclination." The vestrymen took it upon themselves to recommend to the minister that he personally extend his thanks to her for her generous offer. Three years later the vestry ordered that a belfry be added to the church, for which in was necessary to add a levy of three pounds of tobacco per person.[29]

Much earlier in Virginia's colonial history, Mrs. Mary Robinson made special provisions for the religious health of Virginia settlers, though at the time of her death she was living in London. Her will, proved in 1618, included 200 pounds towards the construction and support of a church building, appropriated for the church at Smith's Hundred on the Chikahominy River. Among the objects she donated for use by the Southhampton Hundred church were "fower divinity bookes wth brasse bosses" and "a treatise of St. Augustine, of the Citty of God translated into English, the other three greate volumes were the works of Mr. Perkins newlie corrected and amended." Two years later, two unnamed donors contributed "faire

Plate & other rich ornaments for two Communion Tables, whereof one for the Colledge, and the other for the Church of Mary Robinson's foundinge." Women were also among the benefactors to Bruton Church, in Williamsburg, at the close of the seventeenth century. Cathcrine Sesouth donated ten pounds for the purchase of a silver plate, and Alice Page donated "one pulpit cloath and cushion of Best velvett."[30]

New Netherland's Dutch churches also benefited from donations from influential women. Judith Stuyvesant, widow of the late Director General of New Netherland, provided for her church in her will, entered in court in 1679. Stuyvesant, "by the form of a legacy," granted to the Dutch Church or its congregation "my . . . church or chapel situated on my Bowery or farmes, Together with all the revenues, profitts, and immunityes." Though she went on to indicate that the congregation might choose to demolish the church and use the building materials elsewhere, Judith Stuyvesant required that her family's tomb be preserved. In addition, Mrs. Stuyvesant left to her cousin Nicholas Bayard and his wife and children a burying place in the tomb, with the provision that should the church decay or be demolished, "from the materials a cover shall be made to the said vault."[31]

Maria Gordon, wife of Domine John Gordon, drafted her will in the face of a long and possibly treacherous journey to England in 1685. In it, she stipulated that the just half of all of her outstanding debts and claims, "due to me from different persons dwelling in the province of New York and the neighborhood thereof, and elsewhere in America," be donated to the Deacons of the Dutch Church in New York City "for the behoof of the poor of the same."[32]

Churchgoers of slightly less ample means than Maria Gordon or Judith Stuyvesant also saw fit to leave their mark on their congregations. Sibout Claasens and his wife Susannah Jans declared that by virtue of the "real love and affection during the time of their matrimony shown to each other, and by the blessing of God yet to be shown," they wished to leave to the deacons of the Dutch Church 1000 guilders to be used for the poor.[33]

women in church offices

For the most part, women in seventeenth-century Protestant churches made their mark from outside church government. For though they lent shape to their churches through their donations of silver or land, played a part in the approbation or choice of a minister, and offered their own interpretations of the journey toward grace through their narratives, few women participated in ecclesiastical decisions as members of the formal church polity. While they did not remain silent within the church walls, women in the seventeenth century were barred from the church's highest offices.

According to John Calvin, no scriptural injunctions stood in the way of women assuming church office. To the contrary, that Jesus appeared first to women after his resurrection provided ample evidence to Calvin that the apostolic office Jesus had bestowed upon men belonged for a short time to women. In a published sermon that included a less-than-ringing endorsement of a woman's apostolic capacity, Puritan divine John Cotton admitted that widows, designated by Paul in 2 Tim.5:9,10 as "servants to the church," should in fact be included in the list of church officers. As assistants to the deacons, women were especially fit to minister to the congregation's poor and sick, services "not so fit for men to put their hands into." Cotton further diminished the import of female offices by adding that, to his knowledge, few women who had attained the age of sixty (the scriptural description of a widow prepared to assist deacons) were "so hearty, and healthy, and strong, as to be fit to undertake such a service."[34]

If widows rarely appeared in church or town records as officers of New England's Congregational churches, it was considerably more common to find them serving as sextons in the Anglican churches of Virginia. Included among those members appointed to carry out the day-to-day operations of the church, sextons were responsible for church maintenance and, in some churches, for ringing the bells calling parishioners to services.

Among those historians who have acknowledged the role played by sextons in maintaining church order, few have recognized the spiritual importance of their duties as established by the Church of England. Admittedly the lowest-ranking members of the church hierarchy, sextons were culled frequently from the ranks of the poor or those on relief, including widows. That fact notwithstanding, the Church of England directed its laity and clergy to pay special attention to the maintenance of the house of God. A homily issued by royal authority in 1571 noted that just as men were best "refreshed and comforted" when their houses were kept in good order, "so when God's house . . . is well adorned . . . and is also kept clean, comely and sweetly, the people are more desireous, and the more comforted to resort thither, and to tarry there the whole time appointed to them." Sextons, women among them, worked on the front lines of those whose duty it was to insure the best possible environment for spiritual pursuits.[35]

Sextons were routinely paid 500 pounds of tobacco and cask per year, regardless of gender. In Petsworth Parish in 1682, Ellenor Hogsden, sexton at the Upper Church, and John Litey at the Lower Church were each paid 500 pounds for the performance of their duties. Hogsden took over as sexton when her husband died in 1682 and held the position at least until 1697. Though many widows were assigned the duties of sexton upon the death of a mate who had held the position, in at least one instance a woman attained the position while her husband was alive.[36]

In New Netherland, too, women were permitted to act in an adjunct capacity as teachers in the church school. In at least one congregation, in Flatbush, the orders for the schoolmaster in 1680 included this exception to the prohibition against women teaching: "In the summertime, namely from May to November...if ten or more children come to the school or if those who do come shall make up the tuition fees of ten," than the schoolmaster must be present. "if not, his wife, if six or more children come may do the same and must give them instruction." One year later, the consistory amended the rules; if the number of schoolchildren was twenty or fewer, the schoolmaster's wife was permitted to instruct in her husband's stead. While hardly a ringing endorsement of women in positions of church authority, the rules did acknowledge the abilities of women to promote pious learning among the community's young people.[37]

* * *

As this chapter has argued, women exercised both indirect and direct authority as members of their community's churches. Far from silent, women spoke out in church on a great many occasions, and ministers, church elders, vestrymen, and fellow brethren listened. Whether they acted as benefactors, their names forever attached to objects used in rituals central to Protestant spirituality, or as regenerate Christians whose duty to God demanded that they challenge the authority of those ministers or elders whose guidance they questioned, Protestant women, like men, helped to set the course for their churches. Their vision—and their articulation of that vision—gave shape to their churches, an institution at the center of daily life in all three American colonies.

* * *

In each of the sites of religious meaning and activity discussed thus far—self, family, and church—the line between what was religious and what was political, social, or economic was admittedly thin. Religion and spirituality infused daily life in the seventeenth century. What was religious was political, economic, and certainly social. As we shall see in the next chapter, during times of local or colonial conflict, those lines were increasingly blurred. The church, the one place where the majority of any community was sure to be found on any given Sabbath, proved fertile ground—literally and figuratively—for the expression of social, political and economic concerns. Moreover, colonists appropriated the language of Christian liberty, morality, and righteousness as they took their concerns from the church out into their communities. Secure in their vision of the regenerate individual and parish, women participated fully in those events that reflected both the fissures and the alliances that marked daily life in their communities.

NOTES

[1] For a discussion of the role of women in affirming ministerial authority in New England, see Laurel Thatcher Ulrich, *Good Wives: Image and Reality in the Lives of Women in Northern New England, 1650–1750*, (New York, 1983), 223.

[2] John Calvin, *Commentary on the Epistles of Paul the Apostle to the Corinthians*, Rev. John Pringle, ed. (2 vols., Edinburgh, 1848), I, 147. See also E. Brooks Holifield, *The Covenant Sealed: The Development of Puritan Sacramental Theology in Old and New England, 1570–1720* (New Haven, 1974), 37. On John Calvin's interpretation of lay and ministerial balance of power, see William J. Bouwsma, *John Calvin: A Sixteenth-Century Portrait*, (New York, 1988), 226, 292n.

³ Norfolk County Deed Book, 1637–1646, Reel 1; C. G. Chamberlayne, ed., *Vestry Book of Christ Church Parish* (Richmond, 1927), 38–39. On the laicization of the Anglican church in Virginia with respect to the power of the state assembly over Anglican ministers see John Frederick Woolverton, *Colonial Anglicanism in North America* (Detroit, 1984), 75–77; for those laws pertaining to the control of the state assembly over church law, see Hening, *Statutes*, I, 180–183.

⁴ Firth Fabend, *A Dutch Family in the Middle Colonies, 1660–1800* (New Brunswick, N.J., 1991), 146; Corwin, ed., *Ecclesiastical Records*, II, 747–748; *ibid.*, I, 345–346; A. J. F. Van Laer, ed., *The Correspondence of Maria Van Rensselaer* (Albany, 1935), 69–70. On the relationship between the churches of the Four Towns—Brooklyn, Flatbush, Flatlands, and New Utrecht—and related demographic information, see Gerald F. De Jong, *The Dutch Reformed Church in the American Colonies* (Grand Rapids, 1978), 68–69. For more on the controversy surrounding the appointment of a minister to Albany's church in 1682, see below, chapter seven.

⁵ Richard D. Pierce, ed., *Records of the First Church in Salem, 1629–1736* (Salem, 1974), 154. On the process of gathering a church in colonial Massachusetts, see Robert Pope, ed., *The Notebook of the Reverend John Fiske, 1644–1678* (Boston, 1974), xi-xii. Women were among the founding members of Puritan chruches in England as well; Katherine Chidley, for instance, was one of the founders of the church at Bury St. Edmunds in Suffolk in 1646: Richard Greaves, "Foundation Builders: The Role of Women in Early English Nonconformity," in Greaves, ed., *Triumph Over Silence: Women in Protestant History* (Westport, Ct., and London, 1985), 78.

⁶ *Winthrop Papers, Part III*, Massachusetts Historical Society *Collections*, 5ᵗʰ ser., I (Boston, 1871), 104. See also Patricia U. Bonomi, *Under the Cope of Heaven*, 116.

⁷ Quoted in Ulrich, *Good Wives*, 219.

⁸ Thomas and Virginia L. Davis, eds., *Edward Taylor's "Church Records" and Related Sermons* (Boston, 1981), 191, 195–196.

⁹ Durand Echeverria, *A History of Billingsgate* (Welfleet, Mass., privately printed, 1991), 58–64.

¹⁰ Thomas, ed., *The Diary of Samuel Sewall*, I, 103–106.

¹¹ For descriptions of the developing parish system in Virginia see George Maclaren Brydon, *Virginia's Mother Church and the Political Conditions Under Which it Grew* (Richmond, 1947), 94–97. Parish duties, as Brydon has described them, included a mixture of the spiritual and the civic, in keeping with the Anglican emphasis on the second table laws. Parish duties included processioning lands, providing for neighborly peace, providing for widows, orphans, the aged, sick, and poor, and the presenting to *civil* court all offenders of moral law. Most of these duties fell to the churchwardens, elected by the vestry in most parishes. Church wardens' duties were delineated by the Virginia Assembly, not a clerical body, in a series of laws passed beginning in 1632: Woolverton, *Colonial Anglicanism*, 75–76. For a discussion of the power of the laity in colonial Virginia, vis à vis England, see ibid., 74, 77–80. See also "Bruton Church," in *WMQ*, 1st ser., 3 (1894–1895): 174.

¹² *VMHB* I (1893): 327; Chamberlayne, ed., *Vestry Book of St. Peter's Parish*, 182. Instances of quarrels between church vestries and their ministers were numerous, though the role of male and female parishioners in those cases is less clear. George Maclaren Brydon cites two cases in the 1690s when vestrymen barred the door of the church against their ministers, and

one when a minister was struck by a vestryman: Brydon, *Virginia's Mother Church*, 234. For additional evidence of vestry/clerical confrontations, see *SPGFP*, Lambeth Palace Papers, microfilm reel 739; *Vestry Book of St. Peter's Parish*, 126; *The Secret Diary of William Byrd*, 96, 116, 192.

13 Corwin, ed., *Ecclesiastical Records*, I, 367; cf. Van der Linde, ed., *Brooklyn Church Records* xi-xiii. For a similar case, involving the objections of the inhabitants of a Puritan town on Long Island a quarter of a century later, see *Ecclesiastical Records*, II, 844.

14 De Jong, *Dutch Reformed Church*, 73.

15 *Ecclesiastical Records* II, 772–773.

16 A. J. F. Van Laer, trans. and ed., *Minutes of the Court of Fort Orange and Beverwyck, 1657–1660* (Albany, 1923), II, 24–25.

17 Van der Linde, ed., *Brooklyn Church Records*, 23. The first schoolmaster, Adam Roelantson, appointed to the school established in New Amsterdam in 1638, was sued for slander, assault, adultery, and a failure to pay debts: De Jong, *Dutch Reformed Church*, 44; See also *Flatbush Church Records*, 29–30, for details of a case brought by the widow of Reverend Polhemus against schoolmaster Jan Gerritez Van Markken in 1681.

18 Records of the Reformed Protestant Dutch Church of Flatbush, vol.1a, Consistory Minutes, unpublished transcripts and transliterations, Holland Society, 53–57.

19 John Cotton, *Certain Queries Tending to Accommodation and Communion of Presbyterian & congregational Churches* (London, 1654).

20 Andrew Hill Hamilton, ed., *History of Old South Church, Boston, 1669–1884* (2 vols., Boston, 1899), 38–39, 50, 65–67; "Public Diary of John Hull," in *Puritan Personal Writing: Diaries* (New York, 1983), 228–229.

21 Porterfield, *Female Piety in Puritan New England*, 121–122. For a discussion of the relationship between childbirth and the need for spiritual strength see above, chapter three.

22 On the admission of Dorchester women to the Third Church, see Hill, *Old South Church*, I, 166. Hill reproduces many of the original records connected to this case.

23 *Ibid.*, 164–166.

24 *Ibid.*, 168; cf. "Diary of John Hull," in *Puritan Personal Writing*, 308.

25 Hill, *Old South Church*, 168, 201–202.

26 *Records of the First Church in Boston*, 73.

27 *Ibid.*, 120–122, 132, 140, 220; Porterfield, *Female Piety*, 120–121.

28 See, for instance, "Bruton Church," in *WMQ*, 1st ser., 3 (1894–1895): 172, 173; Edward Lewis Goodwin, *The Colonial Church in Virginia* (London, 1927), 59–60; *VMHB* 4 (1897): 377; McIlwaine, ed., *Minutes of the Council and the General Court of Virginia*, 167; Van der Linde, ed., *Brooklyn Church Records*, 101; Porterfield, *Female Piety*, 132. In Virginia, women were also paid for sewing the surplice, the ornamental robes worn by Anglican ministers, rejected by more Calvinist denominations. See for instance Chamberlayne, ed., *Vestry Book of St. Peter's Parish*, 205.

29 Van der Linde, ed., *Brooklyn Church Records*, 63; Chamberlayne, ed., *The Vestry Book of Petsworth Parish*, 70; Chamberlayne, ed., *Vestry Book of Christ Church Parish*, 137; ibid., 163; Chamberlayne, ed., *The Vestry Book of St. Peter's Parish*, 175, 182, 186.

[30] *VMHB*, 29 (1921), 301–302. Perkins, it may be noted, was a renowned Puritan scholar and teacher from Christ College, Cambridge; Julia Cherry Spruill, *Women's Life and Work in the Southern Colonies* (Chill, 1938), 247. See also Goodwin, *The Colonial Church in Virginia*, 58–60; Brydon, *Virgina's Mother Church*, 56.

[31] *Ecclesiastical Records* II, 934; cf. *Abstract of Wills, 1665–1707* New York Historical Society *Collections* 25 (1892), 139–140.

[32] *Ecclesiastical Records* II, 909–910.

[33] *Abstract of Wills*, 107.

[34] Bouwsma, *John Calvin*, 138 and 270n; John Cotton, *The Way of the Church of Christ in New England* (London, 1645). The Town of Dedham's instructions to its new church in 1637 included widows among church officers "rightly elected & ordayned by the Church in the name of Christ." Don Gleason Hill, ed., *Early Records of the Town of Dedham* (6 vols., Dedham, 1886–1936), I, 4.

[35] "Homily for repairing and keeping clean, and comely adorning of churches," quoted in Yates, *Buildings, Faith, and Worship*, 1. See also Upton, *Holy Things and Profane*, 8.

[36] Chamberlayne, ed., *The Vestry Book of Petsworth Parish*, 20–21, 24, 31, 32, 33, 35, 38, 41, 43,49; In 1678 Mrs. Thorntone held the position of sexton at the Petsworth Church, where her husband served on the vestry: *ibid.*, 8. For additional examples of women serving as sextons, see *ibid.*, 86, 88, 103, 108, 152, 154; *The Vestry Book of Kingston Parish*, 17; *The Vestry Book of Christ Church Parish*, 154, 156; *The Vestry Book of St. Peter's Parish*, 188, 189, 200, 203, 210, 217, 220.

[37] Flatbush Church Records, 49, 39–40.

Part IV

CIVIC LIFE and COMMUNITY: RELIGIOUS CULTURE IN THE PUBLIC SPHERE

Chapter Seven
Gender, Religion, and the Public Voice

I N THE COURSE OF THEIR DAILY LIVES, PROTESTANT WOMEN MADE PERSONAL CHOICES regarding the practice of their faith, exercised authority within the bonds of marriage, directed the religious lives of their children, and wielded informal influence over the affairs of their church. Within the bounds of their religion, women also found outlets for authority and influence in arenas that few historians have explored. Acting as faithful Christians, women took their concerns about private and public piety and morality to the community; they turned to their church, the courts, and to public rituals as forums within which to articulate those concerns. Men and women in all three colonies understood that, as Christians, they were obliged to monitor and contribute to the stability of their communities. The behavior of any one individual reflected upon the whole. Private quarrels—between husbands and wives, between neighbors, and between civic leaders and common people—threatened the stability of the entire town, and women as well as men regarded it as their God-given right to call attention to community dissonance. Whether Protestant men and women acted from sincere piety, or simply couched their civil concerns in pious language is in most cases difficult to discern from the existing evidence. What is clear is that their Protestant faith provided them with the language and the authority to address their concerns in the public sphere.

The language women used to frame their public concerns reflected in many instances the language of their faith and, more specifically, that of their denomination. In Calvinist Massachusetts, colonists often articulated their grievances within the context of their community's duty toward God. The entire community acted in covenant with God. Issues or events deemed an affront to God—witchcraft, Sabbath-breaking, antinomianism or other sectarian threats dominated many of the most vocal community discussions, discussions in which women played an active and authoritative role.

In Anglican Virginia, where concerns with the demands of the laws of the second table (duty toward man as well as God) held sway, men and women focused on issues of public order and the maintenance of their sometimes fragile community bonds. Charges of slander far exceeded charges of witchcraft; forthrightness in contracts of all sorts dominated community concerns. In New York, where Dutch Calvinism developed amid the challenges of ethnic diversity and political upheaval, a compelling mixture of concern with public order and personal piety prevailed.[1]

In all three colonies, the line between public and private authority was blurred. Dedicated to religious convictions and aware that the language of faith might be used to support public actions, women—rarely associated with contributions in the public sphere—voiced opinions, made charges, and attracted the attention of neighbors, civic administrators, and religious leaders. Though barred from formal participation in civic life, nonconformist and Anglican women relied upon religious structures, language, institutions, and ideas to facilitate the transition from their domestic worlds into the public sphere.[2]

THE CHURCH AS SETTING FOR COMMUNITY UPHEAVAL

Colonial men and women aired community concerns and quarrels in a variety of public spaces. Chief among the venues open to colonial women was the church. Horse races and taverns, popular gathering places for men, were not suitable for seventeenth-century women. But the church provided a socially acceptable setting in which to air opinions, redress grievances, and challenge local religious and civic authority. In all three colonies, the church constituted a locale for the dissemination of civic as well as religious information central to colonists' daily lives. In a representative example, the meetinghouse door in Ipswich, Massachusetts was used to post public notices, including the periodic updates of the laws of the General Court, and the latest criminal charges against Ipswich residents.[3]

In Virginia, the church played a central role in colonists' struggles to create communities and maintain kinship networks. Along with the courthouse and gaming sites, it provided colonists—women especially—with a much-needed place for socializing, gossiping, and exchanging opinions about community concerns. County and parish sheriffs and other local officials relied on church services for the dissemination of local news; public proclamations and local or colonial ordinances were frequently pinned to church doors. Secular concerns shared the stage with the sacred.[4]

Some church-based gatherings were politically and economically motivated. In December of 1673, when residents of Lawne's Creek Parish in Surry County met to protest Governor Berkeley's decision to raise local levies to cover expenses incurred during the Third Anglo-Dutch War, they did so at the parish church. According to the sheriff and several justices, who appeared in church to collect the levies from parishioners, fourteen men, "A Certaine Company of Giddy-Headed & turbulent Psons," had congregated there. They refused to disperse when ordered by the sheriff to do so, and were arrested for illegal assembly, contempt, and obstruction of justice. Though no women were named in the court records, the events of the 12th of December—a Friday—were brought up at the church on the following Sabbath, when women were a party to the discussion.[5]

Though men dominated the Lawnes's Creek incident, other church-centered events featured women. In one case, stunning in its detail, several local women in York County, Virginia, took control of their community's religious space, the Marston Parish church, and appropriated civic and religious language to express their dissatisfaction with certain church leaders. In what might be interpreted as a parody of the practice of posting local news on church doors, the three women collaborated in a scheme to distribute written testimony about the character of local church officials. They could identify no more appropriate place to disseminate their "written lybells" (as they were labeled by the targets of the attack), than at the parish church, during the Sabbath service. There they could reach those neighbors sure to be most interested in their gossip.

The details of the case surfaced in court when church officials decided to pursue legal action against the alleged libelers. In October of 1658, Churchwarden Robert Cobb presented to the county court three female members of the church at Marston Parish "concerning several lybells, dropt in the parish church tending to the scandell and abuse of several spouses named in the sd. Lybells, and to the disturbance of the whole congregation and the worship of service of the Almighty God." In response to Churchwarden Cobb's accusations the court ordered the husbands of the three women—Mrs. Elizabeth Wood, Johannah Poynter, and Elianor Cooper—to post bond to guarantee their wives' good behavior until the next meeting of the court.

According to court depositions, including several taken from the accused women and their families, Elizabeth Wood, perhaps with the help of the other two women, had drafted a letter addressed to the gentlemen of the congregation. She made several copies and deposited them in church pews. Though the records provide no clues to the root cause of the animosity between Elizabeth Wood and the church vestrymen and their wives (there is a brief reference in one of the depositions to a dispute between Elizabeth's husband, John Wood, and one object of the libel, Thomas Bromfield), her letter, which bears repeating at length, makes use of a few choice slurs in an attempt to sully the vestry's reputation:

> Gentlemen: this is to give you all notice that we have a fine trade come up amongst us, one of our vestrymen [has] turned mirken maker, Thomas Bromfield by name and also his wife and also goodwife Cobb one of our churchwarden's wife. They mayd one very handsome Mirking amongst them and sent it to one of the neighbors for a new fashioned toakin [token] . . . and soe I leave it to the consideration of the beholder hereof whether men of such carriage be fitt to have any charge in church business, yea or noe.

Not only did Elizabeth Wood appropriate the space used by local officials to distribute her missive (one deposition claimed that Wood said "she would have it set upp at the church door"), she pointedly borrowed from the language of official documents: she "gave notice" to the town's gentlemen, and she finished with a request for a vote, "yea or noe," on the issue of the vestry's suitability. Her choice of slur was most deliberate as well; a mirken maker designed what amounted to pubic hairpieces for victims of the small pox, many of whom lost their body hair as a result of the disease. The choice of what was undoubtedly among the lowliest of professions in the seventeenth century, replete with sexual overtones and linked to disease, would have been an insult to any member of the community, most especially those involved in church administration.[6]

The hierarchical arrangement of Anglican church seating lent itself to local confrontations over class and social status as well. In the summer of 1689, one such dispute disrupted a Sabbath service at Christ Church Parish, in Middlesex County, and carried over into the county court. A local serving woman, Mrs. Ann Jones, undermined the church practice of seating wealthy community leaders in special pews apart from their slaves and indentured servants. In an effort to register her animosity toward the church leaders and her master, himself a member of the vestry, Ann Jones took her seat in the pew reserved for the family with which she served.

Jones, servant to Christopher Wormley, had born two children out of wedlock. Already on shaky moral ground when she attended church services without approbation from the warden or the vestry, she compounded her sins when she deliberately chose a pew "above her Degree." To make matters worse, when churchwarden Matthew Kemp dutifully attempted to "displace" Jones, to escort her from the church, his actions prompted "Disorder and Rudeness" among some parishioners in Peankatanke Church. By Kemp's own account, he was forced to bear the sting of the parishioners' "hard Words" for simply performing the "just and honest Action" of removing the profligate Ann Jones. Though parish leaders stood by Kemp in his decision to remove Jones from the church, other worshippers felt differently, and registered their support for the serving woman. Though according to church records Ann Jones never revealed the name of her children's father, her attempts to humiliate her master, Wormley, or establish her own claims to the family pew, might provide clues to the paternity. Ann Jones chose well the stage on which to challenge the church—and community—hierarchy, and to assert that her own soul was equal to any other Wormley family member's in the eyes of God.[7]

The church served as the stage for pitched social and political battles in New York as well as in Virginia in the seventeenth century. When, for instance, Mrs. Polhemus, widow of the Rev. Polhemus, fell into a land dispute with her neighbors in 1681, she aired her grievances in church. When several surveyors failed to resolve the conflict in her favor, the widow Polhemus brought pressure to bear on her enemies by publicly renouncing her association with her congregation. For a time she withdrew from the Lord's Supper, until another surveyor vindicated her claim. Because the widow had chosen as her forum one of the community's central rituals and key public spaces, the unlucky minister who replaced Polhemus, Caspar van

Zuuren, was drawn into the dispute. His attempts to smooth ruffled feathers failed, and Mrs. Polhemus turned her venom on the cleric. So influential was the widow that van Zuren complained to the Classis in Amsterdam that he was "accused by great and small, by English and Dutch, by the Lieutenant-Governor of the land as well as by the Rev. Consistory of New York, of having said that she did not fairly own the land, and that I had therefore made out her late husband a thief, and her children rogues."[8]

Especially in the years following the English conquest of the colony, when many Dutch residents perceived the English as a threat to their culture, disgruntled men and women aired their grievances in church, often at the time of the Sabbath service. And though evidence rarely singles out women specifically among the participants in such battles, we can glean from both court and church records the degree to which secular concerns crossed over to sacred space, into places where women, at the very least, would have been privy to public controversy. Though not necessarily actors in their community's political culture, neither were women entirely excluded from public debates. For example, women were among the mourners at New York's Dutch Church in 1698 during the ceremonial—and politically charged—reburial of the executed martyrs, Jacob Leisler and his son-in-law Jacob Milborne.[9]

GENDER, RELIGION, AND THE COURT

In 1651, Mary Parsons of Springfield, Massachusetts joined her neighbors in the county court to testify against her husband, Hugh Parsons, accused of witchcraft. With their witchcraft accusations, the townspeople marked Hugh Parsons a threat to their community and its covenant with God. Mary, herself an accused witch, provided key testimony in her husband's hearing. When Mary proclaimed her own innocence and impugned her husband, she made it clear, vocally and publicly, that she had no intention of remaining outside of the covenant with him. She used her moment in the court's spotlight to juxtapose her own piety with her husband's wickedness, and to prove that she intended to be instrumental in wresting a confession out of him. "I told him," Mary proclaimed, "that if he would acknowledge it I would begg the Prayers of Gods People on my knees for him, and that we are not our owne, we are bought with a Price, and that God would redeem from the Power of Sathan." Mary Parsons had in effect preached God's redemption to her husband in the privacy of their home, a fact she lost no time presenting to the crowd assembled at the court house.[10]

Women identified the colonial courts as forums in which they could address their private and public concerns or share in political and social issues central to the community's health and well-being. In Virginia, New York, and Massachusetts, Protestant women entered the court as witnesses, as defendants, as observers, and, in a few instances, as impaneled jurists. There they participated in a process central to maintaining a stable community. They sat in judgment of their neighbors; they offered their observations on behavior, morality, and transgression. They knew that their opinions carried weight. In a world where God's hand was seen in every event

and action, women, as bearers of soul equality, spoke with authority and righteousness in courts across the colonies. For the colonial court, above all its other duties,
enforced God's laws, laws that all members of the community, male and female,
were commanded to uphold. Colonial men and women each had a responsibility to
identify and weed out evil from their midst; each had a role to play in the struggle to
win and sustain God's favor.[11]

WITCHCRAFT TRIALS IN COLONIAL NEW ENGLAND: A CASE STUDY IN GENDER AND RELIGION IN THE PUBLIC SPHERE

As standard-bearers of piety and virtue, women participated in all manner of civil
and criminal court cases. They testified in cases of adultery and slander, infanticide
and bastardy, murder and rape. In seventeenth-century Massachusetts, single
women over the age of eighteen (the age of majority) and widows had standing in a
court of law: they could sue and be sued, convey property, and write and enter their
wills into the public record. And though the laws of coverture governed married
women—they could press suit only with the consent of their husband—their access
to court was assured.[12]

Among the cases which attracted the most attention among neighbors and religious and civic leaders in colonial Massachusetts—and no small amount of attention
on the part of scholars, from the seventeenth century to the present—were those
that involved accusations of witchcraft. And though they occurred far less frequently than other types of court cases, witchcraft trials provide an opportunity to compare and contrast the interplay of gender and religion.[13]

Witchcraft trial evidence in New England documents the religiously-
sanctioned participation of women in the public sphere. Within the bounds of the
community's covenant with God, women monitored the behavior of their neighbors. Even as its doctrine counseled submission for its weak-willed daughters of
Eve, Puritanism encouraged women to play out their covenanted roles not only in
the home, as wives and mothers, but in a public forum. Women could be depended
on to identify members of their town who stood outside the covenant, those who by
their actions threatened family and community stability. Women were, after all,
especially attuned to interruptions in patterns of domestic life. And any breech in
domestic tranquility or public morality might signal potential evil bubbling below a
town's godly surface.

Part of a female network of communication that was in its own way as public as
their husbands', Puritan women monitored the behavior of their neighbors for
signs of a breech in their community's moral and spiritual health. The line between
public and private life was permeable; colonial New Englanders needed to look no
farther than their own homes or in the street before their front doors to find fuel for
local gossip. Private godliness and public behavior were two sides of the same coin.
Seventeenth-century New England architecture reflected this concern with public
godliness: in many seventeenth-century houses, the front door opened directly into
the hall, where the family cooked, ate, slept, socialized, prayed, and read. In the hall

midwives and neighbors gathered to accompany an expectant mother through the labors of childbirth. There they met to read scripture. There they gossiped, and their words, the stuff of seventeenth-century court records, reflected Puritan attitudes about good and evil, and the correlate demand that the godly ferret out evil and challenge it wherever they might find it.

Women who took accusations of witchcraft from the domestic sphere to the courts responded to tensions inherent in the Puritan vision of the female role. On the one hand, as heirs to Eve's weakness, women were unable to control lustful desires, sexual and material. They served as vessels for Satan's evil. Raised with those images, women feared their own discontented spirits and those of their female neighbors. At the same time, on the other hand, they recognized their own capacity for piety, godliness they demonstrated daily as wives and helpmeets, mothers, and church members.

A New Haven court case of 1653 against Elizabeth Godman illustrates this tension. In her deposition against Godman, accused of witchcraft, Goodwife Larremore used language that reveals both the source and the nature of the criteria used to identify a witch. She demonstrated her conviction that she was capable of employing Puritan doctrine to recognize evil in her neighbor:

> as soon as she saw [Godman] come in at Goodman Whitnels she thought of a witch; once she spoke to the purpose at Mr. Hookes; and her ground was because Mr. Davenport, about that Time, had occasion in his Ministry to speak of Witches; and showed that a froward discontented Frame of Spirit was a Subject fitt for the Devill to work upon in that way, and she looked upon Mrs. Godman to be of such Frame of Spirit.

Larremore consulted the Rev. Thomas Hookes. She heard the Rev. John Davenport deliver a sermon on the subject of witchcraft. She digested the contents, and applied its lessons to a neighbor in whom she identified those qualities most often associated with the daughters of Eve.[14]

In 1648, at the court in Hartford, accused witch Mary Johnson confessed that she had entered into a compact with the Devil to escape the drudgery of her daily chores as a servant in Wethersfield, Connecticut. Johnson's confession, the first in New England, underscores the multiple meanings the accused attached to her crime: she understood the religious implications—she had colluded with the Devil—and revealed her notions of the way evil functioned on a local, domestic level, attached to the fabric of daily life. Cotton Mather noted that Johnson confessed that her familiarity with the Devil "came by discontent; and wishing the devil to take that and t'other thing; and, the devil to do this and that: whereupon a devil appeared unto her, tendering her the best service he could do for her." Whether her confession was freely given or forced (the record is silent on this point), Johnson's deposition reveals the tensions between godly work and the worldly desires to which women were, according to scripture, especially susceptible. There could be no more appropriate appeal for a serving girl to make to the Devil than to save her from some of the trials of domestic labor. On the basis of her confession, Mary Johnson was executed for witchcraft.[15]

Increasing tensions—population pressures, increased opportunities to acquire wealth, and a more fluid movement between towns—tested the ability of pious Puritans to maintain their covenant with God in the mid-seventeenth century.[16] Tensions pervaded women's domestic sphere as well as the meetinghouse and market place. And though town leaders often illustrated most vividly the conflict between godliness and worldliness—their access to fine clothing, grander dwellings, and a greater degree of material wealth singled them out in town—it was considerably less disruptive to target alleged criminals, sinners, or outsiders who could provide an outlet for the town's anxiety without challenging its fundamental social order. Godly people of both sexes singled out women who through their behavior, appearance, or demeanor seemed to reflect the town's instability or avarice. And who better to recognize a "devil's handmaiden" than others of the same sex?

In the course of their daily activities as keepers of the home and hearth, women were more likely than men to come in contact with and recognize an ungodly woman and target her for persecution. Trial evidence reveals women-centered networks of friendship and animosity at work in the months before formal accusations of witchcraft were made by one woman against another. Within the bounds of a woman's covenanted duty to sustain her family's and the town's godliness, gossip proved to be an especially potent tool of social control.

Fortified by their roles as keepers of the covenant at home and among their neighbors, women accused supposed witches of behavior and actions that they deemed a threat to those spheres over which they exercised some control. Women who compromised the reputation of a neighbor, exhibited unusual or unfriendly behavior toward children, or threatened domestic order or economy were particularly vulnerable to accusations of witchcraft. Women regulated other women to preserve their domain. To do so, they aired their grievances in public, and often framed their concerns in language that reflected their piety.

Abigail Wescott of Stamford, Connecticut testified in the trial of Elizabeth Clawson that the accused frequently acted out of malice and jealousy. According to Wescott, while the two were walking in the street, Clawson

> Took up some stone and threw at [me] . . . and asked me what I did in my chamber last Sabbath day night . . . and at another time . . . contended with me because I did not com into the house caling of me proud slut what ear you proud on your fine cloths and you look to be a mistres but you never shal by me.

Abigail Wescott found Clawson's language particularly provoking and malicious, as it would have been to any pious woman. Only an evil and discontented spirit would wrongfully accuse another of lascivious behavior on a Sabbath day night. That Clawson accused her of false pride, and exhibited jealousy over her clothing was proof enough to Wescott that Clawson was discontented with her own lot, and thus fair game for the devil. And in Wescott's mind, it took someone with especially ungodly intentions to threaten that she would never marry, would never be mistress of her own home. Marriage was the highest godly estate to which a young woman could aspire in Puritan society; the charge that one would never marry could not be taken lightly.[17]

Many alleged witches had reputations as child haters. To a godly woman, no sentiment could be more threatening to the Puritan social order. The family was the core unit in Puritan society and women and men alike were expected to act in positive ways to shape and control it. According to Increase Mather, families were the "Nurceryes for Church and Common-wealth, ruine Families and ruine all. Order them well and the publick State will fare better." Raising children, then, was one way a woman could contribute to the health and welfare of the "publick State." When a suspicious neighbor threatened to undermine that responsibility, concerned women sometimes expressed their grievances against the suspects with accusations of witchcraft.[18]

In Mary Godfrey's deposition against Rachel Fuller, accused of witchcraft in the death of Godfrey's baby, Moses, in 1680, she testified that when Rachel visited her and her ailing son, and took the child by the hand, she feared the worst, and "put her Hand off from the Child and Wrapped the Child's Hand in her Apron." According to Mary, Rachel "made ugly Faces...and would have looked on the Child, but I not suffering her she went out." Mary also testified that Rachel Fuller had encouraged her children, Mehitable and Sarah, to practice magic to combat witchery, leading them to "lay sweet bays under the threshold," an act that allegedly prevented witches from entering a house. As Mary Godfrey reported, Rachel Fuller herself then studiously avoided coming in contact with the bay leaves, and entered the house "crowded in on the side where the bays lay not." Elizabeth Denham, another witness in Fuller's trial, testified that she became suspicious when Fuller pressed her for information about Godfrey's sick child, and went so far as to call her own child Moses. Rachel had encroached upon Mary's domain. She had undermined her authority in her own household, and interfered with her relationship to her children.[19]

While men referred in their depositions to alleged acts of witchery that threatened their control over financial resources outside of the home—their fields, tools, grazing animals—women's depositions reveal their concerns with threats to domestic economy. Sarah Edwards testified that alleged witch Hugh Parsons, upon being denied the purchase of as much milk as he desired, successfully bewitched her cow. The animal, which "at that Tyme...gave three quarts at a Meale," soon after "gave not above a Quart, and it was as yellow as Saffron."[20] Elizabeth Smith of Weathersfield testified in 1668 that accused witch Katherine Harrison "did often spin so great a quantity of fine linen yarn as did never know nor hear of any other women who could spin so much." Women recognized certain accepted levels of production in the home; they presented evidence that a neighbor interfered with or surpassed those levels as an indication of witchcraft. Their sorcery, especially when born of avarice or jealousy, was an affront to God.[21]

Within the bounds of their religious culture, Puritan women helped to define standards of morality for their communities and measured their neighbors against those standards. They identified those women and men whose behavior marked them as outsiders. In 1651, Mary Parsons joined the townspeople of Springfield Massachusetts as they identified Hugh Parsons as an outsider. In addition to using the occasion of her accusation against her husband to proclaim her own piety, Mary Parsons framed her accusations in a way that demonstrated her sensitivity to the interference of a witch in the town's economic health. She testified that she suspected her husband to be a witch because "all that he sells to Anybody doth not prosper. I am sorry," she went on to say, "for that pore Man, Thomas Millar, for two days after my Husband and he had bargained for a Peec of Ground Thomas Millar had that Mischance of that Cutt in his Leg." Whatever her personal goal was in testifying against her husband (undoubtedly related to the charges pending against *her* for witchcraft), Mary recognized that her words would carry weight if she could prove her husband a threat to the town's prosperity, a prosperity which stood as evidence of God's favor. By so doing, Mary extended her sphere of influence beyond control over the domestic economy into male-dominated economic relationships.[22]

More often than not, however, women leveled accusations of witchcraft against other women linked in a tightly-woven fabric of female communication. In the case against Elizabeth Garlick of East Hampton, women's gossip was at the core of the evidence against the defendant. Already the focus of suspicious behavior when she moved into town, Garlick made an especially vulnerable target. When Elizabeth Howell, the daughter of a prominent townsperson, died in 1657, women's gossip helped to focus the town's fear and hostility on one person.

Seven out of ten depositions taken in the case against Goody Garlick were from women. As the women gathered around Elizabeth Howell's sick bed—which had recently been her child bed—they discussed the suspicious Goody Garlick. They transformed their gossip and suspicions into public participation in the town's legal and economic structure when they chose to present their evidence against the alleged witch in court.

The female accusers traveled in a tight circle of friends. The similarity in their testimony reflects their shared spheres and the power of gossip. Three of the women testified that they had heard the victim call Garlick a "double-tongued woman." Goody Garlick, they swore, had provoked the epithet when she laughed in Goody Howell's face when she came to fetch her husband at Garlick's house, where he was threshing grain. The same three witnesses implied that Goody Howell suspected both Garlick and her husband of collusion in business affairs, and might have been close to making a formal accusation to that effect. Four of the witnesses mention the names of at least two others. All seven mention at least one other woman with whom they witnessed peculiar incidences, all signs of witchcraft: a pin fell from Garlick's mouth, a black cat caused Goody Simon to have a fit in Garlick's presence, and several women who had come in contact with the accused found their breast milk had dried up in the process of nursing. Once again, the alleged witch's acts undermined her neighbors' control over domestic tranquillity, and threatened to deprive them of an act that stood at the heart of godly nurture: breast-feeding.[23]

Across New England, town leaders, local judges, and state magistrates listened to complaints against suspected witches. A substantial number of those complaints came from women, many of whom otherwise might never have surfaced in the public record. Female accusers and witnesses from every level of society voiced their concerns and the ruling elite listened and recorded their words.

In New England, then, the story of witchcraft is more than a story of misogyny; the trials reveal a society grounded in the assumption that all its members would maintain respect for the covenant and the pious order that it represented in their daily lives. Participants in extensive networks of gossip, bolstered by Puritan notions of fostering the religious health of the community, women extended their spheres of influence to encompass public spaces from which they were usually excluded. Whatever their conscious or subconscious motivations for identifying a specific person as an outsider, women wielded power as monitors of their town's social covenant, as protectors of the "inside" of their holy commonwealth.

Gender, the Court, and Religion in Virginia

In their struggle to create a godly society, Virginia men and women, like their Calvinist neighbors to the north, attempted to control crimes that they deemed a threat to their society. When duty called, Virginia's Anglican women and men took their concerns to court. And as in Massachusetts both men and women, as agents of community control, used the courts. What form that control would take, however, was shaped in part by their respective religious cultures.

Anglican culture placed a premium on the sacred bonds between men. Neighbors honored God when they honored one another. Any breech of order, any sin committed by one man against another, was as grave as a sin committed against God. Thus slander—the act of destroying another's good name and reputation—was as dangerous as witchcraft in a society that placed an emphasis on social order. False accusations of any sort robbed a society of the tenuous threads that bound neighbors to one another, and a community to God.

Civic codes were inextricably tied to moral control in Virginia. Unlike in England, where charges of slander and defamation were handled in the ecclesiastical courts, such charges in Virginia, which had no religious courts, were brought before local county courts or, in extreme cases, the colony's general court. Moreover, while ecclesiastical courts in England had discouraged men and women from bringing charges of defamation, instituting deliberately burdensome standards of proof, Virginia lawmakers cast aside those restrictions, making it easier for colonists to bring suit and obtain redress. As early as the 1630s, the Virginia legislature passed a law protecting colonists from those among them who "shall abuse their neighbours by slanderinge, tale carrying or backbitinge."[24]

The 1655 Norfolk County law illustrates public concern about scandal and libel with regard to witchcraft accusations. The same year that the Particular Court of Connecticut sentenced Lydia Gilbert to hang by the neck for witchcraft, the Norfolk court singled out "Divers dangerous & scandalous speeches," false accusations of witchcraft against innocent colonists "whereby theire reputacons have been much impaired and their lives brought into question."[25] Whatever the specific incidents that prompted the passage of the Norfolk law, it was in fact grounded in Protestant theology. John Calvin's exegesis of the ninth commandment highlights the importance of truth in language, and the danger in falsehood. He instructed Christians to "neither violate the character of any man, either by calumnies or by false accusations, nor distress him in his property by falsehood, nor injure him by detraction or impertinence." Drawing on the lessons taught in Exod. 23:1,7 and Lev. 19:16, Calvin cautioned that "our tongue, by asserting the truth, ought to serve both the reputation and the profit of our neighbors...For if a good name be more precious than any treasures whatever, a man sustains as great an injury when he is deprived of the integrity of his character, as when he is despoiled of his wealth."[26]

Women played a role in controlling slanderous speech in their communities, a goal as vital to community health as monitoring and reporting aberrant behavior. In dozens of cases before the county and general courts, single women and husbands and wives in tandem struck out at neighbors whose idle gossip threatened their names and reputations. And the courts responded, often providing for punishments that reflected the religious context of the accusations. Men and women convicted of slander were frequently ordered to appear before parishioners during Sabbath services, often wearing a white sheet, and publicly beg the forgiveness of the victim and the entire community.[27]

As early as 1624, a Virginia woman, Alice Boyse, lodged a petition with the general court against Joane Vinsone. According to Boyse's petition, Vinsone had "most wrongfully and unjustly slandered" her, by circulating the rumor that she had born a bastard child, "which she cannot approve (for that is the most false Accusatione)." When Vinsone refused to submit to the recommended punishment for slander— standing before the church congregation wrapped in a white sheet and begging forgiveness from the victim—Alice Boyse appealed again to the court. Vinsone continued to slander her, she complained, by reporting that she and her husband had made "an arsewarde Bargaine before we were maryed, and that there was that greate love borne by Mr. Jurden." The pain Vinsone's slander caused spread by association; her words besmirched not only the Boyces' moral standing, but that of the Jurdens as well. Mrs. Boyse begged the court to commiserate with her over all of the "unchristian wrongs" committed by Mrs. Vinsone. She beseeched them to demand that the accused appear before them. Though the outcome of the case does not appear in the record, Boyse's words are clear. She refused to let go unchallenged damaging words that had put a wedge between her and her husband, and damaged her standing in the community. To do so would have been to ignore accepted standards of morality and to compromise the stability of her town.[28]

Alice Travellor did receive satisfaction from the Accomack county court when she lodged a complaint against Robert Wyard in the winter of 1643. His punishment too reflected the relationship between civic law and religious culture. The court ordered Wyard to "stand three severall Sundayes in the tyme of devine service before the face of the whole Congregation in a white sheete with a white wann [wand] in his hand . . . and aske the said Alice forgiveness." According to the testimony of a neighbor, Rowland Mills, Wyard bragged to him that he had "sucked Alice Travellor." Such "base and ignominious Language," the court agreed, "hath taken away the reputation of the sayde Alice." Soon after Wyard made his boasts, another man, George Vaux, accused Alice of dallying with Captain Francis Yeardley. The court ordered him to apologize to both Yeardley and Travellor. That one of her alleged liaisons was the son of the former governor of the colony, George Yeardley, may have strengthened Alice's case. Whether or not Alice Travellor was a pillar of the community is irrelevant; base accusations made without sufficient proof threatened to undermine community order. Alice Travellor knew that her reputation deserved the same protection as any other parishioner's.[29]

Richard Buckland's punishment for defaming Ann Smith by distributing a libel in the form of poetry seemed to fit his crime: rather than stand before his congregation wrapped in a sheet, Buckland stood "from the beginning of the 1st lesson untill the second be ended with a paper upon his hat." As befit one who defamed in writing, the paper was to be inscribed in capital letters with the words "Inimrius, Libellos." The court demanded that Buckland beg forgiveness of God and "also in particular the aforesaid defamed." Time and again, the court and its petitioners made the link between slander and impiety; an affront to one's neighbor was an affront to God.[30]

Virginia's assembly and its courts were by no means blind to gender when they passed and enforced laws relating to slander. Laws against slander and defamation silenced women as well as men. Civic leaders and lawmakers acknowledged that scandalmongering and gossip prevailed primarily among groups of women. Ministers reinforced the image of the fishwife, who in her "unquietness" disrupted religious, economic, and civic affairs. But such laws also left room for the notion that the importance of a "good name" and "credit" extended to women as well as men. And Virginia's female colonists learned to use laws passed to control female behavior against others of their sex, or against men, if it served their purpose. In Surry County in 1677, Margery Thompson petitioned against Thomas Hux Senior and his wife Ellen, "for Endeavouring to take away her good Name & fame." She charged that by their slander the Hux's had so "damnified" her reputation that she was due five thousand pounds of tobacco and cask, for which sum she sought redress in the courts. The jury found for the plaintiff, though they reduced her award to eight hundred pounds of tobacco and cask. They ordered Thomas Hux to pay that sum and court costs, with the stipulation that if he refused to do so, his wife would be punished according to the act of assembly that provided against *women* causing undue scandal.[31]

Women who themselves had been charged with defamation or slander also used the courts to clear their own names. When Richard Flynt accused Sarah Bowyer of defaming him and his wife and mother in 1653 in Northumberland County, Sarah requested that the case be brought before a jury so that she might clear her name of the slander charges. In spite of the fact that three witnesses—Joan Gamblin, Sarah Bishop, and Thomas Hopkins—all testified that Sarah had defamed Flynt by spreading the word that he and his mother had kept a bawdy house in England and that his wife Dorothy had committed adultery with another young man, the court carefully considered the evidence in the trial and found in Sarah Bowyers' favor. The jury heard evidence that Cyprian Bishop (husband of one of the witnesses against Sarah Bowyers) had done as much to spread gossip about the Flynts as anyone else in the community. They found "no sufficient proofs" that Sarah had been especially malicious, and attributed the charges made against her to an unrelated dispute. The court ordered Flynt to pay damages to Bowyer.[32]

Men who wished to press suit for slander recognized that while women's gossip might itself cross the line between idle chatter and defamation, the very fact that they were connected to intricate networks and privy to confidential conversations might prove helpful in their own cases. Male colonists did not hesitate to call upon female witnesses to provide appropriate testimony. When John Waltham lodged a complaint in September 1637, against two female neighbors for abusing him and his wife "by most vyle and scandelous speeches," he called upon a third women to testify to what she had heard. Anne Wilkins recalled that when she met Anne Williamson and Anne Stephens at the cow pen she heard them "in a jeering manner abuse Grace Waltham." Mrs. Stephens and Williamson taunted the plaintiff's wife, Grace, by saying her husband John "had his Mounthly Courses as women have, and that the said Anne Stephens [said] that John Waltham was not able to gett a child." The women had impugned John Waltham's morality. They attacked his masculinity, and implied that he was able to fulfill neither his conjugal responsibilities nor the biblical imperative to father children. And by slandering him, they brought shame upon his wife, crimes he was unwilling to let go unpunished. The witness Anne Wilkins, by her proximity to the most damaging gossip, provided Waltham with all the ammunition he needed to seek justice from the court. The court ordered Anne Williamson and Anne Stephens to be ducked, and to beg forgiveness of both husband and wife before the church congregation.[33]

In a similar case in Northumberland County in 1653, John Barnes accused John Ashton of defamation, and called upon a half dozen witnesses—three of them women—to testify on his behalf. Barnes claimed Ashton had robbed him of his good name and credit when he spread the word that Barnes had impregnated his [Ashton's] maid and left her with a fatal case of the pox, a disease recognized as punishment from God for sins of a carnal nature. In this case, the women's testimony was particularly important because of their proximity to the household servants.

Phoebe Kent was the first witness to testify on Barnes' behalf. A single woman of apparently low birth, Kent swore that when she helped Ashton bury his then-deceased servant she noted that the body was "cleare Course and free from the pox." Hugh and Hannah Lee each testified that Ashton had visited them in their home and accused Barnes, in the presence of another woman, Mrs. Rocke. Hannah Lee added that she herself had questioned the maid about her relationship with the defendant, specifically whether "Barnes had promised to marry her and persuade her to run away." The maid had assured her that Barnes had made no such request, and that she "wished the ground might open and she sinke in if ever Barnes did say any such thing to her but she was a poore servant and she must und'rgoe what her Mr and Mrs would report." Hannah Lee's testimony is especially tantalizing; she shared with the court evidence that served to clear not only Barnes of the charges against him, but repair the damage done to the dead maid's honor. The poor servant, who believed herself in no position to challenge her master's false accusations, had an able defender in Hannah Lee.

In spite of the fact that Charles Ashton brought in two of his own witnesses—both prominent male citizens—to swear that the maid had admitted that Barnes had led her astray, the court ordered Ashton to pay the plaintiff three hundred and fifty pounds of tobacco "for the reparacon of the said Barnes his Creditt." In the end, two women, one who through her participation in the burial could testify to the maid's chastity and the other who could testify to the maid's moral righteousness, had contributed to the success of Barnes's suit. They relied upon their ability to prove that the woman with whom Barnes had allegedly dallied was honorable to add credence to the case against Ashton.[34]

Defending against and promoting accusations of slander were not the only opportunities women had to participate in the legal process. In spite of efforts on the part of colonial leaders to restrict women's access to the court, women continued to play a central role in the adjudication process, especially when they could demonstrate that they had the spiritual or moral health of their community in mind. Laws against slander notwithstanding, if sufficient evidence for a crime existed, women did not hesitate to play a role in the prosecution of criminals, and the courts acknowledged the valuable contributions they made to the legal process.

Even among those few accusations of witchcraft that made it as far as the county courts, women testified to protect the accused. When Jonathon Samon filed a complaint in the winter of 1676 against Alice Cartwrite, whom he accused of bewitching his child and causing its death, the Lower Norfolk County sheriff impaneled an "able Jury of women to attend the Court," to search Cartwrite's body for evidence of witchcraft. The examination proceeded, one of the few cases in any colony where such a group of women was referred to as a "jury."

The female jury appointed Mrs. Mary Chichester as forewoman to speak on their behalf. In open court, the twelve women "upon their oathes declare that they having delegently Searched the body of the sd Alice Cann find no Suspitious marks whereby they can Judge her to bee a witch; butt only what may and Is usuall on other women." Based on the jury's testimony, the court acquitted Alice Cartwrite. Thus an able jury of women weighed evidence that they themselves had generated, and in so doing protected the accused's good name and reputation.[35]

Several years later, in nearby Accomack County in 1679, women again played a public role in a trial, instructed to examine a young girl and her parents accused of murdering an infant. Trial records offer compelling evidence of the active participation of a twelve-member female panel. The case also illustrates the peculiar mix of popular and elite impulses that shaped Virginia's religious culture in the seventeenth century.[36]

The incident, which unfolded in the Accomack County Court in the spring, began with a coroner's inquest into the death of an infant, and resulted in charges of infanticide, murder, incest, and obstruction of justice. Some time in late January or early February, Mary Carter, daughter of Sarah and step-daughter of Paul Carter, gave birth to a baby boy. Testimony differed on whether the child was born dead or alive. All three of the defendants did agree that the baby, who lay between mother Mary and grandmother Sarah through the night, was dead by the following morning, and was buried under an outbuilding shortly after daybreak. Mary, Sarah, and Paul Carter were charged with the murder of the baby in March. Testimony taken during the inquest reveals a case even more lurid than it first appeared.

Paul Carter was first examined in closed chamber on March 1, when he related some of the details of the birth and added that Mary had confessed during labor that the baby's father was a man named James Tuck. On the same day, Mary testified that she had indeed consented to sex with Tuck after he behaved violently, but that her step-father "did do in like manner and both of them lay wth her and that she did keep it from her Mother," until her mother discovered she was pregnant. Mary "thought in her conscience Paul was the Father." She testified that Paul and Sarah buried the child first in "the old house," then moved the body to the garden.

Court records next relate a particularly gruesome examination designed to reveal innocence or guilt in those charged with murder. In this case, a panel of twelve women examined both Sarah and Paul Carter, who were instructed by the women to touch the disinterred body of the baby. "We caused Sarah…to touch, handle and stroake the childe, in which time we saw no alteration in the body of the childe." When Paul Carter was called upon to touch the corpse, however, "the black & sotted places about the body of the childe grew freshe and red so that blud was ready to come through the skin of the child." Paul Carter paled, a detail that did not escape the panel's notice. In addition, the women observed that the baby seemed "very much neglected" and appeared to exhibit evidence of violence by his throat, which was blackened as if he had been strangled.

Two weeks later the inquest continued in open court. Each of the three defendants was examined before a panel of judges. Questioning served to reinforce information gathered in the pre-trial hearings, though several new details surfaced. Had you no idea, the justices asked of Sarah Carter, that your husband had engaged in carnal acts with your daughter? Sarah admitted that she had seen her husband "hugg and kiss her daughter and took her daughters coates up to her knees, and that she rebuked him for it and charged him with debauching her daughter." Upon her husband's assurances that Mary had come to no harm, however, Sarah Carter had dropped the matter.

Two women added to the evidence uncovered by the "ordeal of touch" conducted on the exhumed body of the baby. Matilda West and Mary Mikell, both members of the panel, testified that they heard Paul Carter admit to paternity. Madam West had taken it upon herself to rebuke Carter, asking "were not you a wicked man to ly wth yr wifes child." Carter answered "I was a wicked man for so doeing and I must goe to God and not to man for forgiveness."

If Paul Carter found forgiveness in God, he was not destined to do so among the justices in Accomack County. Both he and his wife Sarah, "not having the feare of God before [their] eyes but being led and instigated by the devill," were charged with murder. Mary was charged with consenting, abetting, and concealing the murder of her baby. Because of the magnitude of the crime, local court officials, in accordance with English law, turned Sarah and Paul Carter over to the Governor and Council for further trial before the General Court. The county court directed the sheriff to "take recognizance" of Matilda West and Mary Mikell, two key witnesses in the inquest, both of whom were to appear at the general trial in James City. In April, the general court ruled that Mary was to be removed from Paul Carter's house to prevent further incestuous acts; the record is silent on the resolution of Paul and Sarah Carter's case.[37]

Of note in the case against the Carters is the degree to which women played a role in gathering and presenting evidence against the two suspects. While the justices questioned the defendants, the female panel—and two of its members in particular—provided the only evidence that any crime had been committed; it was their word against the Carters', and they prevailed. In addition, the panel's method for gathering evidence reveals a peculiar mixture of the empirical and the magical: the women took stock of the condition of the infant's body, in search of forensic evidence of a crime; at the same time they employed techniques that undoubtedly were popular among the county's cunning people in the seventeenth century. As they supervised the ordeal of touch, they participated in a process that in another colony might itself have been considered witchery.

Most cases that came before the county courts in Virginia were not as sensational as the inquest into the murder of the Carter baby. But as in the Carter case, women played an active role as accusers and witnesses in trials of people suspected of a breach in morality. And, as in New England, women participated in a network of gossip that reinforced their ability to regulate their community's moral order. Pious individuals, especially women, formed the sinews of communal control in Virginia as in Puritan Massachusetts.[38]

Several cases illustrate the concern with breeches in morality that colonial Virginia's women articulated in public, and the degree to which they depended upon the support of their neighbors to validate case. Women turned to the courts for protection from violence, often challenging the behavior of their economic and social superiors. When Grace Grey turned to the court, and Governor Berkeley, for protection from her violent and godless husband, whom she had "diligently served…with all possible care paines love loyalty & true obedience" for twenty-four years, she threw herself at the mercy of "the Report of all good people & neighbors whether they be rich or poore, who hath been eyewitnesses hereof not fearing but they will speake the truth notwithstanding their great engagemts to him as a mcht [merchant] (of whom they stand in feare & may Bias som of them[).]" As influential as her husband apparently was in the community, Grace Grey counted on the fact that her neighbors would support her charges against him, action rendered necessary by the absence of laws to protect wives. Civil laws, Mrs. Grey offered, were perhaps useless in the face of such evil; only the devil could persuade a man "to abuse a Loveing & obedient wife" and thus reject sacred matrimonial symbolism. For good measure, Grace Grey called on her churchwarden to accompany her to her home in a futile attempt to reconcile with her husband.[39]

In York County in the 1660s, Elizabeth Potterd took the stand as a witness on behalf of a complainant, the wife of Robert [*illegible*: Poiere?]. Potterd informed the court that she had "a quarrell against" the defendant, Poiere, accused of abusing his wife solely as a consequence of gossip circulated by Mary Floyd. She chastised the defendant, claiming it was "no part of an honest man in you to take another womans parte agaist your wife before you know a cause." Indeed, Mary Floyd should herself be prosecuted, for there was "as little honestie in her to make strife between a man and wife." In Potterd's eyes, Poiere's crime lay as much in his failure to trust his potentially innocent wife and his acceptance of the slanderous gossip about her as it did in his abuse of her. Nor did Potterd flinch at publicly challenging the moral rectitude of Poiere and the woman who attempted to destroy a healthy marriage.[40]

Husbands were not the only perpetrators of abusive, unchristian behavior toward women. Though some female servants hesitated to charge their masters or mistresses with wrong-doing (witness the timidity of the young servant whose master alleged she had contracted the pox by having repeated sex with a neighboring landowner), many others came forward to complain. Mary Rawlins, servant to John Russell, took her complaints about her master straight to the governor, William Berkeley. John Russell had treated her with "unChristian like usage and vulgarfull correction," and Rawlins was willing to submit to examination by the governor to prove the same. Though the transcript of her testimony is not available, it was apparently compelling enough to convince the governor to fine Russell forty pounds, a bond "for his keeping the peace and good bearing towards all his majesty's lieges…and especially towards the same Mary." Russell had a history of fractious behavior, but it was Mary's decision to prosecute him that ultimately held him in check.[41]

In Surry County in 1677, Mary Fletcher complained to the court of her Master George Lee's ill usage, "not fitt for a Christian." The court questioned Lee, and found sufficient cause to remove Mary Fletcher from his service. She was to remain with a Captain Spenser until the next meeting of the court. Upon her request, the court chose to protect the plaintiff. This, in spite of the fact that Mary Fletcher bore a bastard child during her service, and had run away from home during Bacon's Rebellion. Though George Lee retained the right to sell Mary's contract to another master—with time added for bastardy and for running away—Mary won the right to remove herself from her master's unchristian care.[42]

Indentured women complained about ill-treatment by their mistresses as well as their masters. Eleanor Rowe presented her case against her mistress, Mrs. Wilkins, to the Accomack County court in 1640. During her testimony, Rowe displayed the piety, humility, and subservience befitting a young woman of her station. To begin with, Eleanor Rowe submitted her petition "in all humble and submissive manner," acknowledging her low status in the household and *vis à vis* the court officials. With her head thus bowed, Rowe testified to Mistress Wilkins' "unchristian like and violent oppression." She complained of her mistress's "continuall strikeing Beatinge and abusinge her with careless resolute Blowes in a manner and most inhumane kindes at that it justly and openly appeared to all mens viewe that her life was oftentymes indangered." Not only did her mistress treat Rowe with unchristian like violence, but she disparaged her servant's character among the neighbors, undermining any hope the girl had of being exchanged to another household. Mistress Wilkins had compromised Rowe's reputation and her good name, a sin that demanded the same attention as the violence inflicted on her.[43]

There is no doubt that colonial leaders in Virginia used the courts to control female behavior. In addition, it became more difficult for women to pursue certain types of litigation as the century progressed. There is ample evidence, however, that in cases where the stability of the community seemed to hang in the balance, where untoward, unchristian behavior threatened to undo the tenuous ties between neighbors and upset the order bolstered by the Anglican church and the state, that women wielded authority in their role as regulators of Christian conduct in the county and general courts.

women, religion, and the court in new york

New York, a colony located geographically between Puritan Massachusetts and Anglican Virginia, set its own particular stage for women actors. Like their Calvinist sisters in Massachusetts, Dutch women found a voice in cases and events that seemed to strike at the heart of their colony's piety and its covenant with God. They found solace and support in the courts, and their voices reflected their religious concerns about community harmony. Moreover, like women in Anglican Virginia New Yorkers pursued alleged criminals whose actions threatened community bonds and neighborly dependence as vigorously as they pursued those who threatened the covenant by compromising the colony's Calvinist foundation. Faced with the diversity of a merchant culture that attracted settlers from throughout Europe and from a variety of religious traditions, and the political and social pressures brought to bear by the English conquest, Dutch men and women sought to control the actions of those residents whose behavior threatened the balance between civic diversity and community piety.

One case, just a hint of which appears in early court records, attests to the unique bonds between diverse groups of New York women, and to the strength with which they challenged civic authority. In the autumn of 1666, in the throes of the restoration of the crown's authority in England, Governor Andros wielded a heavy hand in the administration of New York. He sentenced to death three British soldiers, Thomas Weale, Richard Russell, and John Matthews, accused of trafficking in stolen goods. The case might have passed unnoticed in the record had not a large group of women chosen to take action on behalf of one of the accused.

On the evening of November 11, a Sabbath day, "a company of the chefe women of the city, both English and Dutch, made suite to the Governor for the condemned man's life." It is not clear which man was the focus of the women's appeal or the specific reason for their interest in the case. Whatever their motivation, they doggedly pursued justice. The following morning, "the same women who came last night, with many others of the better sort, and a greater number of the ordinary Dutch women, did again very much importune the Governor to spare him." The women recognized that the soldiers had committed a crime; death, however, was too harsh a punishment, they agreed. Several days after their appeal, the governor pardoned all three soldiers. The women had used a well-known tool, petition, to make their point to the highest civic authority in the colony, taking their lead perhaps from the large groups of women who had done the same at the height of the civil war in England. Moreover, in the name of moderation and peace, the women had crossed religious, ethnic, and class lines to express their concern with public justice.[44]

New York women exhibited an equal concern for issues of personal justice and piety. Though fornication and birth out of wedlock constituted a crime in this colony as in others, records reveal a surprising number of instances when women chose to expose their personal problems in an effort to implicate the man and restore their own good name and credit among their neighbors. Women approached the court on their own, or enlisted the help of an attorney, to seek redress for false promises of marriage, to charge a reluctant father with paternity, and to battle defamation and slander. They did so secure in the knowledge that they could prove themselves victims of crimes as objectionable to God and the court as their own transgressions of adultery or bastardy.

The church and courts recognized that young women were especially vulnerable to false promises and the resulting public dishonor. In September 1652, at the request of his young Dutch maid, Cornelis de Potter lodged a complaint against an Englishman, Ralph Clark, who had backed out of a promise of marriage. The maid, referred to only as Willementie, said that Clark had promised marriage in a series of letters to her, written in English. Willementie was at a clear disadvantage; a Dutch serving girl preyed upon by an Englishman. The council referred the matter over to the town's ministers, who, as commissioners of matrimonial affairs, bore the most direct responsibility for adjudicating cases of that nature. Their authority, more-over, was grounded in clear theological tenets: John Calvin's exegesis on the seventh commandment made specific reference to the vulnerability of young girls. Drawing on Exodus 22:16, Calvin warned "if a man entice a maid that is not betrothed, and lie with her; he shall surely endow her to be his wife."[45]

Dissatisfied with the ministers' progress in the case Willementie petitioned the court on her own behalf three months later. Despite the fact that custom and law assigned ministers the right to supervise the union of a man and a woman, the court agreed with the plaintiff's demand for satisfaction from Clark, who had so dishon-ored her. In spite of the fact that Clark's letters had been written in English, such cultural differences were not enough to prevent Willementie from taking the Englishman at his word, or from pursuing him in court when he seemed likely to break his sacred promise of marriage.[46]

Occasionally, women pursued men who not only reneged on a promise of mar-riage, but also further jeopardized their moral rectitude by denying the paternity of a child born out of wedlock. They called upon other women, most often those who had been present at the birth of a child, to attest to paternity accusations made at the time of labor. In all colonies, the court accepted the testimony of women who had heard confessions made during childbirth as evidence of paternity. In New York, the court not only accepted it, but sought it out and arranged for it. Confessions exchanged during labor were more than simply rumors, and neighboring women in these cases were more than rumor mongers; they were regularly counted on to pro-vide evidence of truths elicited during moments of extreme pain or near death, and related moments of contrition and piety.

Women charged by the courts with the responsibility of attesting to a neigh-bor's labor-induced confessions could not always expect their testimony to be used on behalf of the wronged mother. In one case tried in Albany in 1670, Cornelis Stevens Muller accused Ida Adriaents of defamation. Muller told the court that Ida Adriaents' accusations that he had fathered her unborn baby were false and slan-derous, and he called upon "God Almighty, who knows and searches all hearts and consciences" to attest to his innocence. He also called for the assistance of the court in appointing a committee of married women to attend the birth of Adriaents' baby, and to whom, "when she is in the pains of childbirth" and in mortal danger, she would be more likely to reveal the truth. Ida Ariaents persisted in charging that Muller had "had carnal conversation with her on a bench in the house of Martin Gerritz, under promise of Marriage." She was more than willing "to give birth to the child on it, if it please God," so sure was she that the words she would utter during labor would implicate Muller. The court thus appointed four Kinderhook women: the wives of Jan Bruyns and Peter van Allen, Dirkie Hermes, and a woman known only as Sary the Swede. Their findings (alas unknown) would be sufficient to direct the court in its decision.[47]

Not all men were as anxious to call upon the services of women to act as exam-iners or witnesses in court. When Grietje Peters and Jan van Gelder brought a dispute over a debt to a New York City court in 1662, van Gelder defaulted on his court appearance because, the plaintiff claimed, he was unwilling to appear before the "good women," a group of female arbitrators appointed by the court. In spite of his protests, the court did order two women to inspect the evidence and settle the case out of court, or to return to the court to report their decision. While the court recognized the value of women arbitrators, "good women" who could be trusted to uncover and reveal conversations that had taken place among their female neighbors, not all of New York's male citizens felt comfortable with the court's trust.[48]

In a Hudson Valley community in the same year, a Dutch woman called upon another group of women, her birthing attendees, to attest to the paternity of her baby. In the fall of 1662, Grietjen Hendricks Westercamp, a resident of Esopus, lodged a complaint in the court against Pieter Jacobsen. The man in question, according to Grietjen, "ruined her" when he denied paternity of the child she had recently borne. She asked the court to order the defendant to "restore her to honor," an honor, it is interesting to note, that had not disappeared when the plaintiff engaged in sex before marriage but only when the man with whom she had dallied refused to take responsibility for the outcome. The latter sin, of course, threatened a wider community disruption. Jacobsen must, she demanded, accept the child and fulfill his promise to marry her.

Pieter Jacobson told Grietje Westercamp and the court that he denied the child because "I have my doubts about it." He also denied that he had ever promised to marry Grietje, and shot off several of his own questions about the alleged time of the baby's conception, and the date the baby was delivered. The plaintiff answered forthrightly, identifying the day and time of conception. The baby had been conceived, she swore, at Jacobsen's millhouse, "eight days before Christmas, 1661." She had delivered the baby "eight days before Kermis [a summer fair]." After Westercamp filed her complaint, the sheriff and commissioners of the court granted the defendant two weeks' reprieve, while ordering the plaintiff to return at that time with evidence that Jacobsen had ruined her.

Westercamp took her assignment seriously. Two weeks later she returned to make her case. With her she brought her "exhibits": a certificate and depositions from seven women who "certify and declare that they were present at the birth of Grietje Westercamp's child, and that she swore 3 times that Pieter Jacobse was the father." Jacobsen brought his own certificate from both male and female neighbors who declared that the plaintiff had a history of untoward behavior. Moreover, the defendant repeated his claim that though he had "conversed and lain" with Westercamp, he had made no promise of marriage. "And besides," he added, he "gave her no money for it, and asks if a woman can be thirteen months and four days in the family way." Jacobsen's exaggerated gestational calculations notwithstanding, both parties were asked to return with more evidence.

In the end, Peter Jacobsen convinced the court that he was not responsible for fathering the baby, nor for Westercamp's ruin, and he was released from the obligation of marriage. The trial, however, ended on a rather peculiar note, with a decision that called into question every detail of the case and cast a shadow over Westercamp's and Jacobsen's relationship. When the court rendered its decision to release Jacobsen from any potential matrimonial responsibilities to Westercamp, it added this stipulation: that because both parties admitted that Westercamp had not been compensated for engaging in carnal relations with Jacobsen, he was bound to "pay her for that service." Was Westercamp a prostitute? We know little more about her than the few details that surface in these trial records. But if she was in the habit of accepting money for sexual favors, then her belief that she had a right and a duty to bring Jacobsen to trial is even more startling. Perhaps, given that on this occasion she had become pregnant, Greitje was driven to attempt to provide for her child and retain a place in her community.[49]

Not all women who used a public forum to restore their moral honor were bringing a cad or bounder to justice. Some turned to the courts to challenge false rumors about their character, rumors that might destroy their good name and credit in a Christian community. In New York as in Virginia, accusations of slander were accorded due hearing in court; one who falsely accused another of misdeeds (adultery, bearing a child out of marriage, fornication) posed almost as great a threat to community stability as one who was guilty of those crimes.[50] In the spring of 1666, Anna Reinhart petitioned the deputy mayor of New York City for permission to summon to the mayor's court three women who resided in New Haarlem. Sara Teunissen, Maeyke Oblinus, and Tryntic Petersen had falsely accused her of theft, a crime against the second table commandment, and she intended to gain reparation of character. The court agreed to her demands, and accordingly ordered the three women to make the journey into town to appear at court. Once there, they protested their innocence. They knew nothing of Anna Reinhart, they said, "except what is honourable and virtuous." Whether slanderous accusations were real or imagined, the court recognized that plaintiffs had a right to use that body to air their grievances. Anna Reinhart took advantage of that public forum to restore her virtue in the eyes of God and community.[51]

* * *

In all three colonies, the courts provided one of the prime arenas in which women exercised their responsibility for community righteousness. Seventeenth-century women were no strangers to this public setting, in spite of attempts to limit their access and undermine their authority there. Nor were women silenced in other public venues. They demonstrated their piety, and in some cases broadcasted it, in their churches, at public rituals to honor the dead, and in countless conversations with neighbors. They committed their piety to paper, in prose and poetry, often clearly meant for eyes other than their own. They had confidence that their piety mattered, that they could contribute to the spiritual health of their communities, and they acted on that confidence in both private and public.

NOTES

[1] For a more complete comparison of Anglican and Calvinist piety with regard to emphasis on first or second table laws, see above, Introduction.

[2] For a compelling discussion of the ways in which gender can be used to redefine conventional notions of private and public space, see Mary Beth Norton, *Founding Mothers and Fathers: Gendered Power and the Forming of American Society* (New York, 1996), 19–24. Also see Joan Landes, *Women and the Public Sphere in the Age of the French Revolution* (Ithaca, 1988), esp. 1–2, 8–9; and Terri L. Snyder, "Rich Widows are the Best Commodity: Women in Virginia, 1660–1700" (Ph.D. diss., University of Iowa, 1992), 202–208.

[3] Waters, *Ipswich*, 109–110.

[4] See, for instance, Warren Billings, ed., *The Papers of Francis Howard Baron of Effingham, 1643–1695* (Richmond, 1989), 102; Goodwin, *The Colonial Church in Virginia* (London, 1927), 89. On the existence of kinship networks in seventeenth-century Virginia, see Darrett B. and Anita H. Rutman, *A Place in Time: Middlesex County, Virginia, 1650–1750* (New York and London, 1984). On the role horse racing played in eighteenth-century Virginia society, see Rhys Isaac, *The Transformation of Virginia, 1740–1790* (New York and London, 1982), 98–101.

[5] Wynette P. Haun, *Surry County, Virginia, Court Records, 1672–1682*, Book III (Durham, N.C., 1986), 23–24. See also Warren M. Billings, ed., *The Old Dominion in the Seventeenth Century* (Chapel Hill, 1975; fifth ed., 1984), 243–244, 263–267. Governor Berkeley eventually remitted the fines imposed upon each of the convicted men: *ibid.*: 266–267.

[6] Vincent Watkins, trans., *York County Deeds, Orders, Wills, Book 3, 1657–1662* (Poquosan, VA., 1989), 54–56. On the church as a center for the distribution of local news, see George MacLaren Brydon, *Virginia's Mother Church and the Political Conditions Under Which it Grew* (Richmond, 1947), 181.

[7] C. G. Chamberlayne, *The Vestry Book of Christ Church Parish* (Richmond, 1927), 62–63. On Christopher Wormely, see Rutmans, *A Place in Time*, 259n.

[8] *Ecclesiastical Records*, II, 771–773.

[9] On the presence of women in the reburial ceremony in the aftermath of Leisler's Rebellion see Michael G. Hall, Lawrence H. Leas, and Michael G. Kammen, eds., *The Glorious Revolution in America: Documents on the Colonial Crisis of 1689* (New York, 1964), 132. Also see David William Voorhees, "The 'Fervent Zeale' of Jacob Leisler," *WMQ*, 51 (July, 1994): 447. Two additional cases illustrate the degree to which secular and religious issues merged in church politics in the years following the English conquest. One, which plagued the Albany church for years, involved a dispute between Lutheran minister Jacob Fabritious and an English colonist, who accused him of making disparaging remarks about Calvinists in his sermons. Though there was no love lost between Dutch Reformed officials and Fabritious (upon their conquest, the English had instituted a toleration for all Protestant denominations, some unacceptable to the Dutch Church), in the midst of rising tensions with the English, the largely Dutch court sided with the Lutheran: *Court Minutes of Albany, 1668–1673* I:243, 247–254, 264. On the conflict between Fabritious and Albany's Dutch Reformed Minister Gideon Schaets, see *Court Minutes*, I: 66, 176, 233. The other case, well documented in the work of several New York scholars, occurred in Albany as well. This dispute went to the heart of Dutch/English relations: Nicholas Van Rensselaer's appointment to

the church in Albany by Governor Andros represented to many Dutch officials, Domine Gideon Schaets among them, the egregious effects of English rule. Van Rensselaer, deemed by many to be in collusion with the Catholic King James, alienated many of his neighbors in the Albany community, both as minister and as patroon. On the Van Rensselaer affair, see Randall Balmer, *A Perfect Babel of Confusion: Dutch Religion and English Culture in the Middle Colonies* (New York, 1989), 16–21; Balmer, "Traitors and Papists: The Religious Dimensions of Leisler's Rebellion," *New York History*, 70, #4 (Oct. 1989): 355–358. For an opposing interpretation, see Robert S. Alexander, "The Strange Case of Nicholaus Van Rensselaer," *de Halve Maen*, 60, #3 (Dec. 1987): 1–4.

[10] Samuel G. Drake, *Annals of Witchcraft in New England and Elsewhere in the United States* (Boston, 1869), 234.

[11] One of the best new books examining gender in colonial history uses as its foundation records of the courts of Massachusetts, Maryland, and Virginia. Though Mary Beth Norton spends startlingly little time on religion (she too seems to fall prey to the belief that Anglican Virginia lacked any piety worth considering in an analysis of gender and power) her book weaves numerous tales from local courts into a rich analysis of the ways women found to maneuver in public and private. See Norton, *Founding Mothers and Fathers: Gendered Power and the Forming of American Society* (New York, 1996). For an analysis of the role court records played in her thesis, and a small sample of the ways the author uses court records to explore the relationship between gender, courts, and power, see *ibid.*, 14–16, 83–87, 174–180.

[12] Several scholars have examined the relationship between gender and law in Puritan New England. Most recently, Cornelia Hughes Dayton has provided a considered, careful analysis of the meaning and use of court records, their strengths and pitfalls, and the role such records might play in our understanding of patriarchal power in colonial New England. Though Dayton's conclusions about gender and public authority stand in direct contrast to my own—she found evidence in Connecticut court records of reentrenchment of patriarchal control by the end of the seventeenth century—her work fills a void in scholarship about the relationship between gender and the courts: Dayton, *Women Before the Bar: Gender, Law and Society in Connecticut, 1639–1789* (Chapel Hill and London, 1995). See also C. Dallett Hemphill, "Women in Court: Sex Role Differentiation in Salem Massachusetts, 1636–1683," *WMQ* 3d ser., 39 (1982), 164–175; Helena Wall, *Fierce Communion: Family and Community in Early America* (Cambridge, MA, 1990), esp. chap. two; Nancy Cott, "Divorce and the Changing Status of Women in Eighteenth-Century Massachusetts," *WMQ*, 3d ser., 33 (1976).

[13] The bibliography on witchcraft trials in early modern England and New England is extensive. Trials—endemic, or epidemic, as they were in Salem in 1692—have attracted the attention of historians, anthropologists, psychologists, and sociologists. Among the best known works on American witchcraft trials are Paul Boyer and Stephen Nissenbaum, *Salem Possessed* (Cambridge, MA, 1974); John Demos, *Entertaining Satan* (New York, 1982); and Carol Karlsen, *The Devil in the Shape of a Woman: Witchcraft in Colonial New England* (New York, 1987). Karlsen is one of the few historians to explore in detail the relationship between gender and the witchcraft trials, though she, like most other scholars, focuses on the accused witches as victims of colonial society's most virulent form of misogyny. Christina Larner had begun to explore a more rounded approach to trial evidence in Scotland, one which extended beyond trials as a tale of misogyny, in her last book, published posthumously: Larner, *Witchcraft and Religion* (New York, 1984). Another recent notable exception, though not the

work of an historian, is Deborah Willis, *Malevolent Nurture: Witch-Hunting and Maternal Power in Early Modern England* (Ithaca and London, 1995). Willis effectively links witchcraft accusations, a high percentage of which were indeed made by women, to the contemporary belief in a woman's ability to sit in judgment of her neighbors, especially with regard to their maternal skills. On witchcraft accusations and misogyny, see Norton, *Founding Mothers and Fathers*, 249, 452–453n.

[14] Drake, *Annals of Witchcraft*, 89–90; cf. David D. Hall, ed., *Witch-Hunting in Seventeenth-Century New England: A Documentary History, 1638–1692* (Boston, 1991), 62.

[15] Hall, ed., *Witch-Hunting*, 24.

[16] For examples of the "declension" interpretation associated with economic changes in New England in the mid-seventeenth century see Perry Miller, *The New England Mind: The Seventeenth Century* (New York, 1939); Richard Bushman, *From Puritan to Yankee* (New York, 1970). Attempts to counter the declension interpretation include Harry Stout, *The New England Soul: Preaching and Religious Culture in Colonial New England* (New York, 1986); Christine Heyrmann, *Commerce and Culture* (New York, 1984). On the relationship between social tension and witchcraft see Paul Boyer and Stephen Nissenbaum, *Salem Possessed* (Cambridge, 1974). If we examine women's roles as accusers in witchcraft trials, and interpret their accusations within the context of religious conviction, we challenge the declension interpretation on yet another level.

[17] John M. Taylor, *The Witchcraft Delusion in Connecticut, 1647–1697* (New York, 1971, reprint of 1909 edition), 106–107.

[18] On the link between witchcraft accusations and child-hating, see Willis, *Malevolent Nurture*; Demos, *Entertaining Satan*, 93–94. Demos notes that the "typical" witch in New England was most likely married, though was most often widowed at the time of accusation. She had few, or even no children. For Increase Mather, see *Jeremiads*, in *A Library of American Puritan Writings: the Seventeenth Century*, Sacvan Bercovitch, ed. (New York, 1984), 91.

[19] Drake, *Annals of Witchcraft*, 150–155; Hall, *Witch-Hunting*, 191–196.

[20] *Ibid.*, 229.

[21] Taylor, *Witchcraft Delusion*, 56. For a comprehensive discussion of the relationship between the practice of sorcery and accusations of witchcraft, see Richard Godbeer, *The Devil's Dominion: Magic and Religion in Early New England* (1992).

[22] Drake, *Annals of Witchcraft*, 222.

[23] *Records of the Town of Easthampton, Long Island...* (5 vols., Sag Harbor, NY, 1887–1892), I, 130–140.

[24] Hening, *Statutes at Large*, I: 156. See Mary Beth Norton, *Founding Mothers and Fathers: Gendered Power and the Forming of American Society* (New York, 1996), 84, 258–9. Norton labels suits for defamation and divorce "anomalous" because they represented the only two categories of civil proceedings in which a woman could approach the bench independent of her husband. Though her point is well-taken, her emphasis undermines the ways in which evidence from such trials can demonstrate the role Virginia women played as moral monitors of their communities.

[25] Edward W. James, "Witchcraft in Virginia," *WMQ*, 1st. ser., 2 (1894): 58.

[26] John Calvin, *Institutes of the Christian Religion [1559]*, ed. and trans. John Allen (2 vols., New York, 1936), II, 444–445. On slander as sin in New England, see Dayton, *Women Before the Bar*, 291. In spite of the religious context for laws against slander, it is tempting to interpret attempts to silence accusations, no matter how false or slanderous, as an effort on the part of the patriarchal elite to control the behavior of the lower orders in society. But though such laws indeed seemed to deprive colonists of one of their primary tools for articulating concern about the health of their community, in fact they merely redirected concerns and shaped a different kind of public role for women.

[27] On the importance of "credit" and "honesty" in English popular culture in the seventeenth century see Ingram, "Sex and Marriage," 150–151. The author cites a quote taken from a Yorkshire women in 1696 who, in her comments about the defamation of another woman remarked "they may as well take her life as her good name from her." Implied in those words is a sly equation of the crime of defamation with that of murder.

[28] H. R. McIlwaine, ed., *Minutes of the Council*, 31.

[29] Susie M. Ames, ed., *County Court Records of Accomack-Northhampton, Virginia, 1640–1645* (Charlottesville, VA, 1973), 235–236, 238. Alice Travellor Burdett was in fact notorious; her name came before the justices several times over a short period. After the death of George Travellor, Alice remarried within the year to Mr. Burdett, who died shortly thereafter. By the summer of 1643 Alice was charged with harboring treasonous activity, based on a rumor that "there was a health drunke at [her] house to the damnation of Pymms God and the Confusion of the Parliament." John Pym (1584–1643) was a parliamentary statesman; clearly there were those on the court sympathetic enough to the parliamentary cause to take offense at his and parliament's disparagement: Ames, *Records of Accomack*, 297. Anglican parish leaders in England also used a white sheet as a part of the punishment of quarreling couples. In some churches, contentious couples had to confine themselves in a specially-designed chair, divided down the middle, where they sat covered in a white sheet: Addleshaw and Etchells, *Architectural Setting of Anglican Worship*, 92–93.

[30] *VMHB*, 4 (1897): 407. "Inimrius" might be a bastardization—or a simple misspelling—of inimicous, an archaic word meaning "averse to God and the Episcopacy" (*OED*)

[31] Wynette P. Haun, ed., *Surry County, Virginia Court Records, Order Book*, Book III (Durham, 1986), 66. Though women were the target of anti-slander legislation, and were often called to court as defendants in trials for defamation, they were as likely to press suit themselves. For instance, in Lower Norfolk County between 1637 and 1675 women initiated about half of the litigation against defamation that came to court: Horn, *Adapting to a New World*, 367.

[32] Northumberland County Records, 1652–1655, Reel 1.

[33] Susie M. Ames, ed., *Court Records of Accomack-Northhampton, Virginia, 1632–1640* (Washington, D.C., 1954), 85, 88. Grace and John Waltham did have a son, probably soon after this case, since John died in 1640: James Perry, *The Formation of Society on Virginia's Eastern Shore* (Chapel Hill, 1990), 83–84, 102. Kathleen Brown suggests that gossip among woman in Virginia functioned as a form of social control, one which competed with formal legal institutions. Through gossip, women could exert control over their neighbors' shameful behavior. And though Brown posits that women acted as the voice of moral authority, especially in the absence of other strong authorities, she omits any discussion of the role that

religious culture played in providing women with the authority to take action against their neighbors: Kathleen Brown, *Good Wives and Nasty Wenches*, 99–100, 145–149.

[34] Fleet, *Northumberland Order Book*, II: 27–28. The third woman to testify, Mrs. Rocke, was twenty-one, and might have been a servant herself in the Lee household. The witnesses who testified on Ashton's behalf included Mr. John Trussell, himself a county court official, and Mr. Walter Weeks, who was later named Northumberland's constable.

[35] *Lower Norfolk Virginia Antiquary*, I, 56–57.

[36] On the persistence of popular religious traditions in the midst of an Anglican establishment in Virginia, including witchcraft, magic, cunning, and folk healing, see Jon Butler, *Awash in a Sea of Faith* (Chapel Hill, 1990).

[37] *VMHB*, 4 (1897): 186–197. Transcripts of the coroner's inquest were taken from the Accomack County Court records, and are to my knowledge no longer extant.

[38] Kathleen Brown suggests that married women were accorded respect by justices "because they constituted an indispensable link between churchwardens, county court officials, and female sexual offenders." They were best suited to the task of verbal and physical examination of women accused of sexual misconduct. To this I would add that women were privy to discussions of offenses of all sorts committed both by and against other women: Brown, *Good Wives and Nasty Wenches*, 97–98. On the role and function of gossip in the seventeenth century see Mary Beth Norton, *Founding Mothers and Fathers*, 253–261. See also Norton, "Gender and Defamation in Seventeenth-Century Maryland," *WMQ*, 3d ser., 44 (1987); James Horn, *Adapting to a New World: English Society in the Seventeenth-Century Chesapeake* (Chapel Hill, 1994), 364–367. On the function of individual and communal controls in non-Puritan communities in seventeenth-century England see Martin Ingram, "Sex and Marriage," in *Popular Culture in Seventeenth-Century England*, ed. Barry Reay (London and Sydney, 1985), 158–159.

[39] Petition of Mrs. Grace Grey to Governor Berkeley, August, 1665, Charles City County Deeds, Wills, Orders, Etc. 1655–1665, Reel 1.

[40] York County Deeds, Wills, etc., Reel 2.

[41] Vincent Watkins, transc., *York County: Deeds, Orders, Wills Book 3, 1657–1662* (Poquosan, Va., 1989), 166. Russell proceeded to forfeit his bond by using "contemptuous and bad language towards Major Crowshaw to the abuse of all magistrates."

[42] Haun, ed., *Surry County Court Records, Book III*, 66,

[43] Ames, ed., *County Court Records of Accomack, 1640–1645*, 22, 26.

[44] *Abstract of Wills, 1665–1707*, New-York Historical Society *Collections*, vol. 25 (1892), 74, 75. One other case illustrates the role women played as conciliators in conflicts between Dutch and English neighbors. In the village of Gravesend, on Long Island, a pocket of English Puritanism, Deborah Moody (who had departed from Salem, Massachusetts in 1643), participated in the nomination of town officials in June of 1655. "In behalfe of the Rest" she and clerk John Tillton nominated citizens for the offices of magistrate and *schout*, men who they trusted "will prove faithfull [and peaceable] indeavouring, to bynde up that which is broken amongst us." The Council confirmed Moody's suggestions, though Dutch residents claimed that they had been excluded from the process: Charles Gehring, ed., *Council Minutes, 1655–1656* (Syracuse, 1995), 59–60, 63–64. For a discussion of petition as a means of redress for women in civil war England, and the relationship between radical religion and

female political action, see Patricia Higgins, "The Reformation of Women With Special Reference to Women Petitioners," in *Politics, Religion, and the English Civil War*, ed., Brian Manning (New York, 1983); see also Keith Thomas, "Women in the Civil War Sects," in *Crisis in Europe, 1560–1660* (New York, 1965), 317–340.

[45] John Calvin, *Commentaries on the Last Four Books of Moses*, Charles William Bingham, ed. (4 vols., Edinburgh, 1852), III, 83–84.

[46] Charles T. Gehring, trans. and ed., *Council Minutes, 1652–1654* (Baltimore, 1983), 34, 59.

[47] *Minutes of the Court of Albany, 1668–1673*, I, 207.

[48] Fernow, ed., *Records of New Amsterdam*, V, 140.

[49] Versteeg Dingman, Kenneth Scott, and Kenn Stryker-Rodda, eds., *New York Historical Manuscripts: Dutch, Kingston Papers* (2 vols., Baltimore, 1976), I, 36–37, 39–40, 52, 55, 57–58. We do know that a decade later Westercamp was still living in Esopus; in 1672 she appeared in court with Barbara Jans for fighting. Westercamp had called Jans "Carouje" [a seventeenth-century Dutch word meaning whore], Jans had slandered Westercamp's son and called her "fatted pig," whereupon Westercamp had responded with "Black Devil." At that point the two fell upon one another. *Kingston Papers*, II, 485.

[50] Punishment for slander ranged from the imposition of fines, to public humiliation, to banishment, depending upon the magnitude of the slur and, presumably, the level of respect typically accorded the person defamed. For instance, when Herman Jansz van Valkenburgh, "commonly called Scheele [cross-eyed] Herman," made the mistake of spreading the rumor that Joannes Dyckman, the commissary's wife, committed adultery, and illustrated his charges by "showing with outstretched arms the size of the horns which were put on the said commissary's head," his sentence included being placed "in the flogging iron, with a few rods hanging from the post above his head and on his breast a sign with the words 'False Accuser.'" In addition, he was banished from the town for six years: A.J.F. van Laer, *Minutes of the Court of Fort Orange and Beverwyck, 1652–1660* (2 vols., Albany, 1920–23), I, 203, 204, 206, 208.

[51] Fernow, *Records of New Amsterdam*, V, 347, 349.

Epilogue
Gender and the Soldiers of Christ

O VER THE COURSE OF THEIR LIVES, PROTESTANT WOMEN IN THE AMERICAN COLONIES heard and read numerous messages that reinforced their notion of soul equality, an equality that transcended home and church and extended into the community. The girl who began her prayers in secret, secure in the notion that God was as likely to listen to her as to any other member of her family, grew into the woman whose marriage and childbirth experiences brought her closer to God, and whose duty to actively protect the piety of her family and community drew her into the activities of the public sphere. There, in an arena rarely identified by historians with the female sex, women monitored and questioned the moral character of their neighbors and ministers, and voiced their concerns about the collective piety of their communities.

Religious language and ritual infused daily life in the seventeenth-century colonies. And while some of that language reinforced patriarchal notions of female submissiveness and perpetuated the image of women as daughters of Eve, the fundamental tenet of soul equality also shaped seventeenth-century understanding. Though soul equality was most profoundly important when women confronted fears about their own salvation and their potential for heavenly peace after death, the language of equality also permeated events and actions of daily life. Women acted as spiritual guides and teachers for their husbands and children, stood and spoke before their church communities as examples of goodness and piety, and challenged the behavior of men and women who, in any other context, might have been considered above their criticism. Soul equality knew no status or gender boundaries.

It is admittedly difficult to plumb the minds of actors in seventeenth-century court documents, church records, and diaries. Women who filed suits against neighbors threatening the security of family and community, challenged the

authority of a minister, or left one church for another might well have acted for reasons other than spiritual ones. What is clear, however, is that Protestant women had
at their disposal a language that projected their voices into the public sphere. It provided them with access to social and political authority, at a time when the religious
and the political were inextricably linked.

In the middle years of the seventeenth century, large numbers of English
women, beneficiaries of the language of soul equality, participated in the events of
the Civil War, as petitioners, as members of crowds intent on disrupting the affairs
of the King, and as willing proclaimers of religious reform. In their churches and
homes, Calvinist women rejected Catholic ritual and those aspects of Anglican ritual that they deemed too closely aligned with Catholicism. By the same token,
English women also challenged Cromwell and parliamentary rule during the interregnum. Women were involved on both sides of the conflict; like men, they helped
to raise forces, contributed financial resources, and built trenches and fortifica-
tions.[1]

The tenets associated with soul equality permeated the speech and actions of
female petitioners in London in the 1640s and 1650s. Though estimates of the
number of participants vary (some scholars have estimated that certain petitioning
protests attracted upwards of 10,000 women), female protesters consistently
employed religious language to justify their actions in the public sphere. "Christ
hath purchased us at as dear a Rate as he hath done Men," the female petitioners
wrote in February of 1642, "and therefore requireth the like Obedience for the same
Mercy, as of Men." Women promoted a 1649 petition on behalf of four imprisoned
Leveller leaders "at Severall Congregational Meetings in and about the City of
London."[2]

The colonists who migrated to America, regardless of their political affilia-
tions, were heirs to this spirit of public protest, and the ideas of soul equality that
motivated women to participate. In Virginia, the diversity of religious practice from
county to county and parish to parish resulted in a number of confrontations
between people on both side of the conflict. In 1653, Mrs. Mary Calvert, apparently
a Royalist in the midst of a heavily Puritan Northumberland County, brought the
wrath of some of her neighbors upon her when she called the "States and Keepers of
the Liberty of England Rogues Traytors and Rebells." Similarly, at a gathering at the
home of Alice Travellor in Accomack County in 1643, "there was a health drunke . . .
to the damnation of Pymms God and the Confusion of the Parliament."[3]

For New England's Puritan colonists, the links between the religious and the
political were patently clear. In their conversion narratives, Puritan women recorded the horrors of their passage to the new world and drew parallels between their
voyage and the voyage of the covenanted people out of biblical Egypt. Few narrators
drew such a clear analogy as Elizabeth Dunster, a member of Thomas Shepard's
Cambridge congregation. "We fled in the night," Elizabeth recounted in 1649,
shortly after she and her family escaped certain persecution by anti-puritan forces
in England's civil war. "The enemy came and took away much of our substance,"

Elizabeth continued, "and because I had been means to forward them in the cause, and I was much satisfied that they that forsake not lands and houses were not worthy of him, and count it all joy when persecuted for righteousness." Dunster encouraged her family to flee to Massachusetts, to seek religious freedom in the name of righteousness and to fulfill God's will for her: "When I came over seas," Dunster continued, "I had God's presence. I was assured I was where God would have me, and so I submitted." Mrs. Jane Holmes, who joined Shepard's congregation in 1638–1639, referred in her narrative to her struggle to find appropriate pious surroundings in England. Having rejected her father and step-mother, Jane sought the counsel of a local vicar who, she soon discovered, was "an oppressor of the truth . . . one that taught free will and opposing openly Puritans." Dorcas Downey, a confessing member of Shepard's congregation in 1649, revealed that "the Lord was pleased to begin with me in England, living under means there. When trouble began, I was inclined to come hither for ordinances." Mistress Smith, who confessed that "seeing my friends affected, I was moved and being persuaded to make much of present time," deserted her troubled England for New England's shores. Puritan women did not merely flee from evil; they fled toward promise, and the responsibility to participate in the realization of a city on a hill.[4]

Neither were women in New York immune to the spirit of public protest born of the religious turmoil in England and on the continent. Witness the Dutch and English women, those of the "better sort" and those more "ordinary," who together presented their petition to the colony's governor and council demanding that three English soldiers accused of theft and sentenced to hang be freed (above, p. 276). In addition, in the tumult that marked Jacob Leisler's brief rein in New York, women were among the rioters who challenged the colonial representatives of the "Popish Tiran," King James. In an effort to warn the insurgents of the potential for violence in the wake of the rebellion, Leisler's "rabble cryed out verraet, verraet, or trayson, trayson, the rogues with sixty men will kill Capt. Leisler, and had the drum beaten in alarm." Anti-Leislerian Nicholas Bayard took pains to note in his journal that "Trijn Jans the wife of Jan Joost was very active in this furie." Even the wife of the beleaguered minister Henry Selyns, a woman who might have been expected to condemn Leisler, publicly rebuked her husband for declaring that the recently executed rebel "was an incarnate devil and there was no hope of his salvation." And in a letter written to the Classis on the occasion of Leisler's and Milborne's reburial under the Dutch Church, Leislerian partisans noted that it would be unnecessary to provide a detailed account of the execution "as this was fully done by Certain women a short time after its occurrence, who went to Amsterdam." Though no other details about the this female delegation appear in the records of the event, it is significant that the Leislerian correspondents took care to note their sex.[5]

If, as this study suggests, we accept that religion infused daily life and activity in public and private, and acknowledge that women's voices were among those which shaped and defined power in the home, church and community, the challenge now is to locate those voices in events and actions deemed more conventionally political. It might be possible, for instance, to reinterpret the upheavals of the seventeenth century—not only Leisler's Rebellion in New York, but the Glorious Revolution in Massachusetts and Bacon's Rebellion in Virginia—with an eye toward incorporating women as actors, as soldiers of Christ. In times of intense conflict, when religious liberty in their colonies seemed most under siege, Protestant women joined men in challenging the power of the crown in the name of religion, and the lines between private piety and public action were irrevocably blurred.[6]

By contrast, over the past decade a number of scholars have concluded that patriarchal organization and power reasserted itself in colonial America by the end of the seventeenth century. Fearing that women had gained substantial power, owing to the resettlement process and demographic imbalances, men, according to this view, reined in the activities and speech of women they deemed a threat to their patriarchal privileges. Yet it seems unlikely that women would summarily relinquish their hard-won influence in the face of patriarchal power. Indeed, considerable evidence suggests that eighteenth-century women, by relying on religious language and tenets to express their concerns with contemporary events, were active participants in American political culture. The key to understanding women's authority in the eighteenth century is to examine the means by which their concepts of private morality and piety were brought to bear in the public sphere.[7]

Within this framework, we are, for example, better equipped to interpret the words and actions of women faced with the hardships of an escalating war in the third quarter of the eighteenth century. When Boston resident Jane Mecom learned that the man in whose home her daughter boarded was a British "majr of the Rigement & is a moderate whig but cant be convinced that we ought not to Pay for Tea," she immediately sent two books written by her brother, Benjamin Franklin, in an effort to sway the officer's opinion. The unidentified books, she proclaimed "have done much to wards Instructing the People of England what sort of Parlement men ought to choes & may God defend there harts from all Bribery & coruption." The major was "mightyle Pleasd" with Mecom's offering. Denied the right to participate in formal politics, Jane Mecom nonetheless acted to shape public opinion in tangible ways. In a like manner, Mecom's niece, Sally Bache, took her own course of action. In the fall of 1780, Sally and four other women organized a subscription for the army, raising 300 dollars, with an additional 100 dollars contributed in the name of "Miss Bache," Sally's three-year-old daughter. When Jane Mecom learned of the women's "Noble and generous" actions, she bemoaned the fact that among her own few acquaintances she was unlikely to raise such a substantial sum. She confessed that she yearned for a time when there was "more Relidgon and less Pride." Sally Bache too expressed her own disillusion with her fellow colonists. Several months after her subscription, when she learned of Benedict Arnold's treachery, she wrote an angry letter to her father, Benjamin Franklin. Though she trusted that there was "still a great deal of Virtue" in the army, "our great folks appear to me to be intirely taken up with trying to raise their fortunes, or endeavouring to gain honners." "This is quite a different place since you left us," she complained, "but all revolutions produce a change of manners, and we are not to won-der at the alterations we now see." Far from content to sit by and watch events unfold around her, Sally Bache, by her own example, challenged her neighbors to match her moral righteousness.[8]

In the eighteenth century as in the seventeenth, the church and the home were often coincident with events in the political arena. Though the reasons to undertake explicitly public roles were of course varied and complex—shaped by economic con-cerns, race, and ideological conceptions of religious and political freedom—women concerned with the behavior of local civic leaders or the actions taken by the crown in the governance of the American colonies employed language which reflected a profound belief that God commanded his people to challenge leaders they deemed impious. A religious context allows us to accept the presence of women front and center, to acknowledge their influence in the public sphere, and, finally, to trace their participation in contemporary politics.

NOTES

[1] For a detailed discussion of the role women played in the English Civil War, particularly on the side of radical reformers see Patricia Higgins, "The Reaction of Women, With Special Reference to Women Petitioners," in Brian Manning, ed., *Politics, Religion, and the English Civil War* (New York, 1973). Also see Keith Thomas, "Women and the Civil War Sects," in *Crisis in Europe, 1560–1660* (New York, 1968); Dorthy P. Widlow, Shaking Patriarchy's Foundations: Sectarian Women in England, 1641–1700," in *Triumph Over Silence*, Richard Greaves, ed. (Westport, CT and London, 1985).

[2] Higgins, "Reactions of Women," 215–220.

[3] Northumberland County Order Book # 2, Reel 1; Susie M. Ames, ed., *County Court Records of Accomack-Northhampton, Virginia, 1640–1645* (Charlottesville, 1973), 297.

[4] Mary Rhinelander McCarl, "Thomas Shepard's Record of Religious Relations of Religious Experience," *WMQ*, 3d ser., 48 (July, 1991): 461, 463, 465–466; George Selement and Bruce C. Woolley, eds., *Thomas Shepard's Confessions*, Colonial Society of Massachusetts, *Publications*, vol. 58 (Boston, 1981), 76–77.

[5] Corwin, ed., *Ecclesiastical Records*, II, 966; *ibid.*, 1255.

[6] On the impact of the Glorious Revolution in Massachusetts, see for instance David S. Lovejoy, *The Glorious Revolution in America* (New York, 1972); Robert Earle Moody and Richard Clive Simmons, eds., *The Glorious Revolution in Massachusetts: Selected Documents, 1689–1692* (Boston, 1988), esp. 1–41; Charles Andrews, ed., *Narratives of the Insurrections, 1675–1690* (New York, 1915). The latter offers dozens of documents relating to conflicts in each of the three colonies.

On Leisler's Rebellion see Thomas Archdeacon, "'Distinguished for Nation Sake': The Age of Leisler in New York City," in *Colonial America: Essays in Politics and Social Development*, Stanley Katz, ed. (2d ed., Boston and Toronto, 1976); Archdeacon, *New York City, 1664–1711: Conquest and Change* (Ithaca, 1975); Randall Balmer, *A Perfect Babel of Confusion: Dutch Religion and English Culture in the Middle Colonies* (New York, 1989), esp. 33–47; Balmer, "Traitors and Papists: The Religious Dimensions of Leisler's Rebellion," *New York History* 70 (Oct., 1989): 341–372; Adrian Howe, "The Bayard Treason Trial:

Dramatizing Anglo-Dutch Politics in Early Eighteenth-Century New York City," *WMQ*, 3d. ser., 47 (1990): 57–89. The most persuasive argument for the religious roots of Leisler's Rebellion can be found in David William Voorhees, "'In Behalf of the true Protestant Religion': The Glorious Revolution in New York" (Ph.D. diss., New York University, 1988). None of the studies address the role of women in the Rebellion.

Some attention has been paid recently to the participation of women in Bacon's Rebellion, though most scholars conclude that their actions most clearly resulted in an increase in patriarchal controls, and a resurgence of negative representations of women as overly emotional harridans: See especially Kathleen M. Brown, *Good Wives, Nasty Wenches, and Anxious Patriarchs: Gender, Race, and Power in Colonial Virginia* (Chapel Hill, 1996); Terri L. Snyder, "Rich Widows are the Best Commodity: Women in Virginia, 1660–1700" (Ph.D. diss., University of Iowa, 1992), esp. 64–91.

[7] Some scholars, Jane Neill Kamensky among them, place the reentrenchment of patriarchal authority even earlier in the seventeenth century: *Governing the Tongue: The Politics of Speech in Early New England* (New York, 1999). Others, like Mary Beth Norton, Cornelia Hughes Dayton, Kathleen Brown, and Susan Juster locate patriarchal reassertion later in the century and extend its impact through the eighteenth and into the nineteenth century. See Norton, *Founding Mothers and Fathers: Gendered Power and the Forming of American Society* (New York, 1996); Dayton, *Women Before the Bar: Gender, Law, and Society in Connecticut, 1639–1789* (Chapel Hill and London, 1995); Brown, *Good Wives, Nasty Wenches*; Juster, *Disorderly Women, Sexual Politics, and Evangelicalism in Revolutionary New England* (Ithaca, 1994). This study suggests that if we reexamine eighteenth- and nine-teenth-century events and redefine what constitutes influence in the public sphere, we will find that women continued to exert authority, relying on religious language and tenets to express their concerns.

[8] Jane Mecom to Benjamin Franklin, Nov. 3, 1774, in Carl Van Doren, ed., *The Letters of Benjamin Franklin and Jane Mecom* (Princeton, 1950), 150–151; Jane Mecom to Sally Bache, Oct. 1780 in *ibid.*, 202; Sally Bache to Benjamin Franklin, Jan. 14, 1781. Though scholars of the eighteenth century have examined women's participation in the American Revolution, they frequently define female roles within private, separate spheres where their influence was indirect at best. See for instance Mary Beth Norton, *Liberty's Daughters: The Revolutionary Experience of American Women, 1750–1800* (Boston, 1980); Linda Kerber, *Women of the Republic: Intellect and Ideology in Revolutionary America* (chapel Hill, 1980); Nancy F. Cott, *Bonds of Womenhood: "Woman's Sphere" in New England, 1780–1835* (New Haven, 1977).

InDex